PATHWAYS
TO PERSONALIZATION

PATHWAYS

TO PERSONALIZATION

A FRAMEWORK FOR
SCHOOL CHANGE

SHAWN C. RUBIN

AND

CATHY SANFORD

HARVARD EDUCATION PRESS
CAMBRIDGE, MASSACHUSETTS

Paperback ISBN 978-1-68253-247-8
Library Edition ISBN 978-1-68253-248-5

Library of Congress Cataloging-in-Publication Data
Names: Rubin, Shawn C., author. | Sanford, Cathy, author. | Highlander Institute.
Title: Pathways to personalization : a framework for school change / Shawn C. Rubin, Cathy Sanford.
Description: Cambridge, Massachusetts : Harvard Education Press, 2018. | Both authors work at the Highlander Institute and collaborated with staff at the institute on this book. | Includes bibliographical references and index.
Identifiers: LCCN 2018028960| ISBN 9781682532478 (pbk.) | ISBN 9781682532485 (library edition)
Subjects: LCSH: Student-centered learning—United States. | Blended learning—United States. | Active learning—United States. | Education—Computer-assisted instruction. | Educational technology—Computer-assisted instruction. | Educational change—United States. | School improvement programs—United States. | School management and organization—United States.
Classification: LCC LB1027.23 .R86 2018 | DDC 371.2/07—dc23 LC record available at https://lccn.loc.gov/2018028960

Published by Harvard Education Press,
an imprint of the Harvard Education Publishing Group

Harvard Education Press
8 Story Street
Cambridge, MA 02138

Cover Design: Endpaper Studio
Cover Image: FrankRamspott/DigitalVision Vectors/Getty Images

The typefaces used in this book are Minion Pro and Proxima Nova.

CONTENTS

PREFACE

This is a book aimed at helping local educators and leaders move away from teacher-centered education models and toward approaches that encourage student self-direction, mastery, and engagement. Despite growing interest in personalizing education, students are still spending too much time learning as a group, passively sitting on the rug in elementary school and in rows at the secondary level. Most of the teachers and leaders we encounter want to improve at meeting the academic and emotional needs of their individual students and engage them as independent learners. Most agree the current system has become somewhat irrelevant but have no process for changing course.

We wrote this book because we have witnessed too many conversations at thirty thousand feet and not enough strategic discussions on the ground where teachers, students, and administrators design, explore, and learn together. We fill this gap by offering a framework for supporting meaningful change that we developed after observing, supporting, and collaborating with close to five hundred teachers and administrators—from more than forty different districts across Rhode Island and the country—over the past five years.

Our framework is also greatly informed by our own experiences as teachers. We both believe that personalization is a critical strategy for providing a meaningful, rigorous, and equitable education to all students. In 2000, Shawn began his teaching career in a multi-age second- and third-grade classroom in a new experimental urban charter school focused on personalized, project-based learning. He and his colleagues had a clear vision for instruction forged through research and best practices that stemmed from Big Picture Learning and the Coalition of Essential Schools movement. There was a strong culture of collaboration at the school, and the small faculty was determined to transform the elementary school experience by putting students at the center of their own learning.

Shawn's first classroom included a heterogeneous mix of students who struggled in their traditional public school, English language learners (ELLs) whose families had recently arrived in the United States, and upper-middle-class students looking for a progressive elementary experience. He had students with moderate special needs next to students who had been reading since prekindergarten. Given significant latitude around curriculum and instruction, Shawn worked with each student to build an individual learning plan around an interest-based project. He managed this effort with a clipboard, homemade spreadsheets, and black portfolio boxes. Planning and executing daily lessons based on individual learning plans while still meeting the needs of his diverse learners quickly became unsustainable for both Shawn and his colleagues.

After three years, school leaders hit the pause button to reflect on the school model. It was clear students were enjoying the personalized nature of their learning. (Shawn still keeps in touch with students from those early years and they continue to tell him that designing and implementing individual learning plans and personalized projects represent the most empowering moments of their K–12 school experience.) However, it was also clear that the small faculty was poorly equipped to handle the workload associated with creating learning objectives, personalized learning plans, activities, projects, and assessments that were tailored to the needs of each student. More than 60 percent of the staff left the school after the first two years and the remaining teachers struggled to maintain the rigor of personalized projects and academic work in their K–5 classrooms. Quickly, the experimental elementary program began to shift back to a school with great culture but a more traditional model. While school leaders had the right vision, staff, and intention, they were not able to create a viable process or a manageable workflow for teachers.

As the school moved from a focus on interest, engagement, and project-based learning to a focus on targeted and differentiated instruction, Shawn transitioned to teaching kindergarten. He began moving students between various centers based on their needs and tracking data with red, yellow, and green crayon on a printed spreadsheet. To differentiate, he made multiple photocopies of six different beginner readers every few days and built scaffolded centers on weekends. He knew that if he could deliver instruction at each student's zone of proximal development, then he had the best chance of moving each child forward, while simultaneously building an ethic of struggle and reward into their learning experiences. While the focus of the school had evolved, Shawn continued to struggle with managing the workload associated with differentiating within a traditional system. Yet, his approach was working. Each fall his benchmarking data would show that over 60 percent of his students were significantly below grade level; by the spring, 95 percent of his eighteen students were performing at or above grade level.

Five years later, when Shawn got his hands on a first-generation iPad, he began to realize how instrumental the device could be in supporting personalized learning approaches by blending digital and face-to-face instruction. He leveraged targeted apps and engaging websites to support students struggling with specific standards and skills. He experimented with screencasting, image annotation, voice-over, and movie creation tools, empowering five-year-old students to demonstrate their learning through creative design, building, writing, and performance. He tried various formative assessment tools to help him identify current levels of mastery and regrouped students to support their strengths and needs.

After ten years of teaching, Shawn was excited to share his new insights and outcomes with more teachers and administrators. He left the classroom to join forces with Cathy at the Highlander Institute, an education nonprofit in Providence, Rhode Island. A former math teacher with experience supporting students with diverse learning styles on both ends of the socio-economic spectrum, Cathy was also keenly aware that one-size-fits-all instructional approaches were not meeting most student needs and that efforts to personalize instruction required an intense level of additional planning. Cathy had been leading efforts centered on building teacher knowledge and school support systems around differentiated approaches to instruction, such as response to intervention (RTI), with the goal of helping schools and districts close gaps for struggling students.

Together, we established a blended and personalized learning arm of the Highlander Institute to support teachers and leaders struggling to figure out how to personalize learning through the integration of new technologies. Looking around the state, we saw a sudden influx of devices in classrooms without a connected vision or understanding of how these tools were a valuable addition to teaching and learning. As an organization committed to the high ideals of personalized learning and willing to test, tinker, and fail forward, our goal was to leverage strong teacher practice and high quality software to develop solutions to the same complex problems Shawn had experienced in his own classroom.

In 2014, we developed a state-level fellowship called Fuse RI, pairing early adopter educators with district leaders interested in implementing blended and personalized learning in their schools and districts. To date, we have trained 105 Rhode Island fellows and partnered with forty-one districts or charter schools across the state. As Fuse spreads nationally, we have worked with an additional sixty fellows, creating a small army of change agents who are scattered across the country. Through our Fuse fellowship, we have seen what works and what does not work when attempting to implement and replicate personalized learning initiatives across a range of school cultures and structures. And, we have come to several important realizations:

- There is nothing new or novel about educational theories regarding personalized learning. They are aligned to the writings and wisdom of great thinkers such as Dewey, Duckworth, Freire, Vygotsky, and Papert. Over the past several decades, many school and district leaders have articulated their hopes for offering more personalized and experiential learning opportunities for their students, but years of standardization, combined with the inefficiency of personalization strategies, has prevented leaders from imagining *a pathway* for realizing these hopes and dreams. Implementation efforts that enable *all* students, not just high achievers or students from wealthy zip codes, to benefit from innovative, motivating, engaging, personalized instruction is the central challenge before us now.
- There is great power residing in schools in the form of creative, motivated, and committed teachers who are best positioned to define, test, and translate the promise of personalized learning in a sustainable way for all students. While education reform efforts have typically been defined by district administrators who look externally for a solution, the most effective personalized learning initiatives that we have observed have been defined by teams of teachers addressing local problems of practice through personalized approaches.
- Implementing and scaling personalized learning across a school or district requires a focus on rethinking change management strategies, not a focus on technology integration. We have observed many creative classroom models that leverage technology, but most have been unable to scale beyond the individual teachers who spend countless hours operationalizing their own visions. Traditional, top-down, change management efforts rarely garner desired outcomes when working with emerging and undefined practices. Instead of adopting

initiatives at scale and working to ensure fidelity across an entire school or district, we have seen the benefit of small, iterative approaches to change. Instead of using testing data to pronounce an initiative a failure or success, we have watched teachers engage in cycles of continuous improvement where multiple measures are used to support the ongoing iteration of promising ideas.

Our field work, coupled with research into the most effective national models, has enabled us to develop our Pathway to Personalization Framework to articulate a more personalized change management process for teachers and leaders. Our framework is beneficial for leaders with a wide range of knowledge and expertise within the field of personalized learning, for teachers who have realized the benefits of personalized learning in their classrooms and are interested in supporting school- or district-wide initiatives, and for policy makers, funders, and others interested in learning and supporting new educational approaches.

This book is a step-by-step explanation of our framework, which serves as an implementation roadmap for determining where to begin, how to target efforts to meet local needs, and how to measure progress along the way. Our framework supports leaders regardless of how far or fast they want to move. For novice leaders who are learning about the potential of various practices, and veteran leaders who have enacted change and are looking to accelerate initial successes, our process offers five distinct implementation phases that can help teams construct a personalized pathway through the work. Chapters guide leaders through change management strategies, using stories and examples drawn directly from districts and schools, both in Rhode Island and across the country.

This is not a book that says, "If you do X, then Y will happen," because we do not suggest stock solutions for implementing blended and personalized learning in schools or classrooms. Our framework combines the wisdom of educational philosophers, lessons from current practitioners, and best practices from industry change management theorists. Through examples, case studies, and tools, this book shares our perspectives in a format that explains the "why" and the "how," not just the "what."

INTRODUCTION

Personalizing the school experience for students can feel like an unachievable goal for educators, but updating our one-size-fits-all system to meet the specific needs of the students we serve could be the most important educational challenge we face. There are no shortcuts when it comes to personalizing education for students. You cannot buy personalized learning. There are no plug-and-play products or platforms for making this shift. Personalized learning is a process and series of decisions schools and districts make to create learning environments more aligned to the interests, identities, and abilities of all students as they achieve mastery of skills and standards at their own pace.

We see vast promise in personalized learning models and believe that new technologies hold the key for making these approaches manageable and sustainable for all teachers to implement. Yet, we find it important to balance the current hype and excitement with the fact that the field is still struggling to develop the right infrastructure necessary to enact authentic change. For educators who want students to progress through standards at their own pace, there is an unfortunate dearth of learning progressions and resources to support these efforts. Leaders who believe the competencies behind self-directed learning and creativity are as important as those connected to math and ELA struggle to articulate, teach, and measure these skills and dispositions. As a nation, the federal Every Student Succeeds Act (ESSA) has helped leaders reconsider traditional testing and accountability practices, yet we are years away from replacing standardized testing with a competency-based model built on performance assessments. Our diverse student populations require culturally relevant curriculum and culturally responsive instruction, but educators lack the resources and will to support these efforts. As we imagine ways in which breakthrough innovations can better support all these instructional shifts, we honor the complexities of experimenting with tools, strategies, and processes not yet ready for primetime. While the journey often leads to as many rabbit holes as breakthroughs, the good news is every day students, teachers, administrators, and researchers are pioneering, implementing, and documenting advancements in this space. We can point to classrooms, schools, and even entire districts that are significantly improving the student learning experience and generating higher student learning outcomes through viable personalization initiatives. Unfortunately, for every glimpse at success we find a myriad of emerging uncertainties, which require ongoing attention. There is no resting on laurels with personalized learning. It is a constant churn of inquiry, experimentation, and iteration.

Across the field there are broad and varied definitions of personalized learning, but it is not our goal to build consensus around a single version. Instead, we encourage readers to work with definitions that resonate and adapt promising strategies to address current problems of practice. You know your students and families best and understand the instructional shifts that are most important to local stakeholders. You may aspire to create classrooms where students feel known, both culturally and intellectually. Or, you may envision classrooms where each student is consistently challenged within his or her zone of proximal development. We hope this book helps you articulate your priorities and build your school or district capacity for implementation, but, more importantly, we hope it drives genuine analysis and discourse regarding the ideal student experience.

In our model, success is directly linked to what local students, families, and educators value. We have supported personalized initiatives focused on student engagement that have yielded significant increases in attendance and decreases in behavior problems without an emphasis on academic outcomes. We have supported initiatives focused on achievement that have led to substantial increases on state test scores. And, we have supported efforts emphasizing twenty-first-century competencies, such as student agency and critical thinking, that have dramatically increased student self-direction and persistence on rigorous academic work. This book helps leaders define their priorities and find their unique voices in the personalized learning conversation by leveraging an intentional and structured approach to change.

In the chapters ahead, we help you articulate a persuasive vision, define what you value, and clarify the specific shifts you want to see in classrooms. We advise you to establish an evidence base by collecting and analyzing both qualitative and quantitative data throughout the implementation process. We offer guidance for cultivating buy-in and ownership across all levels of the system as teams build a replication plan that supports all stakeholders. From start to finish, we advocate for adapting our process to meet local needs and moving at a pace aligned to your conditions. Across iterations, pauses, and do-overs, we offer tangible ways to learn from mistakes and build on successes.

Empowering Local Change Agents

This book is designed for education change agents—leaders at the classroom, building, and district level—who believe in the power of personalization and are looking for guidance to effectively implement a new vision for teaching and learning. If you are an education change agent, this book can serve as a road map for transformation. However, first we ask you to check in regarding a few key aspects of this work. Do you believe it is possible to further personalize the current school experience for your students? Do you have the mindset and resourcefulness required to trailblaze a uniquely tailored path? Finally, and most importantly, do you believe in the power of relationships as the engine of change? If your answer to the majority of these questions is no, we advise you to close this book and spend time observing and getting to know the stakeholders in your system before engaging with our framework. If you currently spend the majority of your day running from fire to fire or task to task with your head down in purposeful service—but without pausing to connect and listen to your students, families, or colleagues—you will have a hard time leading this initiative. Relationships are the core of this work. We encourage you to contemplate your relationship readiness before engaging with our change model.

Our framework relies on three central leadership roles. The first is the *lead change agent*, a catalyst for change in a school or district and the point person spearheading the personalized learning effort. The second is the *design team*, a highly engaged group of five to twelve members who are deeply committed to serving as the brain, heart, and soul behind the initial phases of this work. The third set of leaders are *pilot teachers*—talented educators who have the skills and dispositions to test and define aspirational practices. Leaders across these roles must respect the different perspectives, cultures, identities, and social-emotional needs of their stakeholders; otherwise, teachers, students, and families will never buy into or believe in the shifts being promoted. In order for a community to adopt personalized best practices in classrooms, leaders must first walk the walk. When leaders are unable to articulate why personalized learning is important or when their actions counteract the ideals they are espousing, teams struggle to start and scale the work. There are many small, technical shifts you can make within a classroom, school, or district, but this undertaking, much like the Golden Rule, requires leaders to treat colleagues the way they want colleagues to treat students.

Consider Yanaiza, principal of an urban elementary school in Rhode Island. Yanaiza assumed leadership of her school as a turnaround effort in 2014 and utilized a blended and personalized approach to support transformation. Yanaiza deeply understands the power of culture building and relationships as the backbone of a change initiative. Every morning from 8:30–8:45 a.m., she stands before her school community of students, parents, and educators sharing positive updates, goals met, core values, and a shared vision for how "success will live within their walls for the day." Yanaiza describes this morning meeting as the heart of her school. Each day approximately sixty parents participate, hearing the same message as the school community. Handshakes are offered at the end of morning meeting to welcome students to the school day with a personal, positive connection. Parents appreciate the direct access they have to their principal, and Yanaiza appreciates the families who are always willing to offer feedback on her ideas. Recently, Yanaiza and her team have been building consensus around a school priority of fully inclusive classrooms. Full inclusion has historically been a controversial topic at the school, and Yanaiza has listened carefully to stakeholder concerns and incorporated this feedback into her pilot planning. She attributes the support she has received from teachers and parents to her constant communication and the trust she has built within her school community. Teachers and families clearly understand the rationale behind this endeavor and believe in the principal they see and speak to every morning.

For schools and districts who start this initiative without a solid culture of respect, communication, and an ability to collaborate, blended and personalized learning will amount to buzzwords, and your colleagues will wait out your initiative with a "this-too-shall-pass" mentality. You can start the work with a small, core team of dedicated educators, but getting to scale with a personalized learning initiative requires knowing and valuing everyone who will eventually engage in this endeavor.

The Pathway to Personalization Framework

For the last five years, we have searched the state and the country for breakthrough examples of blended and personalized learning. By unpacking comprehensive redesign efforts, amazing data stories, and successful edtech initiatives, we have found solutions of all sizes. We have observed and vetted countless blended and personalized learning strategies, which has enabled us to identify key patterns and groundbreaking approaches that have become the foundation for our Pathway to Personalization Framework.

What has become clear to us through this process is that innovation in the field is not about shiny new products or isolated classroom examples of amazing teacher practice. Instead, innovation is found in a user-centered approach to change management that empowers teachers and students to design, test, and codify their own locally defined personalized learning strategies. Specifically, innovation centers on how leaders learn what aspects of personalization are making a difference for their students and how they create systems to facilitate and expedite faculty adoption of these initial successes.

Divided into five phases—plan, pilot, refine, grow, and network—our framework provides change agents with a sequence of decision points and action steps, along with the tools needed to move from visioning to piloting and testing to replication and scale. While our framework builds on both the successful and failed efforts of pioneer leaders across the state and country, it has also been shaped by lean startup methodology and improvement science research. Consequently, the perspectives of leading change management theorists across various sectors have both validated and enriched our process.

Eric Ries, author of *The Lean Startup*, may seem like an unlikely influencer for a book focused on new pedagogical models, yet our framework is connected to many principles of "lean thinking," including the piloting of "minimally viable strategies" responsive to "customer" wants and needs; continuous iteration; an understanding of whether to persevere or pivot; and action research loops using solid evaluation cycles.[1] Ries makes the case for a new discipline of entrepreneurial management that can be adapted to fit the managerial challenges of supporting complex and transformational educational change. We integrate components of his vision-steer-accelerate process in our plan and pilot phases.

Much of our change process relies on the leadership of early adopter teachers. The concept of an early adopter was introduced in the 1960s by Everett Rogers, a communication theorist and sociologist who originated the diffusion of innovation theory. Rogers described the spread of good ideas as a social movement, and we leverage his theory throughout our book as leaders contemplate the strengths and needs of teachers who sit at different places along the diffusion of innovation curve. Geoffrey Moore created a more contemporary lens from this foundation of work. As the author of *Crossing the Chasm*, he uses the diffusion of innovation curve to chart the adoption of innovative technologies and suggests that in order to find mainstream success, products must cross the chasm between early adopters and individuals on the other side.[2] We use the concept of a chasm to reinforce the idea of a tipping point in the adoption of personalized practices, as well as to demonstrate how practices must be packaged and communicated in order to scale.

Several elements of our framework have been grounded and enhanced by the work of Anthony Bryk, Louis Gomez, Alicia Grunow, and Paul LeMahieu, authors of *Learning to Improve: How America's Schools Can Get Better at Getting Better.*[3] The authors identify key missteps—such as top-down management, a focus on quick fixes, and the lack of collective practitioner knowledge base—that have plagued education reform. Calls to action by the authors include the refinement of promising practices, attention to local contexts, variability, and the collection of expertise that can accelerate how a field learns to improve its core work. We lean heavily on the plan-do-study-act (PDSA) cycles advocated by Bryk and colleagues throughout our pilot and refine phases and also employ their crucial concept of networked improvement communities (NICs) as the culminating phase of our framework.

In their 2016 book, *Innovation and Scaling for Impact: How Effective Social Enterprises Do It*, Christian Seelos and Johanna Mair argue that innovation is not simply the creation of something new, but the connection of a valuable idea to a process for scaling and generating impact.[4] Many education "innovations" have died on the vine over the years, and the demise of promising strategies can be linked to innovation uncertainties that Seelos and Mair discuss, as well as to innovation pathologies that limit an organization's capacity for impact. The frameworks Seelos and Mair developed to diagnose potential stumbling blocks—as well as their emphasis on "learning as the main requirement for productive innovation"—closely align with our process for change, and we return to their lessons in the refine and grow phases of our framework.

The final piece of inspiration for our framework comes from John Kotter, retired professor of leadership at Harvard Business School. Kotter has studied how over one hundred companies have made fundamental shifts in their businesses to cope with changing market environments. In his white paper, "Leading Change: Why Transformation Efforts Fail," Kotter outlines eight steps for successfully transforming an organization and how critical errors at each level can derail a change initiative.[5] The majority of his steps translate very well into an education realm and help us emphasize the importance of essential moves across elements of our framework.

This combination of ideas and theories has enriched our process for change and encouraged us to experiment with high-impact practices that have revolutionized other fields.

How This Book is Organized

After introducing readers to the five phases in our framework in chapter 1, subsequent chapters are organized into five sections, corresponding to each phase of the framework. Each chapter in the book highlights a series of sequential decisions and activities, enabling lead change agents, design teams, and pilot teachers to operationalize relevant and meaningful personalized learning initiatives. We support these steps by providing essential templates, timelines, examples, and artifacts to help teams accomplish this work, as well as offer engaging examples and case studies of successful implementation. We have also created a resource website that provides live links to the specific organizations and resources discussed in each chapter. References to the website, which can be accessed at pathwaystopersonalization.com, are made within chapters.

Our Goal

Personalized learning models seek to transform and revolutionize an educational system that has been entrenched for almost two hundred years. This is a daunting and formidable undertaking. We deeply believe in the promise of personalized learning and, simultaneously, we believe change management approaches to transformation must also be personalized. Yet, there are no quick fixes or silver-bullet solutions within these pages. We recommend navigating this book slowly and taking time to react, respond, and discuss our tactics and how they align to your reality. We encourage readers to learn the process in its entirety before assembling a team and identifying a comfortable starting point. Our framework is not an all-or-nothing proposition. We encourage change agents to adapt, test, and use our process to design a path forward that is aligned to local strengths and needs. Simultaneously, we hope readers will push themselves and their colleagues to undertake some of our more challenging framework elements. It is our hope that stakeholders across educational ecosystems who are ready to reimagine education will find guidance and support for realizing their aspirational visions in this book. There has never been a more exciting time to be working in this field.

THE PATHWAY TO PERSONALIZATION FRAMEWORK

The terms *blended* and *personalized* learning remain largely amorphous and have the power to energize or polarize depending on the audience. Some claim we need a universal definition of these terms, while others attack any definition as limiting or antithetical to the concept of personalization. We have observed "personalized learning" classrooms ranging from self-directed learning, in which students spend a majority of their time working independently on devices, to device-free instruction, in which students blaze their own trail in Montessori-like environments. Some claim personalized learning is overly individualistic and lacking in human interaction and community. Others call it squishy and open-ended without enough curricular structure and accountability. Some focus on fully learner-centric models, making it seem like an impossible dream to achieve within traditional school systems. Others claim victory prematurely after simply shifting from paper to digital worksheets. Within the field, it is still rare to find thought leaders or practitioners who completely agree on the semantics and scope of personalized learning. This is OK. The field is evolving too quickly to require fidelity to a single concept. Definitions of personalized learning will and should continue to mature in the years ahead.

We see this gray area as an opportunity for leaders to consider essential elements, tailor semantics, and customize their own scope of work. We do not believe casting our judgment of what is or is not personalized learning will help you implement a more rigorous model within your local context. Instead, we support process-oriented, best-fit decisions and focus on design and development along a thoughtful trajectory. Shifting schools and districts away from teacher-directed class-room models of instruction to more student-centered learning environments requires intentional action steps. For this reason, we value a systematic process that starts with a grain of inspiration, grows through documented success, and leads to self-sustaining schools and districts that are able to evolve as the field continues to shift and change.

REFRAMING THE IMPROVEMENT PROCESS

There is a temptation on the part of educators to want to "keep up with the Joneses" and adopt the latest in exciting innovations. Consider Natalie, a former teacher in the late 1990s who has been the director of curriculum in a small district serving three thousand students for the past fifteen years. Without the experience of teaching with devices, software, and a robust internet, Natalie is uncertain about how to change course in support of more student-centered learning models, but her colleagues across the state and region all seem to be focused on this work. She wonders what Twitter accounts she should be following or what blog posts she should be reading. She struggles through stacks of books and articles to curate research, theory, and practice. She wonders what grant opportunities she has missed or whom she should be adding to her professional network. Her anxiety is fueled by pressure and a constant churn of uncertainty.

Natalie must work within tight budget constraints. She struggles with the increasing needs of her student population. She is under pressure to improve test scores. She is in desperate search of "the solution." When she reads about the amazing student outcomes attached to a district on the other side of the country—one that resembles her own district in size and composition—she decides to throw all her energy into replicating this effort. She focuses on the "nouns" behind the successful personalized learning initiative, advocating for an investment in the specific platform and consultant team referenced in the article. She glosses over the details—the specific roles, policies, systems, training, and support that have made the solution viable in this particular district. She concentrates on the achievement growth described in the article and downplays her lack of clarity around how this approach aligns with the current problems and challenges facing her students and teachers. After doing some initial research, she realizes her district cannot afford the resources leveraged by the district in the article, but she is now convinced that technology is a crucial cornerstone for success. She issues a vendor request for proposals (RFP) and ultimately settles on a more affordable software suite that has been adopted by several neighboring districts. She does not fully understand the nuanced features, details, or capabilities of this software, but the demo was promising and her procurement process requires immediate action if she wants to implement it in every classroom by the fall. Her teachers roll their eyes and grit their teeth as they await the next new thing being forced into their classrooms without proper vetting, explanation, or support.

We have witnessed this process over and over again with predictably ineffective results. Leaders with the best intentions advocate for tools they do not completely understand and demand fidelity once dollars have been committed to the effort. It is time to pause, reflect, and consider a better process to support well-intended leaders. It is time to start looking internally, not externally, for the seeds of change. Personalized learning should not be leveraged for the sake of technology or innovation; it should be connected to a specific problem of practice. In our experience, the best approaches to personalized learning have centered on challenges articulated by key stakeholders. Consider the teacher who states, "I know I am not challenging the brightest students in my class"; the student who states, "Nothing I am learning about seems relevant to my life"; or the parent who states, "My child is smart but is falling behind—he needs a different approach to reach his potential." We advocate for starting this work with an internal audit of your most pressing needs before looking externally for a resource or model. First and foremost, this work is about building relationships with students and teachers and identifying their pain points. Who is thriving under the current system? Who is struggling, and why? What are the barriers students and teachers are facing in their quests to be successful? We have learned the hard way that effective school and district redesign does not start with top-down restructuring. It starts with student, family, and teacher voices creating a tangible reason—a *why*—for personalized learning.

FAILING FORWARD

Highlander Institute's first statewide effort to scale personalized learning was launched through a fellowship program called Fuse RI. In the summer of 2014, we trained twenty-five committed educators as Fuse fellows to act as change agents across twelve districts interested in moving toward more personalized approaches. Our initial thinking and guidance to leadership teams was built on a competency model that emphasized the need for immediate shifts in administrator behavior. Our assumption was that district administrative roles were built to support traditional classroom models, and an important first step was redesigning administrative roles and responsibilities to better support personalized learning initiatives. For example, in many traditional districts we noticed a strong bifurcation between curriculum and technology departments. We saw shifts to blended and personalized learning models requiring joint decision making regarding curriculum, devices, and software, which meant both sides of the district office needed to improve communication and collaboration. Over the course of three months, we researched and curated strategic administrative practices from thought leaders such as the Council of Chief State School Officers; The New Teacher Project; Friday Institute; International Society for Technology in Education; Consortium for School Networking; the Technology, Pedagogical, and Content Knowledge Framework; and the Planning for Quality Guide from the Evergreen Education Group. We culled a collection of over 650 district- and building-level practices into what we considered to be the forty most important competencies for school and district leaders. After each district team self-assessed their own readiness with regard to our massive list, we created personalized action plans for each district.

After eighteen months, we realized our focus on administrator behavior and the immediate redefining of district-level responsibilities was misguided. Our push to restructure traditional bureaucratic systems was an unwieldy and ineffective first step when district administrators had not yet established a rationale for this work. Starting a redesign process at the top of an organizational chart was the wrong approach. Over the course of six months, we completely pivoted to center redesign efforts within the student experience, leveraging the expertise of knowledgeable teachers who were already leading great work in their classrooms and schools.

THE RATIONALE BEHIND THE PATHWAY TO PERSONALIZATION FRAMEWORK

As we modified our focus, we witnessed firsthand the importance of personalizing the change process for educators. Despite the level of urgency associated with initiating change efforts within a school, teachers consistently possessed various levels of interest and capacity for shifting their instruction. Simultaneously, once teachers and leaders uncovered a central problem, they all had the same question: "What do we do now?" While we knew the recipe for success would differ across our varied school and district partnerships, we realized we needed a process that would help design teams answer this critical question for themselves. Consequently, we developed the Pathway to Personalization Framework to articulate our preferred change management process. Over the past four years, this framework has continuously evolved and become an immediate value-add for school and district redesign efforts in three key ways.

First, we root our approach in a student-focused, user-centered design experience. Like all states, Rhode Island is driven by state standards and course accountability. Our state test scores fall along socioeconomic lines, similar to those highlighted by Sean Reardon in the 2016 *New York Times* article on money, race, and success across districts. Reardon found, "Children in the school districts with the highest concentrations of poverty score an average of more than four grade levels below children in the richest districts."[1] Rhode Island has outlier schools and classrooms similar to Reardon's data set; but, in general, when we connect our personalized learning conversations to state testing data, especially in urban districts, we have a hard time shifting the conversation away from the deep-rooted societal inequities associated with poverty, race, and immigration. Concurrently, suburban districts often possess a swagger around testing success that prevents further exploration of blind spots regarding student engagement and preparedness. Rather than starting with test scores, our framework focuses on defining the current student experience in classrooms, expanding the conversation without necessarily losing the emphasis on accountability. Through activities such as student shadow days, building rounds, student focus groups, and teacher surveys, we help administrators develop a strong rationale for personalized learning methods that is relevant to all stakeholders across classrooms and schools.

Second, we encourage districts to rethink their concept of a pilot. In education, the traditional concept of a pilot references boxed curriculum evaluation as pilot teachers test a product with fidelity to inform district purchasing decisions. In our framework, we repurpose the word *pilot* as a space for teachers to explore high potential, personalized practices with an emphasis on improving the student experience. With time and support to explore and expand new practices, pilot teachers lead the research and development of a localized model for change and identify promising practices for replication.

Third, we emphasize the importance of building an evidence base around pilot efforts before taking personalized learning to scale across a school or district. The work undertaken in pilot classrooms must be connected to varied measures and be supported by learning cycles to quickly determine whether changes are leading to improvements. No longer content with throwing spaghetti at the wall and hoping something sticks, our approach to learning has become much more targeted. This emphasis on pilot accountability helps school and district leaders feel more confident about identifying and replicating valuable practices.

FIVE PHASES TO CHART YOUR OWN PATHWAY

Divided into five distinct implementation phases of plan, pilot, refine, grow, and network, our Pathway to Personalization Framework includes a midpoint where leaders shift from a focus on research and development to a focus on replication and scale. The various phases are depicted in figure 1.1 and described in the following sections, offering leaders the chance to align current implementation efforts with the right entry point in our framework.

FIGURE 1.1   **Pathway to personalization framework**

PLAN	PILOT	REFINE	GROW	NETWORK
Build knowledge	Recruit pilot teachers	Create pathways	Align communication and strategic scaling	Accelerate through collaboration
Lay the groundwork	Structure the learning process		Contemplate the curriculum challenge	
Design your plan	Evaluate the pilot		Personalize the professional learning	

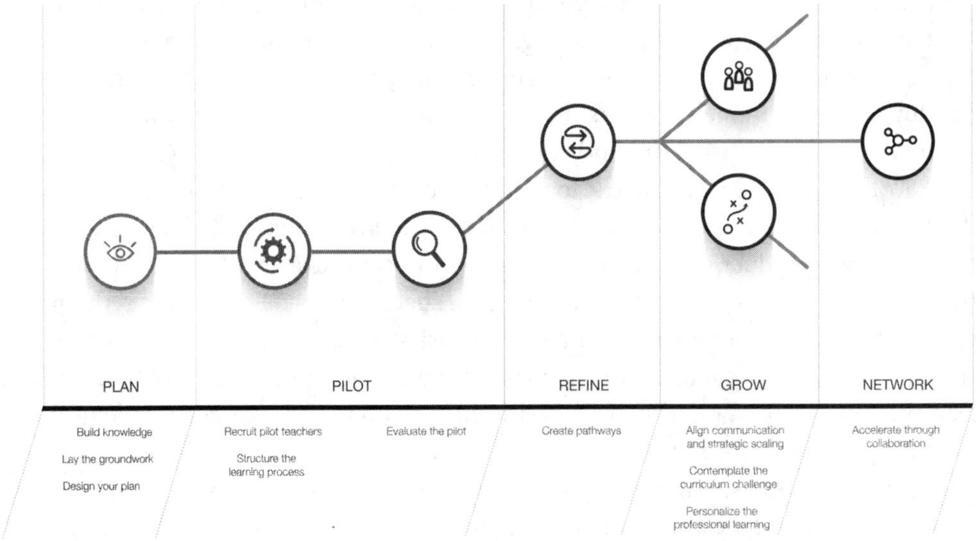

The Plan Phase

The plan phase launches with a focus on knowledge building. To begin, leaders take a deep dive into the critical elements and terminology behind personalized learning as they start to craft their own arguments for change. During this phase, a lead change agent as well as the design team—consisting of students, parents, teachers, and administrators—are identified. Together, they launch planning efforts with a self-study to assess readiness around systems, infrastructure, and relationships, as well as to explore the current student experience. The goal of this process is to connect data and evidence to current strengths as well as uncover important problems of practice. These elements become the rationale for the work and the basis of a vision statement for pilot classrooms. The team then identifies three to five priority practices, which become the backbone of the plan, pilot, and refine phases. As the foundation for forward movement, the plan phase supports the development of an initial direction and enables leaders to effectively articulate the initiative.

The Pilot Phase

Selecting the right teachers to run pilot classrooms marks a critical decision point for the design team. Launching personalized learning initiatives is messy and often inefficient; identifying teachers with grit and problem-solving skills to battle uncertainties and challenges will enable the design team to effectively study the systems and conditions necessary to nurture promising approaches. In this phase, pilot teachers join the design team to further define priority practices and connect practices and associated strategies to a set of data measures. The expanded team outlines data collection plans, builds consensus around launch points, and defines how pilot teachers will be supported. As pilot classrooms get up and running, successes, challenges, and ongoing data collection are discussed at periodic midpoint meetings, and implementation plans are updated as pilot teachers learn and iterate in their classrooms. The pilot phase concludes with a formal evaluation. The expanded team sorts and summarizes three different types of measures to develop a balanced picture of pilot impact and documents the critical barriers pilot teachers face during implementation. The goal of the formal evaluation is to identify high-impact strategies and communicate conditions required for effective replication. In most cases, some practices will require further study, and some will be ready to send to the refine phase.

The Refine Phase

During the refine phase, design teams switch gears from testing new practices to codifying successful practices and building buy-in with a larger base of stakeholders. With the continuing help of pilot teachers, design teams organize pilot information to create four separate deliverables. Broad lessons learned and a rationale for moving forward are compiled into a pilot story to inform and engage stakeholders. Implementation pathways are built through the collection of pilot classroom artifacts—in the form of lessons, activities, routines, protocols, tools, and reflections. Each implementation pathway is tied to a successful priority practice, offering guidance and support to new teachers as they join the effort. Next, teams consider how to embed successful practices within curriculum to reduce the planning burden associated with implementation. While pilot teachers may have the inclination and capacity to build their own materials, most of their colleagues do not, and a sustainable initiative will rely on a viable curriculum plan. And finally, teams develop a proposal for formalizing pilot classrooms into an ongoing research and development engine. Together, these elements become the foundation for replication efforts.

The Grow Phase

The first half of the grow phase explores the intersection of communication tactics, ongoing relationship building, and strategic scaling decisions. Feedback from teachers and students is used to understand "bottom-up viability" for replication, while discussions with district leaders and governing boards help articulate "top-down viability." At this point, the design team engages more fully with the existing school or district leadership team to align the personalized effort with competing initiatives and to study current obstacles and conditions for success. This combined team then defines what scale should look like within its local context, proceeding at a pace that best positions efforts for success. We offer four common scaling scenarios for consideration, including a return to a second pilot phase, a focus on additional early adopter teachers, a cohort model, or a full implementation across an entire school or district. Once teams have developed a scaling strategy, our focus returns to communication tactics and messaging for internal stakeholders. We recommend developing several critical communication artifacts and engaging in ongoing efforts to build relationships and support collaboration and sharing. The goal is to rally a strong coalition of support for scaling efforts.

In the second half of the grow phase, combined teams consider how the universal challenges of curriculum, platforms, and professional learning will impact scaling efforts. Most design teams will have already wrestled with these factors during pilot implementation, but there are particular challenges to consider within each that will impact replication and scaling efforts. In terms of curriculum, aligning high quality lessons, activities, playlists, and performance tasks to priority practices is one of the stickiest challenges facing wide-scale school and district adoption. In short, traditional curriculum has a personalization problem and personalized learning has a curriculum problem. In order to make our aspirational shifts viable, teachers must have everything they need—data, lessons, extensions, assessments— at their fingertips. Next-generation platforms are coming closer to this ideal, but combined teams must often establish their own approach to integrating current curriculum and assessment resources with software programs and homegrown materials to support teachers who are making this shift. Our overview of the current status of platforms and software discusses how these tools are supporting personalized learning implementation as well as their current limitations.

Next, design and leadership teams contemplate how to organize professional learning activities to support teachers as they join the initiative. For far too long, teachers have sat through stand-and-deliver, one-size-fits-all, traditional professional development presentations that are not differentiated by skill, paced to learning needs, inclusive of their voice, or built around multiple modalities for engagement. Leaders must model priority practices, creating professional development systems that reflect the pedagogy and learning environment they envision for students.

The Network Phase

Transitioning to blended and personalized learning is a heavy lift for all involved. In Rhode Island, we have worked to reduce challenges by creating intentional opportunities for schools and districts to collaborate in order to enhance our overall capacity. The network phase is introduced through the story behind Rhode Island's blended and personalized learning movement, which has set the stage for strategic partnerships. We break down twenty years of work across our educational ecosystem and identify common themes around shared leadership, teacher autonomy, technology experimentation, and cross-district collaboration in pursuit of more student-centered learning models. We connect these themes to our current readiness to solve universal problems through the formation of networked improvement communities (NICs). NICs align partners around a central problem through the lens of improvement science, supporting continuous learning cycles across diverse environments to test the validity of potential solutions. We present a current example of how multiple partners are tackling their curriculum challenge through a nascent NIC and contemplate how the NIC model can accelerate learning as design teams across city, state, and country lines collaborate to solve common problems.

USING THE FRAMEWORK: A SAMPLE TIMELINE

When it comes to creating a project timeline, we believe in the strategy of going slow and learning fast. Timelines for moving through the framework will depend on local conditions present in a school or district and will often require significant adjustment as design teams learn, cycle back, or skip ahead. In some cases, multiple aspects of the framework can run simultaneously, depending on resources and capacity. Timeline estimates also hinge on how much dedicated time a lead change agent is given to tackle this work in addition to performing concurrent responsibilities. Figure 1.2 outlines an example timeline across the five framework phases that is realistic for most schools and aligns with the ebb and flow of a typical school year. In this example, the plan phase lasts approximately three months. The pilot phase, which includes recruiting pilot teachers and evaluating the pilot, could take up to eighteen months depending on the readiness, scope, and complexity of

FIGURE 1.2   **Example timeline across the framework**

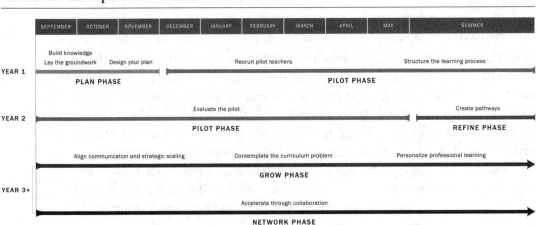

the pilot. We dedicate three months to building the four deliverables that are part of the refine phase, which could be expedited if a design team has been collecting artifacts and engaging the next wave of teachers and administrators throughout the pilot phase. The pace behind initiating the grow phase depends on the quality of implementation pathways, the complexity of identified obstacles, and the availability of resources and infrastructure. Bringing additional teachers and schools into the project is a process of continuous improvement that extends in perpetuity as design teams and teachers continue to test, learn, and improve. At the same time, the search for external partners and collaboration opportunities in the network stage begins in earnest at any point when larger challenges are defined and capacity allows.

Blazing a Trail

There are still a variety of uncertainties and unknowns within the intersection of blended and personalized learning. Our framework is less of a trail map through a state park and more of a process for bushwhacking through unchartered territory. Conditions within each school and district will result in multiple pathways through our framework. There is no singular aspect of the framework that is mandatory. At each phase, we explain the nuances of the work and why it is important, but, ultimately, it is the choice of lead change agents and design teams to determine what is gained and what is sacrificed by blazing an alternate trail.

Ultimately, shifting instruction toward more student-centered, personalized practices is about equity and improving the school experience for all students. No matter your current level of pride in the work you do on behalf of your students, it is always possible to better meet the needs of all learners. As you begin this journey, heed the words of Ta Nehisi-Coates as he describes James Baldwin's measured optimism during the early stages of the civil rights movement: "You should be aware that failure is a distinct possibility."[2] As you find an entry point within our framework, do not fear failure. Fear inaction and propel your efforts forward to improve the school experience for your students.

PLAN

Pathway to Personalization Framework

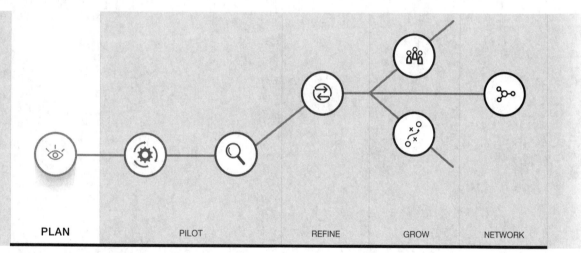

PLAN   PILOT   REFINE   GROW   NETWORK

Build knowledge

Lay the groundwork

Design your plan

BUILDING
KNOWLEDGE

The concept of personalized learning is practically as old as the United States' public education system itself. The first free, tax-subsidized public high school was opened in Boston in 1821, and by 1889, Preston Search, superintendent of schools in Pueblo, Colorado, introduced a plan to enable students to move at their own pace.[1] In 1916, education theorist John Dewey published *Democracy and Education,* advocating for a student-centered approach to education that fostered individual growth.[2] Lev Vygotsky developed his theories around the zone of proximal development in the 1930s. James Comer focused on the power of student-teacher relationships to dramatically raise achievement levels of low income students in 1968.[3] And, constructivist Seymour Papert explored how computers and technology could be used to empower children to experiment, explore, and express themselves in the 1970s.[4] The tenets behind our modern conceptions of personalized learning are not new, and research meta-analyses over the past twenty years have established large effect sizes for practices often associated with personalized learning.[5]

In a 2015 report entitled, "Blended Learning Research Clearinghouse 1.0," Saro Mohammed from The Learning Accelerator highlights instructional approaches that have been shown to have a large, positive impact on student learning.[6] Using the commonly held baseline that a typical teacher has an effect size of 0.4 on their students over one academic year, the report makes the case for pursuing several key strategies that show remarkable growth in effect size, including:

- Reducing group size (to one to one if possible)—effect size of 2.0
- Using formative assessment data to inform instruction—effect size of 1.13
- Providing instruction aligned to student needs—effect size of 0.82
- Offering students opportunities for guided and independent practice—effect size of 0.77
- Facilitating learning in which students have control over learning goals, pathway, and pace—effect size of 0.61[7]

Despite the enduring legacy and historical evidence behind personalized learning, educators have struggled to implement these aspirational practices at scale over the past 150 years. The advent of digital technology and mobile devices has ushered in a new era of possibilities for scaling high potential personalized practices, yet the current promise of breakthrough technology as a catalyst for our most ambitious hopes for public education is as utopian as it is auspicious.

Regardless of your vantage point within our current education system, we can likely agree that the majority of our classrooms are not reflecting critical twenty-first-century shifts in this emerging digital age. We are finding a growing disconnect between the traditional school model and the demands and opportunities of the evolving workplace. The argument in support of school and system transformation is often messaged as an economic imperative—and for good reason. The discrepancy between the current school experience of most students and employer expectations for individual agency and problem solving—among other skills—is real and compelling. However, there is a social justice imperative at the heart of personalized learning that is equally powerful and urgent.

All students do not have equal access to high quality learning opportunities. Too many high school graduates enter college or the workforce unprepared for success. A growing number of disenfranchised students describe school as boring, frustrating, irrelevant, a waste of time, exhausting, and unnecessary. Cell phones, social media, and search engines enable students to tap into the world around them at an earlier age and an increasing rate, making siloed coursework, teacher-directed assignments, and chapter tests less meaningful every year.

Additionally, our US population continues to diversify, highlighting the ineffectiveness of our one-size-fits-all education system. Over the last thirty-five years, the number of low-income families has increased by 7 percent, the number of

English learners has increased by 5 percent, and the number of students diagnosed with disabilities has increased by 6 percent.[8] A recent survey shows a growing number (20 percent) of millennials identify as LGBTQ; taken together, these statistics demonstrate how essential it is for our schools and classrooms to treat students as individuals with multifaceted identities and needs.[9]

The state of Massachusetts presents a particularly interesting case study. The state has long been considered a national leader in school reform, with a strong accountability system and globally competitive standardized test scores.[10] Yet, Massachusetts had some of the largest achievement gaps in the country when 2015 NAEP test results were disaggregated by race, income, and language.[11] In a fascinating 2017 study by the Center for Collaborative Education, Dan French and Diana Lebeaux uncover the realities within one of our most revered state education systems: "No longer can a one-size-fits-all education system, that currently does not adequately educate [Massachusetts's] diverse student body, educate every one of our students; in fact, it never has. Our increasing student diversity is unmasking the urgent need to differentiate our practices and how we organize our schools."[12]

Education in the United States has always been heralded as the great equalizer. When we consider achievement gaps across race, income, language, and learning needs that have continued to persist and grow through the various incremental school reform efforts of the twentieth century, we must acknowledge our most underserved students will continue to be marginalized without an intentional change of course.

There is promise in the scaling of personalized models as they empower teachers to understand, value, and support the unique, multifaceted nature of students. If our goal is to provide every public school student with an education leveraging individual strengths, identities, and interests in order to produce learners who feel engaged, inspired, and motivated, then school must look and feel fundamentally different. Our students are ready for this transformation. We need to be ready, too. Before embarking on a plan for a new personalized learning initiative, it is important for educators to build their knowledge of the core elements of personalized learning, learn about the various practices associated with each element, and understand the major shifts involved in increasing instructional personalization for students.

CRITICAL ELEMENTS OF PERSONALIZED LEARNING

Personalized learning marks a change in the way we educate students that is inherently learner-centered. Based on our work in schools and districts across Rhode

Island, we frame personalization as a learning paradigm that can be stretched and configured to local conditions while centering on core elements. (See figure 2.1.) Over time, three core elements of personalized learning have emerged through our efforts in partner schools and districts:

1. We can personalize learning by differentiating and scaffolding learning for students based on current proficiency levels, cognitive skills, and social-emotional profiles. We call this element *differentiation*.
2. We can personalize by enabling students to progress through competency-based progressions or a well-sequenced curriculum at their own pace without waiting for their teacher or peers. We call this element *pacing*.
3. We can personalize by emphasizing self-directed learning and student ownership; by offering students increased voice and choice; and through a focus on individual identity, interest, and ability. We call this element *agency*.

Our core elements organize central concepts of personalized learning while reaffirming research-based learning principles outlined in seminal works including *How People Learn,* edited by John D. Bransford, Ann L. Brown, and Rodney R. Cocking and *Inside the Black Box: Raising Standards Through Classroom Assessment*

FIGURE 2.1   Core elements of personalized learning

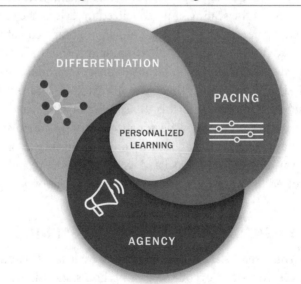

by Paul Black and Dylan William.[13] We see a common through-line across our core principles that emphasizes the importance of teaching with student "preconceptions" and "initial understandings" at the forefront of instructional design. Ultimately, this reduces the concept of personalized learning to one essential theory: in order to maximize learning, our schools and districts must meet students where they are. The field has generated enough research and experience to demonstrate that this concept, above all others, should drive personalized learning decisions and implementation. This position is further articulated in a 2017 white paper from CompetencyWorks entitled, "Meeting Students Where They Are." Authors Antonia Rudenstine, Sydney Schaef, and Dixie Bacallao state that mature student-centered learning models require "that we begin with a commitment to know our students in profound ways—academically, cognitively, culturally, emotionally, linguistically, physically, behaviorally—and not where a grade-based standard or a district-mandated course sequence suggests they should be."[14] We use our three core elements to frame conversations and focus on what truly matters in this work; we define them next.

Differentiation: Initiatives in this element generally focus on adjusting instruction, content, classroom support, and opportunities based on current student proficiency levels. Differentiated instruction models, such as Universal Design for Learning (UDL) and response to intervention (RTI), embrace this element of personalized learning. The collection and analysis of student data is a hallmark of this element, leading to data-driven decision making, customized instruction, and differentiated content. How we define data is a critical caveat to consider. While our system assigns a lot of weight to nationally normed assessments, we believe there is also power in the qualitative and informal information routinely collected by teachers to drive instruction and better understand unique student profiles.

Pacing: Traditional classrooms require students to move in lockstep through a problem, lesson, unit, and grade level. The element of pacing changes the classroom experience by allowing students to move ahead when they are ready and spend more time on a concept when needed, prioritizing mastery as a core principle, rather than seat time or task completion. Central to this element is consistent student access to the curriculum, both in and out of school. Initiatives around competency-based learning progressions, flipped instruction, and adaptive software allow students and teachers to play with pacing. A critical caveat to note within this domain is the importance of student-to-student and student-to-teacher relationships in learning. Opportunities for group dialogue, debate, and collaboration are essential and must be intentionally built into models that support pacing and self-directed learning.

Agency: Classrooms that shift to support increased student voice, choice, and agency empower students as individuals with unique strengths, interests, and identities. Efforts within this element seek to improve engagement and motivation by infusing the curriculum with relevance and purpose for each learner. Practices such as student goal setting, individual feedback loops, multiple assessment options, student-created curriculum, and project-based learning increase student choice and ownership. Our caveat in this domain is the challenge of maintaining appropriate rigor when incorporating elements of student agency. Current resources have not yet caught up to new demands.

CONNECTING THE BUZZWORDS

If mastery is the goal and personalization is the challenge, then blended learning is a key strategy. We use this statement to describe how we view the interaction between three distinct terms that are often confused and used interchangeably: mastery, personalized learning, and blended learning. Even though this sentence has become Highlander Institute's call to action, it was originally written to explain the interplay of these overused buzzwords because we often fielded the questions, "What is the difference between blended learning and personalized learning?" or "How does personalized learning support mastery-based progressions?" Our statement, while not comprehensive, is our best attempt at illustrating the relationship between these three terms as well as our personal "why" behind this work.

We believe mastery of essential competencies is the goal of education, and personalization enables mastery for more students. Pockets of "offline" personalized learning exist, but these models are difficult to achieve at scale and are often only effective with small cohorts of students who do not struggle academically.[15] It is our contention that when aligned to stated goals and leveraged in connection with strong teaching, the use of high quality education technology can enable previously elusive aspects of personalization to become sustainable and replicable through blended learning strategies.[16]

Mastery is the Goal

One can argue mastery of core competencies has always been the goal of educa-tion. However, implementing mastery models in schools that still operate within age-based cohorts and performance benchmarks is inherently complicated. Stu-dents have had to learn effectively within stand-and-deliver classrooms and navi-gate pacing constraints that are established by the system and operationalized by their teachers. Over time, students with different learning preferences and pacing needs have not pursued higher levels of math, science, writing or (name any subject here). Continuous gaps in their foundational knowledge have resulted from years of attaining minimal to moderate proficiency levels but still advancing to the next grade or course based on the school-year calendar. Students hit a wall when these gaps become overwhelming, disengage, decide they "aren't good" at the subject, and pursue other options.

The revised goal of education must become mastery of core competencies for *all* students. Personalized learning approaches must align to the unique potential, pacing needs, and passion areas, empowering anyone with the requisite desire and persistence to design, create, research, and compete within their fields of interest. On-demand content, adaptive software, and flipped learning strategies have begun to address long-standing and legitimate excuses about the complexity and unsustain-ability of guaranteeing mastery for every student across domains. Yet, as we consider how to unravel legacy constructs such as bell schedules, grade levels, and seat time, a new challenge is emerging. Namely, determining what competencies are most impor-tant for students to master and whether all students should master all competencies.

The Partnership for 21st Century Learning frames key subject-level content within the context of career and life skills: the four Cs (critical thinking, commu-nication, collaboration, and creativity) and digital media and technology skills.[17] Model standards for Career Technical Education in states such as California have explicitly linked competencies to industry standards and have developed standards in partnership with industry leaders.[18] The Collaborative for Academic, Social, and Emotional Learning (CASEL) has outlined a framework for social and emotional learning competencies.[19] The International Society for Technology in Education (ISTE) has created standards for students, highlighting competencies such as stu-dent voice, student-driven learning, creativity, and discovery within a lens of digital skills.[20] The Stanford Center for Assessment, Learning, and Equity (SCALE) con-nects the concept of student competency to performance tasks scored by rubrics.[21]

Dispositions for learning—such as persistence, motivation, and grit—are gaining traction, as well as competencies around student civic engagement.

There is no shortage of perspectives on the most important competencies for students to master. Educators are in the difficult position of having to straddle a policy environment where traditional competencies continue to be measured and publicized as new competencies emerge and must be prioritized. There are simply too many competing demands for our current system to manage. As federal and state leaders grapple with codifying next-generation standards and competencies, educators and leaders have some freedom to explore this new frontier. Amidst the confusion, leaders can start small by focusing on the development and evaluation of a few critical competencies that would make the most impact on their specific student populations.

Personalization Is the Challenge

The complexity of personalized approaches is the central challenge to transforming instruction at scale. Students require different conditions, delivery models, opportunities, support, and environments in order to be happy and successful at school. We are left with a huge design challenge—how to support a massive range of learners across a massive range of competencies. Most educators would agree that redesigning school to empower a range of unique individuals is worth the effort, but they are unsure where to find the solutions necessary to support this concept.

The Universal Design for Learning movement is a powerful framework for personalization that exemplifies this design challenge. Consider the three UDL principles emphasizing the primary neurological networks impacting learning:

1. The recognition network affects *what* students learn, with effective instruction giving learners various modalities for acquiring information.
2. The strategic network mediates *how* students process information, with effective instruction providing learners alternatives for demonstrating what they know.
3. The affective network regulates student *attitudes and motivations*, with effective instruction tapping into student interests and offering the right level of rigor.[22]

Implementing these UDL tenets can vastly improve the student experience in any classroom, but in order to do so, teachers must redesign large components of their curriculum, including goals, methods, materials, and assessments. Lesson-plan guidance developed by leaders at CAST, an organization that incubated UDL as a framework for improving teaching and learning, offers teachers thirty checkpoints across nine guidelines when considering how to instruct students.[23] In an average elementary classroom where an educator teaches four subjects a day to twenty-six students, implementation quickly becomes infeasible when it falls on the shoulders of individual teachers. There is just not enough time in the day to effectively sort content by the modalities, pathways, assessment strategies, and engagement models while also considering diverse learning preferences, student trauma, special needs, and language barriers. The complexity of this approach is a sticky challenge and significantly impacts implementation, replication, and scale.

We would like to take a moment to reinforce that personalization is the challenge, not the solution. We strongly believe that achieving any personalized model at scale requires the savvy integration of blended learning.

Blended Learning Is Our Key Strategy

At the end of the day, nothing changes at scale in education without efficient systems to support teacher practice and workflow. If we cannot design something at least 90 percent of a teaching faculty can successfully implement, then our lofty visions for personalized learning will become another smoldering log on the hearth of education reform. We must create what Jon Deane, Deputy Director at Chan Zuckerberg Initiative, once described as "a system that drives behavior."[24]

Differentiating instruction, customizing approaches, planning curricular extensions, setting individual goals, supporting student-developed tasks, and managing project work requires efficiencies only digital solutions can offer. Scaling these approaches depends on seamless, user-friendly, interoperable products that allow teachers to change the way they spend time rather than adding additional demands to their already taxing schedules and job descriptions. As schools and districts identify the facets of personalization they aspire to deliver, we believe leaders must "hire" blended learning to support implementation. Blended learning has incredible power and potential when it is aligned to a specific personalization problem and integrates high quality face-to-face instruction and targeted digital curriculum—with student data driving instructional decisions.

Let's revisit the UDL approach. In a high-functioning UDL classroom, technology serves as a catalyst for making learning accessible to all students. Imagine a learning management system that includes a bank of high quality performance tasks, all tagged to academic standards and UDL principles. Teachers could quickly search for and assign tasks to students based on learning profiles, interests, and proficiency levels. Depending on the activity at hand, students could use a device to write an essay, dictate an audio file, create a visual representation, develop a mind map, record a performance, or prototype an invention, all to demonstrate mastery of a single core standard or competency. Simultaneously, the teacher could conference with individual students and run mini-lessons, emphasizing executive-function strategies targeted to the needs of specific students. Blended learning is presently our best shot at moving beyond our current human capacity challenges and workflow issues and toward coherent and sustainable personalized practices.

The Blended Learning Universe has defined several blended learning models such as station rotation, lab rotation, individual rotation, flipped classroom, flex, a la carte, and enriched virtual.[25] These are important starting points for leaders to consider as they align technology to personalized approaches; however, we do not recommend schools select a model and call it a day. Rather, we encourage school leaders to explore different approaches and continuously combine or remix models based on local priorities. In the chapters ahead we often combine terms, using *blended* and *personalized learning* to demonstrate the value of technology integration in the implementation of personalized practices.

Our traditional education system is just starting to be unbundled and reconfigured. During what will certainly be a lengthy and messy process, education stakeholders at all levels must get used to living in an uncomfortable space—where our lack of control over the larger system meets our actual control over the smaller systems we interact with on a daily basis. While mastery, personalization, and blended learning are complex terms requiring deeper exploration, we are encouraged by the ways pioneering leaders, design teams, and individual teachers are integrating these three concepts—even within traditional systems—to create better learning environments for students. Jason illustrates the kinds of shifts that are possible at the classroom level as teachers explore the interplay between personalization, mastery, and blended learning.

Jason's Story

Jason is a veteran high school math teacher in a high performing suburban school district in Rhode Island and is one of Highlander Institute's first Fuse RI fellows. He is responsible for delivering content on a timeline developed by his math department and administering common assessments on the department schedule. As a caring and dedicated teacher, Jason was pleased that most of his students were successful in his courses but constantly looked for ways to support and engage his struggling students beyond providing after-school help.

In June of 2013, Jason received an iPad for Father's Day and immediately started playing around with various screencasting apps. He made an exam review video for his algebra course and posted it on YouTube as an optional resource for his students. A few days later, his students stayed after class with praise for the video concept, articulating how powerful it was to be able to pause and rewind the teacher as they reviewed concepts. One student described his learning preference, explaining how he liked to consider how to approach a problem and determine what he understood and what he didn't before Jason walked him through the solution. Jason's traditional class model never allowed the time or space for this approach, which was infinitely frustrating for this student. The student feedback was a pivot point for Jason, allowing him to see the potential of technology to increase personalization for his students.

Over the next summer, Jason pitched the idea of "flipping" his geometry classroom to his math chair. His teaching schedule was reconfigured so that he only had one prep (geometry), which freed him up to create videos and related activities for students to watch and complete on their own schedule and at their own pace. Through trial and error he iterated on the "flipped model," handing more control to students over when and how they worked through a unit. With the department pacing guide and common assessment schedule still intact, Jason set soft deadlines and actively supported the daily progress of students as they moved through lessons at their own tempo. Students worked independently or in a small group and could maximize class time to eliminate homework. Some watched videos at home while doing problems in class, while others worked exclusively in class, or through some combination that met their needs.

In year two, after wrestling with resources and data that spanned spreadsheets, an app, a web-based program, and a learning management system, Jason moved his curriculum into a single platform that he researched and vetted with his principal. Now he loads his content into one place, instantly views student progress, and identifies patterns of incorrect answers for an individual student or across the entire class—while students receive instant feedback on the problems they complete. Jason consults the class data frequently as he roves around the classroom in his rolling office chair, meeting with students to game plan, clear up misconceptions, answer questions, or conference with students who may be falling behind. Groups convene around a whiteboard for more formal mini-lessons or discussions. Extensive resources are organized into digital playlists of lessons, problem sets, and supplemental activities that clarify the "bare bones" work that all students must complete to be ready for unit tests and that offer additional levels of practice and challenge, depending on what students may need.

Student feedback on Jason's new instructional model has been uniformly positive. Students appreciate the independence to complete work on their terms, develop skills at their own pace, and ask questions in a small tutorial setting. With 24/7 access to playlists, they can get a head start on challenging lessons and spend extra time on practice problems when needed. From Jason's perspective, the model is "no worse than the traditional model for anyone, and it is a significant improvement for many."[26] He has found that he has developed much stronger relationships with his students through the two-way dialogue that accompanies small tutorials versus the one-way dialogue that was a hallmark of his lectures. He has significantly reduced boredom and frustration—chronic enemies of strong classroom culture—while building student persistence, confidence, and grit. Students can't sit passively in class anymore. If they aren't doing anything, they aren't learning anything.

School and district leaders need to be on the lookout for teachers who are exploring ways to integrate mastery, personalization, and blended learning in their pedagogy. There are many ways to approach the work in support of students at all levels—and we have found pioneer teachers experimenting in every single one of our partner schools. While traditional systems do not need to be dismantled for the work to start, leaders must understand that replication and scale will require a restructuring of the larger system and be prepared and willing to tackle that challenge. Otherwise, they will be forced to settle for isolated examples of strong practice.

A PERSONALIZED LEARNING PROGRESSION

In order to help school and district leaders understand the key shifts required to move away from traditional, teacher-centered classrooms and contemplate how to plan personalized learning initiatives, we developed a personalized learning progression (figure 2.2). The progression leans heavily on the blended learning models developed by the Christensen Institute as well as iNACOL's initial Blended Learning Teacher Competency Framework, which articulates teacher competencies that are necessary to support blended learning implementation.[27] It focuses on the core elements of differentiation and pacing, outlining the benefits and potential drawbacks of deepening implementation in these two areas.

Our progression helps leaders envision change by determining where they are, where they want to go, and what initial strategies and systems are necessary

FIGURE 2.2   Personalized learning progression

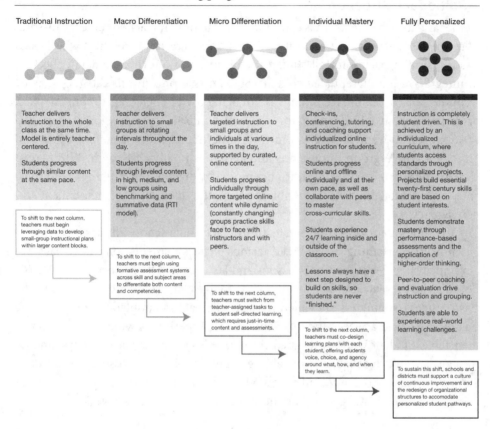

to support their shift. The path a district takes through the progression is not necessarily linear, and the goal is not necessarily to land every school or district at the far right in the "fully personalized" stage. The decision to aim in one direction or another across the progression impacts the scope of work. Next, we preview the progression and provide a classroom example at each stage. We consider the progression again in chapter 4 as a resource for establishing a design team vision for personalized learning pilots. We are careful to emphasize this is a non-judgmental progression. The goal is to trigger a conversation in which all stakeholders, including students, parents, and teachers, have a chance to build a collective vision for blended and personalized learning and pave the way for effective strategic planning.

Traditional Instruction

At the far left of the spectrum is traditional instruction or teacher-centered instruction. In this category, the majority of classrooms are implementing whole-class lessons, similar pacing for all students, and little to no formative data collection or integration of differentiated content. Some classrooms in this category may be technology-rich, but the technology is not being used to personalize content, pace, or instruction. It is important to note that while this progression is designed to support a movement away from traditional instruction, there are times and places for whole-group discussions and activities in any classroom. While most classrooms operate within a traditional model by default, this design is not inherently bad; personalization is possible through the integration of elements of student agency.

YouTube videos are a common feature of Jack's high school physics lessons, giving him an entertaining way to make various physics elements come alive. Jack has developed slide decks for all his lessons and lectures that he projects on a SMART Board as he presents. Students sit in pairs at tables and take notes for most of the class. Student volunteers are called up to participate in simulations during some classes, and once a week students replicate an experiment with their partner at their table. Student work is assigned through a learning management system and students are able to collaborate on lab reports and problem sets using the platform. Students are quizzed every Friday and take a chapter test every three weeks. Extra help is available for struggling students after school three times a week.

Macro Differentiation

To the right of traditional instruction lies macro differentiation, which is an actionable starting point for teachers looking to begin to differentiate through a blended learning approach. The focus is on utilizing formative data to establish three instructional groups and deliver targeted instruction in a small group setting—essentially an RTI approach. Many teachers implement the station rotation model during this stage, with differentiated instruction delivered through both online and teacher-facing methods. A red flag to look out for in this model is enduring proficiency-based groups that prevent interaction or collaboration between students across competency levels. It is important to regroup students frequently and find time for heterogeneous group activities. Across groups, all students should engage in appropriately rigorous curriculum.

Leslie organizes daily literacy instruction for her first-grade students around three centers. Each week she builds groups based on interim assessment data, information collected from adaptive software programs, and a review of student work. Each day, Leslie leads differentiated instruction tailored to the needs of each group by using a station rotation format. While one group works with Leslie, another group works at the computer center on an adaptive software program that allows them to work on the specific phonics skills they need to build. The third group engages in a collaborative activity that is differentiated to support their current reading level. Students at this station consult their personal binders to confirm their level for the week, find a partner with a similar level, gather the appropriate materials, and then move forward with the activity. At the end of a twenty-minute period, Leslie rings a bell to signal students to get ready to transition. A minute later, she rings the bell again and students move to the next station.

Leslie provides explicit scaffolding to support the differing needs of each group as they transition to the activity center. Some groups have more structure and some have more choice and independence; some activities may support remediation, while others may focus on challenging applications. (If all students are completing the same exact work at each center, there is no differentiation present and this would not be an example of macro differentiation.) To help with classroom management, an "ask me" lanyard is worn by student leaders at each center, who issue bathroom passes, help with questions, and troubleshoot technology issues to prevent teacher interruptions. At the conclusion of center time, students engage in common experiences, including read alouds, discussions, and collaborative activities.

Micro Differentiation

This phase of the progression is a natural next step as classrooms begin to leverage formative assessment data to make more targeted and frequent decisions regarding differentiation around more nuanced skills and competencies. The regular use of online assessments and observation allows teachers to move beyond a three-group approach to establish smaller—or more micro—clusters of students based on cognition, proficiency, interests, identity, or social emotional needs. Teachers use data to frequently regroup students into different configurations to maximize instructional time—including student feedback data collected through exit slips or surveys. Some micro-differentiation strategies include one-on-one tutorials; peer tutoring; interest-based activity groups; and small-group instruction. Instead of sitting through lessons or content they have already mastered, or continuing to struggle without necessary scaffolding, students receive targeted daily instruction through a combination of online, teacher-directed, and peer-collaboration activities.

In Mike's fifth-grade ELA classroom, each unit starts with a whole-class introduction and a pre-assessment. Students are assigned to one of four playlists based on their pre-assessment results. Each playlist is connected to a set of missions and teacher-led mini-lessons. Playlists are differentiated in terms of vocabulary, reading levels, and challenge levels. Struggling students have more skill-building tasks and start each day in a teacher-led session where they are supported through application tasks that require scaffolded information or vocabulary. Students working at grade level have a mix of skill-building and application tasks and meet with the teacher three times a week. Advanced students have more application tasks and conference with the teacher two times a week. Students have some choice over the activities they complete and can work individually or with a partner. Mike tracks the progress of all students through quick exit tickets at the end of mini-lessons, daily student reflections, and submitted work. Students can also designate a red, yellow, or green status update through a website on their laptop, and Mike tracks these designations in real time on his iPad, inviting "red" students to meet with him between mini-lessons and connecting "yellow" students to peers for support. Students who fall behind, finish early, or have problems are identified to meet with Mike first thing the following morning for redirection and support. Students come together periodically to engage in whole-class activities. At the end of each unit, students transition together to project-based learning activities and conclude the unit with assessments or performance tasks.

Individual Mastery

The shift to individual mastery is perhaps the most challenging within the progression, requiring significant school infrastructure and policy shifts that allow students to transcend the limitations of grade-based cohorts. In this phase, the school and classroom evolves, allowing students to move through content and develop skills at their own pace. Students receive support through preferred modalities, which can include online content, teacher-directed small-group support, peer collaboration, and self-directed work time. Assessment dashboards alert teachers and students when competencies have been mastered or when additional help is required. Whole-group activities and student-led presentations are facilitated at the discretion of the teacher and also punctuate the learning environment. Because students are able to move at their own pace, it becomes increasingly difficult for students to find peers to work with and for the teacher to support a wide range of potential questions. This model is extremely difficult to implement without a comprehensive, sequenced, multi-grade curriculum (including assessments) that can be managed digitally. Schools without this infrastructure are not ready for a self-paced model. Individual teachers cannot be responsible for designing and building curriculum on top of implementation.

Students enter Deb's fourth-grade classroom and gather for a morning meeting, where they greet each other and are presented with the daily agenda. Deb shares the lessons, discussions, or group work that will reunite the class over the course of the day and releases students to their first main work block. Students consult their playlist tasks across reading, math, and science and review their personalized learning goals, determining what they will work on, who they will work with, and when they will consult Deb in order to meet their weekly goals. Tasks are varied and differentiated and include formative check-ins, both electronically and in-person with Deb, so both she and her students know when they are ready to move on. As students approach the end of a unit, they have the option of taking Deb's assessment, creating their own assessment, or developing their own performance task to demonstrate mastery. Oftentimes, these finished products are added as playlist resources for peers.

Much of Deb's time in the classroom is spent checking in, conferencing, and clearing up misconceptions with individual students. Between conferences, she keeps an eye on the individual progress of all students on her laptop and calls small groups together in real time to add challenges, build skills, or facilitate discussions. Homework is not formally assigned, but students can access all class resources and curriculum at home and can use the extra time to catch up, practice, explore, or move ahead in the curriculum. Individualized weekly goals help students determine how much time they need to spend on assignments each day.

Fully Personalized

In fully personalized classrooms, most legacy school constraints—grade levels, bell schedules, single-subject courses, grades—are deconstructed at the school level, resulting in environments that more closely resemble adult and professional learning. The balance between online and face-to-face instruction loses uniformity and the need for established blended learning models decreases. Each student is guided by a personalized learning plan rather than a structured classroom workflow. Students in this phase demonstrate skill mastery in unique ways and focus on opportunities and topics that resonate most with them. Curriculum can be student designed or co-created and is articulated in a learning plan that serves as a road map for building knowledge and competencies throughout a term. Teacher check-ins with students are less frequent but longer in duration, focusing on content clarification, ongoing performance assessment, and tailored goal setting. There is a heavy emphasis on individual proficiency, which can be tracked through real-time data dashboards or manually by students. A defined system of accountability informs all stakeholders of student progress toward the mastery of learning goals and competencies.

Students enter Beccy's high school advisory on Mondays, Wednesdays, and Fridays and get settled for a forty-minute whole-group learning session that begins and concludes each of their days on campus. This time is teacher-directed and includes goal setting, exposure to different fields and content areas, conversations about current events, Socratic seminars, critical thinking exercises, and/or direct instruction at Beccy's discretion. Students spend the rest of the day—with the exception of a one-hour math seminar—working on the individualized project work connected to their internship.

Beccy helps negotiate interest-based internships for each of her advisees and supports them as they design and manage related project work, which forms the backbone of their curriculum. The projects are varied in content and scope. One of her students worked in the visitor education department of the New England Aquarium. Once she became certified on the animals and ecosystems in various galleries, she was scheduled to support guest inquiries on her internship days. She was also asked to develop a live animal presentation. She researched an animal, tailored her message in a way that was engaging to children and adults, and practiced in front of her mentor. Once the presentation was polished, her animal talk was printed on the aquarium schedule each day she was on site.

With no formal courses and no "teachers," all students work toward custom learning goals aligned to their internships. They also engage in common experiences. Each of Beccy's advisees must complete three narratives, three research papers, and three exhibitions each year. They are also responsible for weekly journal assignments and regular math work. At the school level, all students must submit a seventy-five-page autobiography by the time they graduate, complete a senior thesis project, and apply to at least one college. Many students earn job-related certifications connected to their internships. Most students leave school with credit from at least one college course due to a close relationship with the community college, which is located a block away from the school.

Beccy establishes deep relationships with her sixteen advisees—who stay with her over the course of four years—and is able to take a long view of their learning and growth. She shepherds them at their own pace, determining when to push academics and when to support personal growth at points in their development. Throughout high school, students control the "what," "where," and "how" of their learning experiences.

Moving Across Progression Stages

At each level of the progression, the use of formative data, differentiated instruction, and elements of student agency are ramped up to create learning environments that are progressively more tailored to where students are and where they want to go. While it may seem exciting to push to the far right of the progression, it is important for teams to set realistic expectations and understand the preferences of local stakeholders. Each phase is a complex transition, and both teachers and students require careful scaffolding and support to successfully shift their roles and responsibilities.

● ● ●

Defining how personalized learning will improve the student experience and support critical student outcomes in a school or district is not an easy task for leaders. We have seen leaders set an agenda based on their gut, their neighboring district, or a particularly loud parent. We have also watched leaders as they study the conditions of their schools and contemplate specific personalization approaches that resonate with their local communities. We believe this is the better path and offer our definitions and framework to support these efforts. Once leaders have begun to grapple with the personalization problem they will design around, it is time to gather additional stakeholders and data before collaborating on a local vision and scope of work.

LAYING THE GROUNDWORK

Prior to 2012, the Highlander Institute team focused on "leveling the field" for students by supporting district reading instruction and narrowing the literacy gap—particularly among underserved students. Generally, our district partners were exclusively interested in increasing student achievement scores on state assessments and initiated collaborative reform projects with us when their current student performance did not measure up to expected local, regional, or state outcomes.

Our point person for these projects was often a district director of curriculum. Curriculum was an important component of our project work, and we encouraged leaders to invest in a comprehensive literacy program that supported tiered instruction. In many cases, new curriculum was purchased and district teachers were provided a certain amount of professional development by the publisher. Subsequently, they were asked to abandon all previous literacy materials in favor of complete fidelity to the newly purchased program.

Our literacy projects were successful—sometimes significantly—at increasing student achievement metrics. However, we were cognizant that our model stopped short of reaching students who did not fit neatly into three instructional groups, whose needs could not be met by a single curriculum, or who did not find the curriculum readings relevant or compelling. Often, the most adept teachers felt hamstrung by their inability to draw on their own wealth of knowledge and expertise. Significant time was spent coaxing reluctant teachers and ensuring compliance with the new curriculum and protocols rather than focusing efforts on how to best utilize new resources to meet diverse student needs. Coaching and professional development were centered on the practices and information that we felt were most important. Consequently, workshops and embedded coaching were relevant to the teachers who shared our perspectives, and less relevant to those who did not. While instruction in some classrooms witnessed large and positive shifts, there was little change in the daily experience for many students. Scale and sustainability were issues across every single one of our district partnerships, with systems often falling apart once our engagement concluded.

As we considered how to refine our change management process, we realized that presenting districts with a relatively scripted solution and a one-size-fits-all training structure prevented teachers from connecting reform efforts to their most pressing needs. Some teachers needed to prioritize classroom management and culture before tackling data protocols and phonics. Others were already adept with our priority skills and were ready for more nuanced support. Furthermore, our well-intentioned efforts to swoop in with all the answers prevented local leaders from owning the initiative and developing the capacity to continue the work once we were gone.

Our shift from supporting traditional district change projects toward guiding personalized initiatives has caused us to redefine the lead role within our reform work, rethink the scope of initial planning efforts and decision making, and redesign the composition and tasks of a project team. In this chapter, we outline the infrastructure necessary to design a successful pilot initiative. We start by defining the most important roles required to enact true and lasting change: the lead change agent and design team members.

THE LEAD CHANGE AGENT

Systems, schools, and classrooms do not redesign themselves. In fact, left alone they do the opposite, sitting in stagnant status quo for decades despite a constant murmur of discontent. Throughout our various partnerships, we have noticed that a key player has often organized and catalyzed early-stage progress in successful endeavors. We call these leaders *lead change agents*, and they possess a range of roles from teachers to building principals, to coaches, to district curriculum or technology directors. We have watched lead change agents clearly take the helm in some cases, as well as step back and allow their team to divide and conquer the work in other situations. Whether designing at the school or district level, the key is to identify at least one person who is passionate about the work, epitomizes leadership, and brings a combination of interest, enthusiasm, knowledge, experience, and political capital to the table. Lead change agents must believe shifts in classroom practice can ultimately improve the student experience and be interested in creating opportunities to actively test their theories.

We have found lead change agents who are closer to the classroom (teachers or coaches) have enhanced credibility because of their deep contextual knowledge of students and families, as well as their ability to speak to current classroom successes and challenges. Administrators are equally adept at tackling the role of lead change agent, but many have experienced the onset of modern classroom technology from afar and not as a practitioners in the trenches. As Heather Lattimer pointed out in her 2012 paper on teacher leaders, "Engaging teachers as change agents not only extends the Principal's capacity for leadership; it also ensures that the change is authentic and appropriate to the context; that it is responsive to the needs of teachers and students; and that it will endure beyond the scope of an individual Principal's tenure or central office reform initiative."[1] Across Rhode Island, we have witnessed powerful examples of grassroots momentum bubbling up through the leadership of classroom teachers.

Whether the lead change agent is a teacher or superintendent, a mindset for change and continuous improvement sets the stage for success. Equally important is ensuring that the lead change agent is recognized and empowered by the highest level of school or district administration to assume this role. Most often we see examples of a single lead change agent spearheading this work, but in some cases multiple leaders with a similar vision collaborate to share the responsibilities of this galvanizing role.

SETTING AN INITIAL DIRECTION

Contrary to the district literacy project approach that was described previously, we do not recommend planning for the full implementation of any personalized learning endeavor at the outset of your redesign process. Bryk and colleagues provide a compelling historical perspective for starting smaller:

By definition, improvement requires change. Unfortunately, in education, change too often fails to bring improvement—even when smart people are working on the right problems and drawing on cutting-edge ideas. Believing in the power of some new reform proposal and propelled by a sense of urgency, education leaders often plunge headlong into large-scale implementation. Invariably, outcomes fall far short of expectations, enthusiasm wanes, attention wanders, and the school moves on to the next idea without ever really understanding why the last one failed. Such is the pattern of change in public education: implement fast, learn slow and burn goodwill as you go.[2]

The nature of blended and personalized learning initiatives provides additional justification for starting small. In a nascent field full of experimentation, change agents do not have the luxury of drawing on a large body of research to help them set a district course on day one. Best practices exist, and early-stage research points to the value of blended and personalized learning practices with regard to student outcomes, but this information needs to be translated into local contexts before attempting broad or prescriptive change.

Our pilot process creates nimble learning environments that are able to shift with changing circumstances, needs, and priorities. The goal is to empower strong teachers to test student-centered methods and learn what works for students, families, and teachers within a unique school or district. A pilot concludes when various stakeholders are convinced that the new approaches being implemented add value for students, and when leaders have gathered enough information about successful approaches to operationalize them in more classrooms. With this in mind, lead change agents have a series of initial decisions to make that will have a significant impact on the pace and success of pilot efforts.

Defining an Initial Pathway

While the course of an initiative will evolve and expand through the pilot process, lead change agents who have researched promising models, visited personalized classrooms, talked to early adopters, attended conferences, and joined professional networks are better positioned to consider relevant and promising initial approaches. Identifying areas of urgency within the school or district, considering an initial focus, and thinking about scope will help leaders effectively communicate their intentions and build the right team to shepherd this work. While these points will be validated by the design team, launching the process with a concept prevents the inefficiency that accompanies a tabula rasa start.

As a starting point, lead change agents can consider major elements of personalized learning—differentiation, pacing, and student agency—and select one or more, depending on alignment with local needs, tolerance for change, and timelines for implementation. Do you feel a sense of urgency to close gaps and support students in achieving better outcomes on state tests? If so, then your blended and personalized learning pilot may hinge on the ability to differentiate instruction for students. Your priority classroom practices may rely on strong assessment, creating targeted instructional groups, and giving students access to their own data so they can set growth goals. If you are more interested in encouraging students to be self-directed learners with the ability to move through content as they master concepts, then pacing may be your initial focus and your work may center on building competency progressions and performance tasks. Perhaps you are concerned by current levels of student engagement or question whether instruction and curriculum are responsive, relevant, and authentic for all students. In this case, you may choose to focus on elements of student interest, identity, and agency. Your initial work may prioritize what the Hewlett Foundation calls "deeper learning," a set of interrelated competencies focused on the integration of rigor and twenty-first century skills.[3] Or, you may focus on increasing student voice and choice in classrooms. Table 3.1 outlines a broad rationale for each element.

TABLE 3.1 **Charting an initial pathway**

CHOOSE DIFFERENTIATION IF . . .	CHOOSE PACING IF . . .	CHOOSE AGENCY IF . . .
• there is a sense of urgency to close academic gaps; • teachers believe in the concept of small-group instruction; • teachers believe in ongoing formative assessment and dynamic groupings; or • there is evidence that current student engagement, behavior, and achievement is connected to one-size-fits-all lesson delivery	• teachers have access to a comprehensive set of competencies tied to scaffolded curriculum; • students are exhibiting the ability to be self-directed and make decisions about their learning; • teachers are ready to offer students flexibility about how and when they can access work; or • there is evidence that allowing students to move at their own pace will improve student outcomes	• student engagement, motivation, and/or twenty-first-century competencies are core priorities; • teachers are ready to co-design curriculum and activities in partnership with students; • there is interest in moving toward student-centered learning practices; or • there is evidence that connecting content to student identity and interests will increase engagement/ attendance/behavior

We have found most leaders select one initial starting point but begin to add elements of the other two as they pilot and build momentum. For example, teachers focusing on differentiation may ultimately explore how to infuse student choice and interest into collaborative or independent work activities. Teachers allowing students to self-pace may think about expanding their focus to differentiate instruction for students at multiple academic levels. And teachers eager to connect curriculum to student interest and identity may also leverage tools to differentiate content by reading level or allow students to access various work choices without waiting for peers or the teacher. We believe there is a synergy between these elements, and the strongest examples of personalized learning often incorporate all three.

It is also possible to establish a pilot initiative with multiple focus areas, depending on the current level of interest and resources. At a high school in southern Rhode Island, for example, administrators defined six initial pathways to personalization and tasked departments with selecting a starting point that resonated most with their subject matter, teaching philosophy, and resources. The World Language department selected pacing, with the goal of creating more fluidity between course levels. The English department chose relevance and is working toward infusing student identity and interests into the curriculum. The Social Studies department focused on inquiry by elevating student voice and the creation of student-driven essential questions to promote ownership of content. Classroom culture, student goal setting, and differentiated instruction were also offered as possible options for department teams. Allowing teachers to have a voice in selecting a priority and designing a plan has been powerful, and piloting several strategies simultaneously has enabled teachers in different departments to learn from each other and accelerate implementation. However, it is important to clarify that schools cannot do everything at once. Ranking priorities and aligning implementation expectations with available resources is important and prevents the frustration often associated with moving too quickly.

In addition to direction, leaders should enter this work with a sense of scope. In some cases, pilots have targeted specific student populations such as English language learners (ELL) or students with individual education plans (IEPs); other pilot efforts have been directed toward specific schools or grade levels; still others have targeted a vertical content area across the district, such as math. An early sense of scope will help inform who should be added to the design team and who should be involved in initial information gathering conversations. It does not make sense to force a pilot implementation into a school where there is strong resistance or a principal who does not believe change is necessary. Aligning the scope of work to local strengths is a key consideration. Understanding where pockets of innovation are being seeded across the district leads us to the next action step for lead change agents: creating a design team.

ESTABLISHING A DESIGN TEAM

In our literacy reform example at the beginning of this chapter, an existing leadership team comprised of district administrators often became the ad hoc literacy project team. In hindsight, this was a mistake. Existing teams already have full agendas and often lack the capacity to take on a whole new realm of work. Most leadership teams are administrator heavy and top down. Not all team members who inherit the project are enthusiastic about its value, and blockers can significantly derail momentum. We believe that intentionally assembling design teams best positions personalized learning initiatives for success.

The term *design team* implies members are actively engaged in creating new and relevant learning models. Members do not simply follow an established task list. They must believe they can make a difference by contributing their experience, knowledge, perspectives, and creativity as they shape the pilot process. In the words of the international design firm IDEO, the work of a design team is "human-centered" (focused on the student and teacher experience), and operationalized through "inspiration, ideation, and implementation."[4] One of the most important decisions of a lead change agent is who to include on this initial team.

Ideal design teams are comprised of five to twelve members and include a mix of diverse and passionate stakeholders with different perspectives on the current system. At least 25 percent of members should be teachers, with at least one building leader and one representative from the district office. All design teams should have a system in place for integrating student voice, which can include student representation on the actual design team.

There are several characteristics design team members should share:

1. They should be leaders with high credibility among peers and colleagues
2. They should be adept at building and forging relationships
3. They should have a high sense of urgency and a desire to make change
4. They should reflect current student demographics including similar backgrounds and/or identities

Ideally, design teams should include members with specific expertise in three key areas. The first is experience implementing blended and personalized learning practices. The second is current and historical knowledge about school or district curriculum. The third is experience with data collection, analysis, and visualization. If a school or district does not have the internal capacity to fill these roles, external experts can be invited to join the team or serve as advisors when needed.

As John Kotter states, "Major organizational change . . . requires a team of people powerful and accountable enough to give credibility to the fact that change is essential."[5] Ultimately, the work done by the design team will only scale if the members are trusted and respected by their colleagues. It is less important to build a design team around the fastest moving and most tech-savvy individuals as it is to include educators and leaders who understand the importance of relationship building and continuous improvement.

In their book *Blended*, Michael Horn and Heather Staker describe four different types of teams: functional, lightweight, heavyweight, and autonomous. Our design team concept would be best described as autonomous, which "allows innovators to step outside of the existing context—including staffing, budget, facilities, and curriculum—to pioneer a new model."[6] Initially, our design team structure requires less authority and stakeholder buy-in than Horn and Staker suggest because the team is initiating a small-scale, rapid learning process. Some administrative participation is required to ensure buy-in, ongoing resource reallocation, and the necessary flexibility to test and try new ideas.

Administrator Voice

When initial pilot designs require additional teacher planning time, curriculum waivers, or funding, it is important to have administrators at the table who can sanction these changes. We encourage including a subset of administrators who are advocates of blended and personalized approaches and have the capacity to prioritize this work. In one of our larger partner districts, eager administrators were identified through a quick survey, which was disseminated by the lead change agent at the beginning of the design team recruitment process. Several questions relating to interest, curiosity, and willingness to learn were included in the survey, which helped the lead change agent identify leaders at the administrative level who possessed the right mix of knowledge, skills, and enthusiasm for this work.

Lead change agents will increase the likelihood of a successful initiative by recruiting as many strong principals to the design team as possible. As we discuss in chapter 11, an effective building leader plays a critical role in supporting pilot classrooms, communicating successes, and accelerating replication efforts. We consider the characteristics of strong principals to include a focus on communication and building relationships with students and teachers, being a visible and accessible presence in classrooms and across the school, and actively supporting and empowering talented teachers as they trailblaze a path toward better teaching and learning. Strong school culture is another key indicator of an effective school leader.

Teacher Voice

When recruiting teachers to the design team, consider factors such as union leadership, grade level, and content area variability, prior experience, the ability to build relationships and influence peers, as well as age, race, socioeconomics, gender, and sexual orientation to ensure diversity. Ideal teacher candidates have several characteristics in common:

1. They persist through challenges
2. They are willing to test and try new teaching strategies
3. They welcome feedback
4. They see students as partners in this work
5. They are comfortable with technology (but don't need to be technology experts)

When thinking about particular sensitivities that make teachers good design team candidates, it is helpful to consider the personality traits of groups across the diffusion of innovation curve. The diffusion of innovation theory was popularized by noted sociologist and communication expert Everett Rogers as a way of defining how innovations are adopted by a group of individuals.[7] Essentially, the theory offers a sequence of adoption based on the classification of individuals across one of five categories: innovators (risk takers), early adopters (visionaries), early majority (pragmatists), late majority (conservatives), and laggards (skeptics). An adapted version of the curve is found in figure 3.1. The theory posits that adoption is spread by "human interaction through interpersonal networks," with each adopter category influencing and guiding adoption for the next group.[8] The adoption of personalized learning approaches tends to follow a similar curve, with teachers across similar categories playing different roles in our change management process.

We have found that teachers who fall in the early adopter and early majority categories are best positioned to contribute to the design team. Early adopters have the mindset and capacity to translate new ideas into successful, concrete practices.

FIGURE 3.1   The diffusion of innovation theory

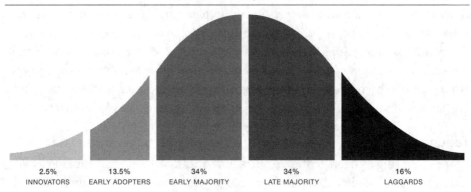

| 2.5% | 13.5% | 34% | 34% | 16% |
| INNOVATORS | EARLY ADOPTERS | EARLY MAJORITY | LATE MAJORITY | LAGGARDS |

Source: Based on Everett Rogers, *Diffusion of Innovations* (London and New York: Free Press, 1962).

More than innovators, who are generally viewed as excessively risky by peers, early adopters are eager to explore an innovation and make a case for change. Early majority teachers will adopt an idea when presented with adequate evidence. Their presence on a design team ensures that pilot work is deemed valuable and viable before the team considers replication. Later, in the grow phase, we will return to all categories of adoption along the curve to help leaders meet different needs of teachers as they replicate and scale the work.

In most scenarios, a few early adopter teachers will participate as design team members *and* pilot teachers. We have consistently found ownership, autonomy, and input are key drivers of a successful initiative, and teachers appreciate the opportunity to shape details of the work they will be running. The personalities and capacity of early adopter teachers position them well for this dual role; we discuss considerations for choosing early adopter teachers to lead pilot classrooms in more detail in chapter 5.

Student Voice

After selecting teachers, it is time to decide how to include student voice on the design team. Personalized learning initiatives are committed to student-centered approaches; consequently, students should be active designers. This may seem obvious, but establishing effective student participation takes thoughtful commitment and planning. Student voice is often first to get steamrolled when logistics get hard. At a recent information gathering session, a local lead change agent convened a diverse group of fifty stakeholders to share their perspectives on the current state of teaching and learning and included ten students. During the highly successful meeting, students were honest about perceived strengths and needs within their schools and helped pinpoint key problems of practice. The session ended with the lead change agent asking for volunteers to join the design team. All ten students expressed interest, but invitations were never issued as district leaders were reluctant to release students from class to participate in ongoing design meetings.

This leads to a second consideration around student voice: continuity. We have witnessed many well-intentioned efforts to include student voice in reform efforts through surveys, focus groups, or student interviews that do not extend beyond quick, initial attempts. Students can be understandably skeptical of these activities, particularly when they already feel marginalized within their school environment or when their input never leads to any noticeable changes in their school or classrooms. Design teams should consider how to continuously engage students in their planning and implementation efforts.

While offering students a seat at the design team table can be a great strategy, often students do not have the context or lexicon to contribute meaningfully to all facets of the process. Do not bring students to the design team table if you do not have the time and capacity to support their active participation. The most valuable efforts we have witnessed dedicate a portion of a design team agenda to soliciting structured student feedback. In a recent design team conversation, a middle school student was asked, "What do you think would make your classroom experience better?" Without missing a beat, the student replied, "We move from class to class with less than three minutes between bells. As soon as we get into our classroom the teacher jumps right into teaching his lesson. It would be great if we could have ten minutes to check in about how we're feeling and whether we're frustrated about something that happened before school, or in the hallway on the way to class. We never get a chance to express how we are doing during the day. People are angry and just want to talk about it."

As we continue to search for effective models for involving students in the design process, we find promise in the concept of co-generative dialogues, or cogens, conceived by Christopher Emdin in his 2016 book, *For White Folks Who Teach in the Hood . . . and the Rest of Y'all Too: Reality Pedagogy and Urban Education*.[9] Modeled after rap cyphers, cogens are structured conversations with a small, heterogeneous group of students with the goal of generating a plan of action for improving the classroom. Governed by explicit norms, cogens launch with students identifying small-scale reform ideas at the classroom level, such as how their teacher could open or conclude a lesson or what collective actions would improve student engagement. As students see the positive results of their participation manifest in the classroom, the group begins to tackle more sophisticated reforms together. The composition of cogens continuously changes as each participating student identifies a classmate to replace him or her and assumes a new leadership role in the classroom on a fixed schedule. While we encourage pilot teachers to use the cogens protocol within each of their own classrooms, we see value in developing a series of design team cogens to effectively integrate student voice into the ongoing design process.

Inviting students into the process requires time and commitment and is worth the effort. It demonstrates the willingness of a design team to break the mold of traditional project management and design in partnership with the primary stakeholders of their efforts. We will return to this concept many times throughout the book as a reminder to keep student voice at the center of this work.

Parent Voice

As we have gained experience supporting design teams, we have recognized the importance of including parent voice in redesign efforts. Families who spend thirteen to twenty years educating their children in the same school system often outlast a fair number of teachers and the vast majority of school and district leaders within a district. Too often, successful reforms disappear almost overnight when dynamic leaders leave for a new opportunity without cultivating a strong base of support. In a 2017 article called, "Notes From the Field: If You Want Great Schools, First Work With Parents to Create 'Actionable Demand,'" author Alex Cortez states, "[I]nnovations cannot reach their full potential without 'actionable demand' that removes the political and policy barriers preventing innovations from being embraced broadly by school systems."[10] Actionable demand can be created by parents who are informed, organized, and empowered, and design teams should consider how to collaborate with parents through the design process.

Parent voice can be incorporated into the self-study process (which we describe in the next section) through focus groups, conversations, surveys, or other means that offer parents a chance to share their perspectives on their children's school experiences. We also suggest that teams offer parents the chance to respond to self-study results and weigh in on the identified challenges and problems of practice uncovered during this process. As Cortez writes, "People don't try to solve problems they don't know they have. In too many school districts and cities, parents are not even aware of the inadequacy of their education systems."[11] We have also found that parents play an important role as design team members. In ideal situations, parents can be tactful but honest about the issues they encounter. There may be some awkwardness as the emphasis on problems of practice often brings focus to the dirty laundry, but parents will not have colleagues they may be trying to protect and are unlikely to sugarcoat challenges that may not otherwise receive the same level of scrutiny. Their perspectives ground the team in reality.

As design teams leverage existing communication systems and parent groups, they should be consistently on the lookout for parent leaders who can act as liaisons between the design team and the larger parent community and have the capacity to organize parents as advocates of the work. We are still in the initial stages of supporting these efforts in Rhode Island and look forward to sharing additional strategies and new breakthroughs in the future.

Communication Considerations

Drafting an informal memo of understanding (MOU) for potential members can help frame goals, member expectations, and benefits to add clarity to the design team recruitment process. It is important for potential members to understand how the work of this team will differ from a traditional project management team. An example MOU is included in appendix A. Lead change agents should also consider how to engage enthusiastic stakeholders who are not invited to sit on the design team. We purposely limit the size of design teams to keep conversations productive and manageable. However, lead change agents can find creative ways to include larger numbers of stakeholders by forming subcommittees or hosting periodic informational meetings to share design team plans and request feedback. We encourage lead change agents to collaborate early and often with anyone who has a similar mindset and excitement for the work. Design teams should never be considered exclusive clubs that only certain people are allowed to join.

Finally, it is important to remember perfection can be the enemy of innovation. The beauty of our Pathway to Personalization Framework is that every phase is additive and allows for cycling back to earlier phases when it makes sense to do so. Your initial design team may gather the wrong players around the table or you may need to restart design work multiple times before you have something worthy of piloting. Learning from mistakes is an important part of the process. In the words of Eric Ries, "If we hadn't built our first product—mistakes and all—we never would have learned . . . that our strategy was flawed."[12] The trick is to learn as quickly as possible. With a design team in place, the next step is to collect evidence on the strengths, conditions, and readiness indicators unique to your school or district.

STUDYING CURRENT CONDITIONS

A design team's first action step involves a self-study. Team members begin by assessing their own knowledge levels and developing plans for deepening their personalized learning expertise. Then, the team reflects on both the system capacities and human capacities currently in place to support the initiative. Finally, the team studies the current student experience.

Design Team Expertise

At one of our first district leadership meetings in a suburban Rhode Island district, administrators and school leaders sat around the table to discuss their vision for blended and personalized learning. One of the school principals interjected with a memorable statement, "I feel like I'm trying to recreate France and I've never been to France." This administrator (and many of his colleagues around the table) did not have enough background knowledge about blended and personalized learning to picture what he was trying to create. The fact that he brought up France was also interesting—an unfamiliar place that is uniformly accepted as worth visiting. It seemed his "why" for undertaking a blended and personalized initiative was not directly connected to a problem of practice within his school, but centered on the idea that "everyone else is doing it and it seems like a good idea." When design team members frame their urgency for change as a movement away from traditional education practices or as a desire to keep up with other districts—rather than as a solution to an identified challenge—productive forward movement is compromised.

Before establishing an initial direction, design team members should be able to articulate the relationship between blended learning, personalized learning, and mastery; identify the major classroom and instructional shifts required in the movement away from traditional practices; and understand some of the models, strategies, and resources available to operationalize these shifts. A wealth of materials has emerged to help educators understand the look and feel of blended and personalized learning experiences. With the abundance of white papers, websites, frameworks, and videos available, the issue is less about being able to access information and more about effectively vetting and curating the overwhelming amount of resources that are available. In an effort to support the curation process, we have included a list of organizations, publications, definitions, and thought leaders that have resonated the most with our team and the educators across our district partnerships. This information is organized and linked on our resources website. Lead change agents have the opportunity to model the use of asynchronous, self-paced learning by combining compelling resources and reflection activities into a playlist that design team members can access and complete online from the comfort of their own couches.

For design team members who still cannot quite picture France, site visits to model classrooms in the region or state are a worthwhile use of time. If you are not sure where to find exemplary classrooms in your area, contact your state department of education, search through the Christensen Institute Blended Learning Universe school directory, check out the list of Next Generation Learning Challenge grantees, or visit us during our annual conference in Providence, Rhode Island every April as we run site visits to model classrooms during the three-day event. When observing blended and personalized learning classrooms, it is important to spend at least twenty minutes in identified classrooms and at least twenty minutes debriefing with the teachers you observe. Note aspects of the classroom environment, instructional strategies, resources, and routines that are supporting personalization and ask about the planning, behavior shifts, and daily workflow required to implement the lessons you observe. Depending on your initial direction, you may want to tour classrooms specializing in differentiation, pacing, or student agency. At the end of the visit, reflect on what excited you most about the observation, what ideas you want to bring back, and what questions you have.

A third way for design team members to build their knowledge involves a personalized action plan. Lead change agents can assign each member the task of creating his or her own plan for deepening knowledge by joining a professional learning network (either face-to-face or virtually on a platform such as Twitter), following blogs, attending conferences (live or digitally recorded events), or leading book studies. Design team members can pursue learning pathways that work for them and report what they have learned to the team. There is never a point in the framework when members should stop building knowledge. The rapid evolution of the field requires members to continually integrate new ideas and best practices into the initiative. As teams deepen their understanding of blended and personalized learning, they should also study the local conditions necessary to support the implementation of effective pilot classrooms.

Studying Systems and Infrastructure

Before crafting a pilot initiative, it is helpful to study local conditions and identify both strengths and weaknesses. As teams survey the systems and infrastructure currently in place, there are several considerations to assess including time—one of the most precious commodities in education. Design teams will need time to create and launch pilot efforts, pilot teachers will need time to plan (ideally common planning time where they can collaborate), and all involved will need time to observe pilot classrooms and reflect on progress. Lead change agents should investigate the policies and procedures behind common planning time, hiring substitutes, scheduling meetings, and any other logistics requiring staff time. Understanding what flexibility exists within your system will be helpful as the work unfolds.

The current level of classroom barriers to personalization is a second category to evaluate. In order to launch pilots that use technology to increase personalization, pilot teachers will need access to adequate hardware, software, broadband, tech support, and increased autonomy. The results of a 2017 RAND study entitled "Informing Progress: Insights on Personalized Learning Implementation and Effects" offers teams a great starting point for reflection. The report identifies several obstacles teachers perceived to have either a major or minor impact on classroom personalization efforts, which are outlined in figure 3.2. Understanding the current impact of these obstacles provides a design team with important insights regarding school or district readiness to plan and launch pilot classrooms. We have adapted this table into a survey, which can be administered to an entire faculty or limited to the perspectives of design team members and/or district administrators.

Leading a successful personalized learning initiative requires a central focus on building, deepening, and managing relationships with a variety of stakeholders. Part of the initial work of the design team is to take stock of the current status of relationships within a school or district, clarify the roles intended for different stakeholders, and establish a targeted plan for cultivating critical advocates of the work. To guide this effort, the Highlander Institute has drafted a human capital assessment that can be tailored to local needs (appendix B). This form asks design team members to rate the current willingness of key stakeholders to engage in plan and pilot phase activities. Scoring occurs twice; once as the initiative is being conceived, and again as the design team prepares to support scaling efforts.

FIGURE 3.2   Obstacles perceived to personalized learning in the classroom

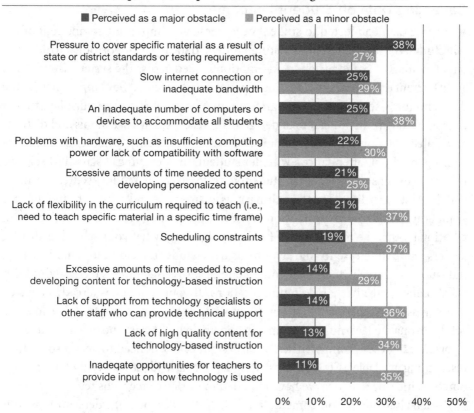

■ Perceived as a major obstacle   ■ Perceived as a minor obstacle

Pressure to cover specific material as a result of state or district standards or testing requirements — 38% / 27%

Slow internet connection or inadequate bandwidth — 25% / 29%

An inadequate number of computers or devices to accommodate all students — 25% / 38%

Problems with hardware, such as insufficient computing power or lack of compatibility with software — 22% / 30%

Excessive amounts of time needed to spend developing personalized content — 21% / 25%

Lack of flexibility in the curriculum required to teach (i.e., need to teach specific material in a specific time frame) — 21% / 37%

Scheduling constraints — 19% / 37%

Excessive amounts of time needed to spend developing content for technology-based instruction — 14% / 29%

Lack of support from technology specialists or other staff who can provide technical support — 14% / 36%

Lack of high quality content for technology-based instruction — 13% / 34%

Inadeqate opportunities for teachers to provide input on how technology is used — 11% / 35%

(Based on the responses of 525 teachers in the national comparison sample)[13]

*For a full list of all obstacles surveyed, download the RAND Survey Results Addendum, Studying Human Capital[14]

After analyzing initial ratings, design team members can begin to evaluate important knowledge and interest gaps, which can inform next steps for cultivating interest and buy-in across the system. The point of completing the assessment is to catalyze efforts to engage low-scoring stakeholder groups. Keeping key leaders in the loop will increase the engagement of all stakeholders when they are needed during the refine phase. Ideally, all scores will improve to the top score of three by the time the team is ready to scale. Feel free to adapt our human capital assessment to reflect your own players, organizational structures, and intended roles.

Collecting Data on Student Outcomes

Analyzing data connected to student outcomes is an important component of the self-study. The first dive into existing student data is an opportunity to identify targeted areas of academic or socio-emotional need across the system as well as to audit current data processes. Existing types of data collected, the completeness of the data, and the ease with which design team members can access and display student outcome data are all indicators of design team readiness. Most schools and districts can collect data on four outcome measures relatively easily: whether students are coming to school (attendance), whether students are behaving at school (discipline referrals/suspensions), whether students are learning at school (scores on math and ELA standardized tests/benchmark assessments), and whether students are graduating from school (promotion/retention/graduation rates). The availability of additional outcome metrics offers further insight into what your school or district leaders value. It is rare to find data measuring student socio-emotional learning, indicators of trauma, or student competencies across the four Cs (critical thinking, collaboration, creativity, and communication). If your school has already collected data across these outcomes, then you are most likely well on your way to developing a solid personalized learning program. If this data does not exist and you are interested in prioritizing these competencies, your design team will need to spend some time researching available assessment instruments. We have identified a list of alternative outcome measures, which we have included in our resource website.

Analyzing student outcome data can help the design team determine who is thriving within the current instructional system as well as who is not. Data sets should be sortable by subgroups so that team members can uncover specific student populations who are struggling, losing ground, or making very little progress. We encourage teams to use a data protocol as they look for patterns within various outcome measures. The ATLAS protocol was created by the School Reform Initiative and supports equity of voice while allowing all members to describe the data, make inferences, and share implications for future work.[15] The process moves from articulating facts to questioning and interpreting data, to discussing the implications for classroom practice. As design teams pore over their student data sets, they should be able to identify student populations who are not currently being well served and articulate related problems of practice.

A recent district design team meeting exemplifies this point. Within this district, the two schools being considered for pilot work both uncovered that Latino/a students were beginning the year significantly lower on interim assessments and making less growth than their peers over the course of the year. Additionally, it was discovered that Latino/a students had a disproportionate percentage of discipline referrals and school absences across both buildings. These findings were surprising to the design team and shifted the conversation, encouraging team members to further explore the current student experience of this subgroup and leverage redesign efforts to address these disparities.

Shadowing a Student

User-centered design focuses on building empathy for the current student experience and considering possible improvements from a student's perspective. Yanaiza, our principal from the introduction, constantly asks her teachers, "Would you want to be a student in your own classroom? If learners had a choice of whose room they could go to each morning, would they choose yours?" These are important questions, and we recommend that design team members deeply contemplate them by shadowing a student.

In 2014, the late Grant Wiggins posted an incredible reflection from a veteran high school teacher turned tech coach, which starts with the statement, "I waited fourteen years to do something that I should have done my first year of teaching: shadow a student for a day."[16] The former teacher proceeds to make three key observations after following and behaving as the host student for two days:

- Students sit all day, and sitting is exhausting
- High school students are sitting passively and listening during approximately 90 percent of their classes
- (As a student) You feel a little bit like a nuisance all day long

These three takeaways clearly establish a sense of urgency for redesigning the student experience. While many shadowing activities lead to the creation of small "school hacks" designed to improve the student experience, we encourage design teams to use the experience to inform the strategic direction of the initiative. Student shadows help to identify larger problems of practice and can form a compelling call to action.

In the previous example, the observer invested two full school days in the shadowing process, collecting evidence from two different students across twelve class periods—including transitions and lunch. Meeting host students at their homes offers additional perspective on challenges students face navigating to and from school. While design team members can determine the amount of time to dedicate to student shadowing, we recommend staying with a student for at least four hours including electives, transitions, and lunch.

Design team members should shadow different students and be intentional about the students they select, ensuring adequate representation across various demographics within the district (different grade levels, high-performing, low-performing, lunch status, ethnicity, ELL, special education, etc.). If you are focusing pilot efforts on a particular grade level or school, concentrate your shadowing activities accordingly and ensure the team selects a representative mix of students, not just those who are high-performing or well-behaved.

For example, Julia, a high school principal in an urban Rhode Island district, took the opportunity to shadow a graduating senior and is now incorporating shadowing as a regular activity for her entire leadership team.[17] The experience deepened her understanding of the daily challenges her students face, such as navigating snowy crosswalks to make the morning bus, searching for friends in a crowded cafeteria, trying to get to the bathroom between classes, and eating lunch in five minutes after a long lunch line. It also broadened her perspectives on learning processes that best meet student needs in the classroom as opposed to rubric indicators of "good teaching" that she usually looks for during classroom observations. The experience challenged Julia to consider and integrate student voice, making her a self-described better person and better leader. For design teams, student shadowing is not meant to be an isolated task that can be simply checked off a list. Rather, it is meant to change the entire narrative behind reform efforts, altering the lens of the design team as it continuously seeks to better understand and improve the student experience.

New resources are providing structure and support for creating an effective shadowing experience, such as the free materials available on the School Retool website.[18] Their templates and guidance can take you from preparation to shadowing, reflection, and action. Outlining your assumptions and establishing learning goals for your shadow day will help you think about the kind of evidence you want to collect through time studies, photos, videos, and student questions. The key element is to stay open to noticing and collecting data with an objective lens—with the goal of finding design flaws and personalization challenges you can address.

● ● ●

Getting started requires the management of many moving parts. Lead change agents have full discretion regarding how much time to dedicate to the tasks of setting an initial direction, understanding teacher interest, establishing a design team, and engaging in a self-study. Supplementing this process with additional activities can further clarify current strengths and weaknesses. Design teams that dedicate time and thought to each of these pieces will be best positioned to create and design relevant and high-quality pilots.

DESIGNING
YOUR PLAN

In our initial year of supporting districts drawn to more personalized approaches, we worked with any and every district expressing interest. This quickly led to some important lessons about readiness and commitment, which informed our later partnerships. In 2014, for example, we were excited to launch a personalized learning redesign collaboration with a particular urban district we had never worked with before. We were aware of several teachers in this district who we already considered early adopters and, during our first meeting, the superintendent and curriculum director committed to sharing the role of lead change agents for the initiative. The superintendent said all the right things to convince us of her commitment to more personalized learning methods. However, as our relationship evolved, we began observing conditions suggesting the district was not ready for this work. Attendance at our first meeting with the full leadership team was spotty, and only the superintendent and curriculum director showed up to meet with our coaches. The new high school principal seemed tuned out and uninterested in the work, and the enthusiastic middle school principal was about to retire.

There were no teachers or students at the meeting, and as we pushed to establish a vision for a pilot, it was clear the administrative team was not unified, and there was no collective desire to implement new models for teaching and learning. The superintendent was unable to articulate her rationale for shifting instruction beyond wanting students to be "college and career ready." It was clear her team was unsure about this new direction, yet we plowed forward, developing a vague vision statement and an overly broad focus for pilot classrooms. Our two coaches stood ready to support pilot teachers as they experimented with new approaches, but poor communication between the district and the building leaders left the teachers frustrated and uncertain about their next steps. Meetings scheduled with the superintendent to get things back on track were canceled due to more pressing issues. Soon after, we pulled the plug on the engagement, realizing the district was not ready to undertake the complexities of this shift.

In general, we have found launching effective personalized learning change initiatives requires a level of planning and project management that vastly exceeds the time and resources most leaders have previously dedicated to reform efforts. At this point, lead change agents should pause to ensure a strong, committed team is at the design table before building consensus around an initial course. Our framework is demanding; we ask a dedicated design team to study local conditions, wrestle with various meanings and nuances of personalized learning, and articulate a rationale for moving forward.

In this chapter, we walk design teams through a series of conversations and decisions that will be used as the foundation for designing a pilot, recruiting pilot teachers, communicating the initiative, and evaluating its effectiveness. It is challenging to quantify the time required to complete the planning phase. Generally, teams have taken between ten and twenty hours to work through the process described in this chapter. School-based teams often move faster than district teams as the organization of initial meetings requires less logistical planning. Experienced teams who have a history of successful collaboration and a strong commitment to the work are also able to move at a quicker pace. Building relationships and reaching consensus are critical components that should not be rushed.

Aside from customizing the planning efforts to meet local needs, there is a second element to our process that increases the time commitment: aligning pilot designs with components of improvement science. In their book *Learning to Improve: How America's Schools Can Get Better at Getting Better*, authors Bryk, Gomez, Grunow, and LeMahieu make a compelling case for connecting reform efforts to an evidence-based process of improvement.[1] Rather than continuing to look for magic bullets and quick fixes, educators need to study the impact of new practices and understand how to reliably replicate quality outcomes. Disciplined inquiry encourages a team to study both quantitative and qualitative data to understand if a change is adding value. Major instructional shifts across diverse classrooms require an understanding of the conditions necessary for a change to take hold, as well as the variability present when the shift is implemented with different populations of students. Documenting this knowledge allows insights to be shared across a district, a state, or the larger field, accelerating all efforts. We have aligned our process for the planning and implementation of pilot classrooms with the six core principles of improvement science, outlined by Bryk and colleagues, and encourage teams to leverage these principles to take a "go slow to go fast" approach.[2] Take time to circle back to the six principles in table 4.1 as you make your way through our framework to ensure that your investment in this process can be fully utilized by leaders and educators to support replication efforts.

For many educators, improvement science can be an uncomfortable call to action. Integrating disciplined inquiry within the constant churn of classroom design can be daunting. We still have much to learn about efficiently aligning improvement science and redesign initiatives. However, we believe this is the right path forward if we are dedicated to making our education system more personalized, relevant, and effective. We have applied the work of Bryk and the Carnegie Foundation around disciplined learning to both our pilot efforts (chapter 6) and our network phase (chapter 12), by adapting their three essential questions:

- What specifically are we trying to accomplish?
- What changes might we introduce and why?
- How will we know these changes are actually an improvement?[3]

TABLE 4.1 **Six core principles of improvement science**

1. Make the work problem specific and user centered. Focus on a specific problem of practice and engage key stakeholders in the conversation.
2. Focus on variation in performance. Understand the conditions under which promising practices can be widely replicated.
3. See the system that produces the current outcomes. Study the current state of affairs to understand how local conditions impact the effort.
4. Establish an evidence base to support replication decisions. We cannot improve at scale what we cannot measure; we should not be scaling practices that are not demonstrated improvements.
5. Use disciplined inquiry to drive improvement. Leverage continuous learning cycles to learn fast and iterate often.
6. Accelerate learning through networked communities. Leverage like-minded partners to develop and test solutions to common problems.

The answers to these questions create conditions for pilot classrooms to reach their highest potential. The process is broken down into three steps: finding common ground, creating a vision and scope, and identifying priority classroom practices.

FINDING COMMON GROUND

At this point in the process, lead change agents should have a strong sense of their own vision for this work and be ready to bring in the design team to build consensus around a shared vision for pilot implementation. The first order of business is building a common definition of blended and personalized learning approaches. Next, the design team must develop a shared understanding of local context and review common obstacles to this work at the classroom level. Once in agreement, the design team is well positioned to hear from the lead change agent on ideas for initial direction, which it will adopt, adapt, or reframe during the second portion of this chapter. Leading questions for the design team to discuss are as follows:

- How do we define key concepts (blended learning, personalized learning, and other buzzwords) that are compelling to the team?
- Which student populations are thriving within our current instructional system? Which are not?
- What do we want to change about the current student experience?
- What is the magnitude of the top three to five obstacles currently facing pilot teachers? Can we move forward to formalize pilots without immediately addressing them?

Developing a Common Understanding of Blended and Personalized Learning

When design teams apply blended and personalized learning approaches to address a problem of practice, it is important to ensure the group has a shared understanding of how these approaches might solve the problem. Team members can reference favorite definitions, frameworks, graphics, or quotes from resources examined during their recently completed learning phase in order to develop a shared vocabulary to describe the work. It is essential to pause and build alignment around language; otherwise, team meetings will become a Tower of Babel where members talk over, under, and around various definitions. Teams can even create glossaries with common terms and definitions. This helps clarify complex conversations and allows new team members to get up to speed quickly as the design team grows over time.

By the end of this phase, teams should reach a common understanding of the differences and relationships between mastery, personalized learning, and blended learning, as well as a shared definition of blended and personalized learning. In table 4.2, we include a sample "definition bank" created by a Rhode Island design team. This team spent an hour reviewing a playlist on blended learning approaches and then ninety minutes working to achieve consensus around local definitions. The team used these definitions to build a vision statement for classroom pilots, which the superintendent included in a short video that explained this initial thinking to all district stakeholders. It is not necessary to share your work publicly as you develop and refine definitions and frame pilots. However, in this small community, the superintendent wanted everyone to be aware of the important work the design team was tackling.

Leveraging the Self-Study

There is a systemic problem preventing good education reform ideas from being effectively replicated and scaled: context matters. There are a myriad of examples of failed redesign efforts generated from a single flawed theory: if (enter a new approach here) has found success at (enter a school or district here), that approach implemented with fidelity should work anywhere. Often, new approaches are successful because they start small with the right group of people, iterate over time, and directly connect to an explicit need. When these successes are turned into stock solutions, they inevitably lose the power generated by true ownership and

TABLE 4.2 **Sample definitions**

Blended learning: Dynamic teaching combined with online curriculum and technology tools, enhancing teachers' ability to reach every student and accelerate student outcomes.

Personalization: Instruction and assessment is tailored to students' learning preferences, connects to students' interests, and allows for voice and choice.

Differentiation: Teachers respond to student learning needs based on continuous formative assessment practices. Instruction meets learners where they are, providing diverse access to the curriculum, and allowing students to progress at their own pace.

Engagement: Students and teachers are actively involved in learning, persist through challenges, and are proud of the work they produce.

Deeper understanding: Students move beyond skill acquisition to meaningful application.

responsive decision making. Reform ideas must be defined and designed within local contexts, which requires a keen understanding of what is going well and what stakeholders wish to change.

During the self-study, lead change agents and design team members gained knowledge, considered the reallocation of time, explored classroom obstacles, assessed the current state of human capital, analyzed student outcome data to find trends or problem areas, and shadowed a student. All this groundwork has helped prepare design team members for deeper discussions regarding local need and focus for this work. As the team discusses their findings, they may be focused on different things. One member might fixate on data identifying a specific population of students who are not being well supported. Someone else might have a classroom video of a blended lesson in the front of his or her mind. Yet another person may be stuck on the scripted math curriculum and its inability to support pacing opportunities. Everyone brings his or her own vision and sometimes baggage to the design team table, which is why it is important to launch this conversation by debriefing the eye-opening and humbling experience of shadowing a student.

Debriefing the Student Shadow Experience

The goal of the student shadow debrief is to build empathy for students, develop a clear understanding of the current student experience, and identify components of an ideal student experience that may or may not currently exist. To prepare for the discussion, facilitators may informally survey team members, collect and share notes and observations, or assign a pre-meeting journal prompt. We have seen facilitators lead discussions by posting four questions on chart paper around the room: How would you describe how you felt during your shadowing experience? What did you observe students doing most of the time? What did you observe teachers doing most of the time? What was most surprising to you about your shadowing experience? Armed with sticky notes, participants move in small groups around the room to post their thoughts on each question.

At one student shadow debrief, the lead change agent began the conversation by asking each participant to share a takeaway. All the design team members mentioned only positive aspects of the current student experience until the lead change agent—who purposely waited to speak last—took her turn. She paused, and then shared a strong criticism of the low level of rigor she saw on most of the tasks her student completed throughout the day: "My student answered close to one hundred questions over the course of the day and I did not see her pause even once to think before writing her answers." After her reflection, the rest of the room sat up a bit straighter and began to engage more deeply in the conversation. The lead change agent elected to go around the circle a second time, and each team member voluntarily shared a concern they noticed over the course of the day. During this debrief, it is important for team members to be constructive, yet critical, of the current student experience.

At the conclusion of the debrief, the team should prioritize suggestions for improving the student experience and look for additional self-study data that will validate—or contradict—these priorities. Drawing on student outcome data to corroborate student experience improvements is particularly important. Connecting subjective observation data to objective outcomes data is a critical skill for design teams to hone as they progress through our framework. There is no perfect protocol for aligning these diverse data sets or deciding which takes precedence, but this type of analysis will be a recurring aspect of the work.

Discussing Key Obstacles

Any classroom pilot of blended and personalized learning approaches will likely face several of the obstacles we introduced in figure 3.2. During the debrief, team members build consensus around the major obstacles pilot teachers may face and determine next steps required to reduce them. Sometimes no action is needed in the short term. Other times, identified obstacles are severe and will not be resolved overnight, such as current bell schedules or a lack of flexible furniture. Reflecting on the magnitude of current obstacles helps teams understand their level of readiness to launch pilots. Occasionally, the presence of multiple obstacles has required teams to pause until they can ensure pilot teachers will be adequately supported. Pilot teachers will appreciate a transparent approach as design teams work to reduce barriers on their behalf. As design teams transition from debriefing and finding common ground to setting a course forward, we encourage teams to review and discuss any additional thoughts or sources of data collected during the self-study.

Introducing Initial Direction

Once design teams have developed a common understanding of current strengths and needs, they are ready to create a vision and rationale for their pilots. Lead change agents can launch this process by sharing the initial thinking that is driving their enthusiasm for this work; however, they must be mindful that the design team is not a rubber-stamp party brought together to ratify their vision. During the next phase, design teams may validate this initial concept or take the pilot work in a completely new direction.

CREATING VISION AND SCOPE

Like many change management theorists, we emphasize the importance of a clearly articulated rationale for change. Leaders should be able to return to it in their hallway conversations, parent newsletters, and meetings. Why is this work important? What is the goal? As teams consider how to articulate their vision, there are several key discussion points to explore:

- Why are you pursuing a personalized initiative?
- What problem are you "hiring" blended learning to solve?
- What characteristics of personalized learning are your priorities?
- What student populations, content areas, or grade levels are you targeting for this work and why?

Articulating the Why

Since the rationale for the initiative will manifest itself within pilot classrooms rather than district-wide, we suggest moving away from creating a long-range vision to developing an initial problem-based call to action summarized as a pilot vision statement. It may be difficult for leaders to get a handle on exactly what they hope to create or the specifics around how they will get there. Eric Ries identifies a parallel situation in the world of startups, where uncertainty plays a significant role in planning. Ries suggests a pivot away from traditional concepts of "making complex plans that are based on a lot of assumptions" toward starting smaller and "making constant adjustments through short cycle feedback loops."[4] An initial rallying cry should resonate with educators and launch a robust learning period.

We have often started this discussion by having each team member write a narrative description of how teaching and learning could evolve to increase personalization. Done in the form of a three-to-five sentence "elevator pitch," this activity allows team members to picture—and then share—an ideal classroom experience. These personal statements often overlap and build alignment among the group, leading to important opening conversations. Sometimes leaders and teachers struggle to be generative and creative writers in a meeting format. Recently, one of our Fuse fellows created a Google form that simply asked leaders to share nouns, verbs, and adjectives describing current as well as aspirational classrooms. She then aggregated the words, identified commonalities, and created a statement representing much of their combined intention.

Another way to begin this conversation is by considering which of the three core elements of personalized learning resonates most with the group. Design teams leaning toward differentiation or pacing can reference our personalized learning progression in chapter 2 to consider how far and fast they want to go in their early stages of transformation. One of our favorite ways to use the progression is to print a poster-size copy and provide team members with three different colored stickers, sticky notes, or markers. Each color relates to one of the following three questions: Where do you think the majority of our district currently lands on this progression? Where do you personally want us to be on this progression? Where do you realistically think we can get the majority of our teachers to be within the next three years? This exercise demonstrates current levels of group consensus.

For schools and districts prioritizing student voice, choice, and agency, our progression—which focuses on differentiation and pacing—is less useful. When discussing themes related to student agency, it is important to prioritize various elements to build common ground. Choices can include culturally relevant pedagogy, interest-based activities, student goal setting, student voice in the instructional process, student choice in instructional content, socio-emotional learning, the four Cs (collaboration, communication, creativity, and critical thinking), deeper learning—or any additional elements that resonate. Depending on the initial level of consensus, the team can take a deeper dive into common priorities or divide into smaller groups to investigate different options and report back to the group. It is challenging to create vision statements around student agency because many of the concepts are abstract. Clarity and focus around priority elements is important to position pilot teachers for success. Supporting resources relating to student agency can be found on our resources website.

One important pitfall to watch out for during this initial conversation is the magnetic pull of blended and personalized learning products. If your design team includes experienced and knowledgeable educators, it may want to discuss tools right away. Be on guard as design team meetings can quickly devolve from a discussion on practices or student experiences to an edtech product demo. Jumping to tools before setting goals is a common misstep in this work.

After investigating areas of personalization that are compelling and building consensus around priorities, design teams are ready to build a vision statement for pilot classrooms. Before we look at exceptional examples of vision and direction, here are a few ineffective launch points to avoid:

1. Abstract and general pontificating about the need for twenty-first century skills and learning: This approach fails to provide tangible and specific reasons for students and teachers to engage with or get excited about this work. Avoid following this example:

   > The world our children face is rapidly changing, requiring new skills and preparation to be ready for college, career, and citizenship. A blended approach enables educators to integrate technology with face-to-face instruction to personalize learning for all students.

2. Focusing on devices: An initiative that is centered on hardware is doomed. Teachers need to understand why devices are necessary as well as the change in instruction they are hoping to inspire. Avoid following this example:

   > Every student will have access to a device to enhance his or her understanding of standards and create opportunities for blended learning.

3. Focusing on platforms or edtech tools: Similar to focusing on hardware, centering the work on software defines the *what*, rather than shifts in the learner experience (the *why*). Avoid following this example:

   > Starting this September, our district will be leveraging G-suite and Google Classroom to digitize curriculum, assignments, and grading protocols. This will build efficiencies for teachers and allow students to access classwork any time and from any place.

4. Emphasizing a specific framework or model: Frameworks are helpful for big picture understanding and models are helpful for establishing entry points for this work. However, neither helps teams define why blended and personalized learning is important. There should be no concepts in your vision statement that require further explanation. Avoid the following example:

   > Teachers in grades K–12 will use the SAMR model (substitution, augmentation, modification, redefinition) as they create tasks that are infused with technology.

Our favorite examples of *why* statements combine an emotional appeal with specific pedagogical actions. The best statements are free from buzzwords, easy for teachers to understand, and aimed at solving authentic problems.

See the following examples:

1. The achievement of every child matters to us. Our traditional model of whole-group instruction is disengaging both struggling learners and high achievers. By leveraging technology to differentiate instruction, we will be able to better match every student with activities and support that meet their needs.
2. Improving student engagement is a key driver of our personalized learning initiative. Teachers will collect student outcome and interest data and align instruction to meet identified needs and passions. Students will work on interest-based projects and tasks to support their development of critical thinking, problem-solving, and communication skills.
3. We believe student engagement is deeply connected to culturally responsive teaching. Teachers will create learning environments where all students feel valued and allow students to make explicit connections between their identity and the curriculum.

Clarifying the Scope of Work

In the next step, design teams define the ideal group of students and teachers to actively participate in the pilot. Some initiatives target particular grade levels or content areas—either because of the emergence of a clear problem of practice or the existence of a high density cluster of early adopter teachers. Some teams apply their analysis of student data to target the initiative toward specific student populations, such as English language learners who are struggling in traditional elementary classrooms or middle school girls who are experiencing an uptick in behavior referrals.

While it is important to match personalized learning pilots with critical areas of need, we have found the most success when design teams target early adopter teachers to lead pilot classrooms. We cannot overstate the importance of teacher mindset for successful pilot implementation and explore this teacher characteristic in greater detail in chapter 5.

IDENTIFYING PRIORITY CLASSROOM PRACTICES

With an initial sense of "the why" and "the who," design teams are ready to identify broad practices in service of the rallying cry—the *how*. Termed *priority practices*, these initial approaches form the foundation of the pilot phase.

In education, we have a history of focusing on nouns as we approach redesign and improvement. We have a vision to increase test scores, so we adopt a research-based reading curriculum. We want our students to be prepared for the twenty-first century, so we purchase a SMART Board for every classroom. Or, we want our teachers to deliver a more personalized teaching approach, so we train the faculty on how to use a specific learning management system (LMS). Each of these action steps is oriented toward incorporating a thing, instead of cultivating better instructional practices. Personalized learning requires a shift in focus toward verbs. Articulating priority practices provides a guidepost for pilot teachers who will operationalize the design team vision.

Reviewing Examples of Strong Practice

Design teams begin this process by collecting and reviewing strong examples of blended and personalized instruction. At the Highlander Institute, we have developed a priority practices tool (see appendix C) organized into four main domains: classroom culture; identity, interest, and agency; differentiation; and rigor and mastery. Each domain is further defined by six to eight core instructional practices. Initially built on the collective wisdom and research of national organizations such as CCSSO, Future Ready, and iNACOL, the tool continues to be informed by our coaching efforts in partner classrooms and is forever a work in progress. At the conclusion of each school year, we update the tool to reflect the new practices, strategies, and resources we have observed across hundreds of classrooms.

Design teams can simply use the Highlander Institute tool or expand the list of practices they would like to consider by investigating additional practice frameworks. We have included some of our favorites on our resource website. If key practices are missing and not included in existing frameworks, the team is encouraged to add them. The review process concludes with the lead change agent assembling a final list of practices for consideration.

Selecting Priority Practices

The selection of priority classroom practices will guide classroom level change as envisioned by the design team. The team is tasked with selecting three to five priority classroom practices, which will serve as the foundation of pilot efforts. Priority practices are used to do the following:

1. Define the scope of pilot work for design team members and additional stakeholders
2. Recruit and train pilot teachers (explored in chapter 5)
3. Guide and measure pilot implementation efforts (explored in chapters 6 and 7)
4. Codify validated implementation (explored in chapter 8)

Identifying priority practices is an important step for design teams. Selections should be closely aligned to the pilot vision and rationale for the work. They should represent the practices the team feels are most vital to the model they are trying to build. Pilot teachers will focus their initial efforts on these practices but will iterate and expand their efforts over time. Design teams can add priority practices to the roster as they observe pilot implementation efforts and see the connections between new practices and the pilot vision. Teams who are new to this work should rank their selected practices and consider starting with one or two.

Priority practices should support actionable and concrete next steps. Consequently, specific and proactive language is important for goal setting and implementation. For example, a practice stating *teachers will personalize work for students through the use of technology* is too vague. This example does not specify which technology-enabled practices could be observed in a classroom, nor does it give a teacher actionable next steps for implementation. What if the teacher is "personalizing work" but not using technology? What if the teacher is utilizing technology, but all students are on the same screen and working on the same problem? However, a practice that states *students are using collaborative dialogue when working in small groups* offers a specific way to operationalize a vision, enabling teachers and administrators to identify the presence or absence of this practice.

In summary, the key checklist for identifying initial priority classroom practices include the following:

1. They align to the vision
2. They are not redundant
3. They are specific and observable

Strong meeting facilitation will ensure all design team members are heard and feel their input is valued through this process. We often project or post the vision for the pilot on the wall and hand each design team member a printed copy of our priority practices tool when we run this exercise with our own design teams. Team members individually circle the practices they believe best align to the pilot vision.

We then collect all the documents, analyze which practices received the most votes, and aggregate these practices into a final table that we share with the entire group. We continue to discuss, refine, and prioritize until we reach consensus on three to five total practices. We have included a sample pilot vision and associated priority practices developed by a local design team in table 4.3

A Note on Local Variability

We should note that depending on the size and experience level of the group, different teams have included pilot teachers in design team meetings at different points in the process. Some teams recruit pilot teachers immediately and include them from the beginning. This offers pilot teachers incredible ownership of the work but, in some cases, has led to unwieldy design teams where reaching consensus is difficult. Other teams create a complete plan before recruiting pilot teachers. This has provided pilot teachers with clear direction but has sometimes impacted teacher ownership of the initiative. We believe the ideal structure falls somewhere in the middle. The process we lay out here encourages design teams to engage in initial planning, recruit pilot teachers (explored in chapter 5), and then collaborate to build the second half of the plan (explored in chapter 6). Often, at least one teacher on the design team will also lead a pilot classroom. As always, we encourage teams to carve a pathway that best meets local needs.

TABLE 4.3   **Example vision and priority classroom practices**

VISION STATEMENT
Pilot efforts will focus on better understanding the unique strengths, needs, and current learning levels of all students, aligning assignments to support these diverse student profiles and providing opportunities for students to take a more active role in the classroom.
PRIORITY PRACTICES
Student learning profiles defining current strengths, needs, skill levels, and environmental conditions for each student drives instructional decisions.
Tasks are differentiated based on student needs.
Students have the opportunity to provide input and feedback on learning experiences.
Students have choices in how they demonstrate their understanding.

MEETING FACILITATION AND GROUP NORMS

The facilitation of key discussions and decision points in this chapter emphasizes dialogue, reflection, and team building over speed. Building consensus on a quality vision for pilots and aligned priority practices requires skilled discussion management, inclusion, and productive forward movement. Often, the team is collaborating and discussing around a large table, with a few slides and handouts to guide and stimulate the conversation. Articulating a set of group norms is helpful to ensure team members feel safe when sharing perspectives that might be controversial—while simultaneously ensuring a single person or statement does not derail the meeting. We have successfully employed a process created by Learning Forward to develop a set of norms with teams who will be collaborating over a long period of time.[5] The process encourages groups to build consensus around priorities and expectations regarding time, participation, listening, confidentiality, and decision making. Establishing ground rules and keeping team members accountable helps maintain momentum and creates a supportive culture where differing opinions can push teams to a higher level of thinking.

For some teams, it may be important to name potentially negative behavior up front to prevent it from derailing the work. For example, we have witnessed many unfortunate examples of student-blaming through the design team process. Statements demonstrating lowered expectations for individual students as well as blatant racism toward entire student populations have undermined core principles of personalized learning initiatives, including student-centered design, inclusivity, and equity. The presence of negative statements is a sign that your group culture is broken and must be remedied before productive forward movement is possible. Norms that explicitly address toxic comments—particularly concerning students and families—may be necessary.

It is important for design team meeting facilitators to revisit team norms at the beginning of each meeting. They can be used to set individual or group intentions for the meeting. We have included the Highlander Institute team norms in table 4.4 and have included additional norms on our resource website.

When preparing for design meetings, lead change agents should trust their gut with regard to local best practices and group expectations. In some schools or districts, strong data practices already exist and design team members will expect student outcomes data to be present in any initial presentation or conversation. In some cases, data will be less crucial, but design team members will require an

TABLE 4.4   **Highlander Institute team norms**

Let's keep our time sacred.
Honor the learning differences/needs of those in the group.
Be aware of your emotions/biases.
Allow all to have both a voice and the freedom to be silent.
Feedback should be specific, kind, and helpful.
Discussions should be solutions oriented.
Find time to build relationships/connections with those in the group.
Learn to thrive in the risk zone.
Build in wait time.
Embrace each person's truth, even when it's different from your own.

explanation or connection between this work and previously prioritized initiatives. For some design teams, leadership and culture may be elephants in the room that must be addressed before moving into aspirational conversations around blended and personalized learning. And, for some teams, iterative change is already the norm, so jumping right into design and ideation will feel natural. Whatever the local environment, take time to honor previous work, build relationships within the team, and frame decision points to be relevant and compelling for the members sitting around the table. In other words, personalize the experience.

● ● ●

In his 2016 blog post on building world-class guiding coalitions, David Ferrabee makes compelling statements that are easily transferable to our design team concept:

> Put simply, the guiding coalition is an easy notion to grasp, but surprisingly hard to do well. Yet the success of a change programme hinges first and foremost on the quality of the team that guides it. . . . In fact, the guiding coalition are the unsung heroes of change management; the team that relentlessly ensures that change is occurring on a daily basis. . . . The coalition should neither be stacked with work and meetings nor starved of vital opportunities to build momentum for the change. . . . Once the guiding coalition has been appointed and has contributed to building the plan and vision, they need to remain actively engaged with it. Without this sustained participation, the guiding coalition will inevitably meet resistance to change.[6]

There is a huge difference between understanding the need for a design team and effectively executing on the concept. A strong design team will create a common language for change with a compelling rationale and well-defined priorities. At this point the team is ready to enter the pilot phase.

PILOT

Pathway to Personalization Framework

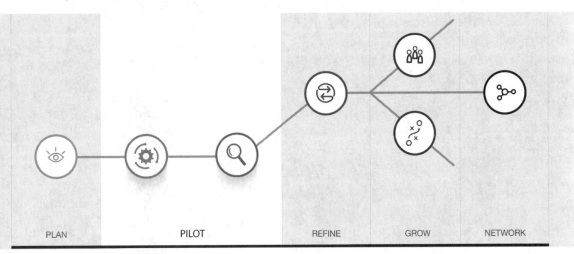

PLAN   PILOT   REFINE   GROW   NETWORK

Recruit pilot teachers   Evaluate the pilot

Structure the
learning process

RECRUITING PILOT TEACHERS

In the fall of 2011, the Highlander Institute launched a series of touch technology workshops for educators interested in strategically teaching with first-generation iPads, SMART Boards, and SMART software. Every educator in those sessions was by definition an early adopter of these new technologies. Armed with their personal or school-issued iPad, they were sacrificing a late August beach day to explore new practices and possibilities.

One particularly memorable teacher—Roshni—sat in the front row taking furious notes. Throughout the two-day workshop she was able to quickly expand on presented concepts and simultaneously troubleshoot technical issues for her fellow participants. Her enthusiasm was contagious. As a second year teacher at a local public charter school, Roshni had just experienced a rough one-to-one iPad rollout with limited guidance on how teachers were expected to use the new devices. But, she saw value and possibility in the new technology to better support her urban students in their quest to learn and felt confident in her ability to identify and develop promising new practices.

As our organization grew and evolved, we kept tabs on Roshni and frequently observed her classroom. Roshni beta tested multiple edtech products on her iPad, offering feedback to product developers. She started an edtech testing club, empowering students to select interesting products and share their perspectives with product developers. Roshni led a school-wide push for competency-based report cards and developed a relationship with a startup competency grading company, working long nights to support a product that would facilitate the grading transition for her school. She believed in the power of collaborating with edtech developers to create user-friendly solutions to move the needle on assessment, differentiation, and student engagement. Her entrepreneurial and collaborative approach united students, colleagues, and companies around promising new strategies and models. Roshni was the epitome of an early adopter.

As we discussed in chapter 3, early adopter teachers play a critical role in our change management process. They are enthusiastic, energetic, creative practitioners who yearn to explore strategies outside their comfort zones and test and develop promising practices. After the lead change agent and design team have established common ground and determined their initial vision and priority practices, it is time to identify and recruit a cohort of early adopter teachers who can execute the vision by leading pilot classrooms. In this chapter, which begins the pilot phase of our framework, we further define the characteristics of early adopters, offer strategies for selecting pilot teachers from your population of early adopter teachers, and describe the support pilot teachers will require in order to position them for success.

DEFINING EARLY ADOPTER TEACHERS

As we translate Rogers's diffusion of innovation theory into an education setting, we have observed that his estimates of 13 percent of people falling into the early adopter category, with an additional 2 percent falling into an innovator category, also applies when considering a teaching faculty in a school or district. Educators who fall into either category are quick to buy into new ideas, practices, and tools, but innovators are more likely to independently blaze their own trail with less concern about alignment to a design plan. Early adopters are more willing to collaborate and compromise as they explore. As Geoffrey Moore explains in his book, *Crossing the Chasm*, "Early adopters, like innovators, buy into new product concepts very early in their life cycle. . . . They are people who find it easy to imagine, understand, and appreciate the benefits of a new technology, and to relate these potential benefits to their other concerns."[1] There are clear parallels in the education realm. While early adopter teachers may not be as technologically savvy as innovators, they are not scared of technology and intuitively see possibilities and potential applications when presented with new strategies and resources. Further, they often have more credibility with their colleagues who feel like the fast and furious pace of innovators is not something they can replicate. Design teams can learn from the struggles, the creative problem solving, and the ingenuity of early adopters during the pilot process, determining pain points—and related support systems—that will be required when taking practices to scale.

We believe excellent teachers can be found throughout the diffusion of innovation curve (see figure 3.1) and are not suggesting early adopter teachers are "best." However, just as technology startups count on early adopters in the marketplace to determine the relevance of new products, design teams can count on early adopter teachers to identify the value and wider application of promising blended and personalized learning practices. These entrepreneurial teachers are best positioned to wrestle with the uncertainties of instructional shifts and fail forward. Empowering early adopter teachers protects the larger faculty from the frustration and stress that can accompany trailblazing redesign. Lessons learned during the pilot phase are baked into a teacher resource bank to ease adoption for teachers further down the curve.

The magic behind early adopter teachers is found in the relationships they build within their schools, as well as the additional time and energy they are willing to dedicate to the work regardless of their negotiated contract or obligated time commitments. They are usually grounded by a deep commitment to doing whatever it takes to support the students in their care; consequently, their students are willing to explore and experiment as trusted partners in their classrooms. They are collaborative and will leverage their emotional intelligence to gain influence and flexibility with school leadership. But, beyond these qualities that are generally found in many good teachers, we look for early adopter teachers who possess specific skills, competencies, and mindsets that position them well to navigate the uncertainties and challenges of pilot classrooms. When identifying early adopters for a design team pilot, we recommend considering their classroom culture, competencies, capacity, opportunities for collaboration, and alignment with design team priorities.

Foundational Classroom Skills

Without exception, the early adopter teachers we have identified across our district partnerships have the demonstrated ability to create strong, respectful classroom culture and effective classroom routines. We have found the presence of several foundational classroom practices is an essential leverage point for supporting the shift to personalized learning environments. Most of the following practices are observable, and quick classroom walkthroughs can help leaders understand the level of teacher comfort and competency within each element. The classroom behaviors listed here are a great starting point and reflect the intention of the first domain of the Highlander Institute's priority practice tool (appendix C):

- Interactions between students are positive, supportive, and promote accountable behavior.
- The classroom culture makes students feel safe and valued.
- The physical classroom environment is safe and organized for learning.
- Students understand and follow classroom rules and expectations.
- Directions, routines, and classroom procedures are accessible and responsive to all learners.
- Classroom resources, including tech devices, are treated with care and used for their intended purposes.

Identifying the teachers who have already established classrooms with these characteristics is a critical first step toward selecting your cohort of pilot teachers. You may have tech-savvy teachers who model strategies and take on leadership roles but still struggle with classroom management. These teachers might make great design team members but are not the right teachers to lead pilots. The fast pace of experimentation and iteration is not a good fit for teachers who struggle with behavior or lack structure; and pilot classrooms will not reach their potential without a strong instructional foundation already in place. The next set of benchmarks includes traits and skills that best position teachers for success in a pilot environment.

Early Adopter Competencies

We often launch a discussion with educators by asking, "What competency is most important for teachers who are leading a blended and personalized learning classroom?" They typically reply with some derivation of "the ability to use technology." Our experiences supporting and learning from hundreds of early adopter teachers over the past five years suggest this is not the case. We have found the most important characteristic of effective blended and personalized classroom teachers is an orientation toward growth and change.

Consequently, much of the Highlander Institute's certification, fellowship, and classroom coaching work is built on the iNACOL Blended Learning Teacher Competency Framework, pictured in figure 5.1.[2] Released in 2014, the

FIGURE 5.1   iNACOL Blended Learning Teacher Competency framework

Source: iNACOL, The International Association for K-12 Online Learning

competencies represent a multi-year, collaborative effort between professional learning organizations, university professors, researchers, and practitioners from across the country.

While there is no established hierarchy of competencies within iNACOL's framework, when we share the framework, we purposely de-emphasize "technical skills"—which include coachable skills such as data practices and the use of instructional tools. In our opinion, the more intangible domains, such as mindsets, qualities, and adaptive skills, should be targeted as the key competencies for identifying pilot teacher readiness with regard to blended and personalized learning implementation. In the next section, we explore each of the domains in the iNACOL framework and provide examples of how these competencies play an important role in the implementation of new instructional approaches.

Mindsets

Mindset competencies include core values or beliefs that align with goals of educational change and mission.[3] In order to be successful amidst the initial uncertainty surrounding a blended and personalized initiative, early adopter teachers need to understand, adopt, and commit to new forms of teaching and learning. Teachers who cannot imagine moving beyond a traditional instructional model have a fixed mindset and will not be able to enact change without highly structured expectations and targeted professional development. These teachers are not well-positioned to lead learning cycles or experiment with new approaches. Alternately, teachers who see themselves as learners will optimize the opportunity to try new strategies and make mistakes. These teachers have been dreaming of a day when their leaders reach out to them and say, "We want you to try new things in your classroom. We will give you autonomy and support and encourage you to fail forward!" Teachers with an orientation toward change believe a new vision for teaching and learning is necessary and have the capacity to reflect on their instruction and build on promising practices.

The disposition for change—and a growth mindset—is difficult to coach. There are a few ways to identify teachers with growth mindsets: Are they comfortable with open-ended and exploratory professional growth activities? Do they tap into social media to generate new ideas? Have they found a mentor (in the building, in the district, in the state, or via social media)? How do they respond to new ideas presented during staff meetings? Do they actively seek out opportunities for professional learning such as conferences, webinars, or peer observations? Are they leading or involved in book groups? Are they the first to tinker with new resources?

In 2013, Highlander Institute partnered with a local nonprofit to launch a design thinking program for educators. The program description for this initiative was extremely vague, which made teacher recruitment difficult. The four teacher teams willing to take a chance on this opportunity were asked to identify a school or classroom problem and then design and implement a solution. Initially quiet and confused, the educators quickly warmed to the design thinking process and used the unstructured opportunity to create a fully customized solution to a building-based challenge that they researched and identified together. The growth mindset of participating teachers enabled them to find value within relatively undefined parameters. These sixteen educators have gone on to become leaders in blended and personalized classroom redesign across the state, with many of them now serving as Fuse RI fellows.

Qualities

The second layer of competencies are less innate and more coachable and include characteristics such as grit, transparency, and flexibility. These competencies represent patterns of behavior that help teachers reduce obstacles, address challenges, and communicate successes as they explore new approaches. A well-rounded early adopter will demonstrate strengths across this category. A teacher who never gets discouraged but who refuses to open his or her loud and messy classroom is not ideal. Neither is a collaborative teacher who only dabbles in safe bets to eliminate the risk of failure.

The best way to identify these qualities is to spend time observing classrooms—particularly when teachers are trying something for the first time. Good pilot candidates are comfortable with observations. They enthusiastically explore new models and are confident enough to change direction mid-lesson in response to an opportunity or classroom need.

We launched our first blended learning school partnership in 2012 after winning a large collaborative grant with a local elementary school. With stacks of devices and boxes of resources arriving on a daily basis, the faculty was excited and ready for a new adventure. However, unexpected adversity was a consistent presence. New SMART Boards would not work with new Chromebooks, software licenses were not syncing properly, and student logins were a nightmare to manage. Originally designed for special education students in the 1970s, the school space was difficult to reconfigure, and heavy cement walls impacted broadband reliability. The hits just kept coming and teachers could have easily given up. Yet, through it all, this close-knit group worked together to reduce obstacles and create workarounds; they laughed, they experimented, and they took advantage of student expertise. They created password necklaces to help younger students access login information and collaborated on lessons and activities, using thumb drives when necessary. Through it all, they stayed positive, supported each other, and celebrated promising turning points.

Adaptive Skills

iNACOL defines adaptive skills as "generalizable skills that apply across roles and subject areas."[4] These aptitudes—which include competence in areas such as collaboration and problem solving—are complex; they help practitioners tackle new tasks or develop solutions in situations that require organizational learning and innovation. They are mastered through modeling, coaching, and reflective practice.

In our experience, creative problem solving and thoughtful iteration are critical competencies of early adopters. Teachers with strong adaptive skills use challenges as teachable moments and find creative ways to address unexpected issues. These teachers have high content, assessment, and facilitation acumen. They capitalize on new insights and ideas as they emerge and quickly pivot toward high-impact practices and approaches.

Adaptive skills can be cultivated, and we have found teachers are more likely to demonstrate these skills when their school leader supports risk taking, transparency of practice, autonomy with accountability, and high quality data practices. Innate adaptive skills are typically demonstrated by teachers who are comfortable with uncertainty and willing to try something new, with feedback from peers or administrators. Teachers with strong adaptive skills are open to data collection, analysis, and data-driven decisions when placed in a system that values this work.

To launch his exploration of blended and personalized practices, the principal of a new Providence middle school selected one team of grade-level partners to receive Highlander Institute coaching. Neither teacher had any training in these teaching shifts, yet both enthusiastically arrived at our 7:00 a.m. coaching sessions ready for feedback and immediately enacted our suggestions. They quickly reconfigured their classroom furniture, shifted their daily schedules, and adapted their scripted curriculum guides. Simultaneously, they identified pain points as they surfaced and pitched potential solutions. They asked for help creating screencasts to provide additional clarity to students in collaboration centers while they led targeted small-group instruction. They quickly made the shift from macro differentiation to micro differentiation, pushing us—their coaches—to create better data protocols using more nuanced formative data that would allow them to regroup students with more frequency. Our observations and targeted feedback were embraced as they pivoted toward high-value practices, which yielded stunning student growth in a matter of months.

Technical Skills

Often perceived by teachers and leaders as the most important, this domain is comprised of the skills, expertise, and "know-how" required to execute new classroom strategies. Data practices, instructional strategies, blended learning classroom management, and instructional tools can all be learned and practiced, and we have seen even the most reluctant teachers make large strides when offered strong coaching. This has caused us to de-emphasize the relative importance of this domain as we believe any growth-oriented, collaborative teacher can be quickly taught how to sign into a learning management system and upload content. Early adopter teachers quickly acclimate to using tutorial videos, discussion boards, and crowdsourcing strategies to develop the technical skills they require—and they recognize and use student expertise to help them learn.

There are a few ways to identify teachers with strong technical skills. They eagerly integrate free classroom apps, quickly see patterns while using classroom software, and immediately understand how to generate and read software reports. Another indicator of strength in this domain is social media presence and online networking. Teachers with strong technical competence can be found troubleshooting projectors during staff meetings and helping colleagues implement a new tool during their planning period.

One of our first consulting entry points in blended and personalized learning was through a competency tracker we built at the Highlander Institute called Metryx. Metryx is a web app that allow teachers to enter specific student skills or competencies and evaluate mastery based on their observations. Adopted school-wide by a Providence-based career and technical academy, an early adopter teacher of automotive shop was immediately drawn to the tool. He had already built a spreadsheet of comprehensive automotive skills aligned to performance tasks across grade levels, so he deeply understood the concept and took to Metryx like a fish to water. His comfort with technology allowed him to quickly upload his information and begin to collect data with little training. While we struggled to coach his colleagues to effectively identify critical skills and independently navigate the tool, our early adopter was already regrouping students and targeting instruction based on demonstrated proficiency in brake pad replacement and fluid diagnostics.

CCSSO Leadership Competencies: The Interpersonal Domain

While mindsets, qualities, and skills are critical, the whole point of personalized models is to integrate systems and learning experiences to provide teachers with enhanced opportunities to understand and empower individual learners. Building a strong culture of trust and respect where students feel known and valued is central to any shift toward more personalized models. Consequently, we have found value in adding an interpersonal domain to the competency framework for early adopters. Identified by the Council of Chief State School Officers, in partnership with Jobs for the Future, the interpersonal domain is highlighted in their "Educator Competencies for Personalized, Learner-Centered Teaching" document, which was released in 2015.[5] The interpersonal domain includes the "social, personal, and leadership skills educators need to relate with students, colleagues, and the greater community, particularly in multicultural, inclusive, and linguistically diverse classrooms."[6] Across the hundreds of diverse K–12 classrooms we have observed and supported, effective blended and personalized practices have consistently been layered on a foundation of strong teacher-student relationships.

Interpersonal skills are intimately connected to teacher awareness and responsiveness to issues of equity and identity and to a dedication to leveling the playing field for historically marginalized students. Teachers with strong interpersonal skills intentionally create positive and respectful learning environments where students feel known and valued. They make an effort to connect with all students, to understand who they are, what is important to them, where they come from, and what they need to move forward. One key indicator within this domain can be observed by how teachers structure their first few weeks of school. Teachers with strong interpersonal skills take time to get to know each student and make connections between the curriculum and what matters most to each child.

While many teachers ask students to complete a "get-to-know-you" survey about themselves during the first week of school, one of our favorite high school ELA teachers implements a comprehensive plan for building student relationships and a trusting classroom culture that evolves throughout the school year. She begins the year by sharing important aspects of her identity and experience with her students, including her strengths, struggles, and pet peeves. Throughout the next few weeks she spends time getting to know individual students—both in and out of class. Simultaneously, she launches her first unit, which is centered on community building. She selects resources, readings, and activities centered on community building within school neighborhoods, the school, and the classroom. As students begin to build trust with their peers, she encourages them to share more about themselves and their perspectives. Often her students are not able to articulate defining aspects of their culture or identity right off the mark, and she teaches them to reflect on how their viewpoints are linked to aspects of their identity and experience. From there, she engages her students in a series of personality assessments and asset-finder surveys. Rather than asking them to reflect on their strengths with a blank piece of paper in front of them, she provides them with survey results and explanations that help them see themselves in a positive light. As activities evolve into individual conferencing and goal setting, students develop a strong sense of who they are as learners and recognize that they are truly valued by their teacher. "I want them to know I believe in them and deeply care about them," she explains, "and I want them to value and care about each other."

Taken together, the foundational classroom practices, mindsets, qualities, adaptive skills, technical skills, and interpersonal skills outlined in this section form a robust set of characteristics to support the identification of strong early adopter teachers. We have found the best way to identify early adopter teachers is to spend time in their classrooms, talk to their students, and compile anecdotal evidence about their priorities, approaches to problem solving, professional growth activities, and feelings about change.

THE IMPORTANCE OF EARLY ADOPTERS

After reviewing the many incredible characteristics of early adopter teachers, you can see how their power and potential can accelerate classroom-level change. In our change management framework, early adopter teachers play a pivotal role in both short- and long-term reform efforts. As potential pilot teachers, they engage in continuous learning cycles within their classrooms. At the conclusion of the pilot phase, they address challenges, explore solutions, and build additional infrastructure to support replication. The ongoing, active involvement of early adopter teachers is essential to a successful personalized learning initiative. This premise may seem obvious, but we have witnessed plenty of examples of unsupported and disillusioned early adopter teachers. It is not enough to simply identify early adopters. They must be engaged and empowered if your vision and priority practices are going to gain momentum. It seems appropriate to pause for a moment and consider why this subset of teachers is not productively leveraged in some districts and actively disenfranchised in others. Consider Sonia's story.

Sonia has been teaching high school English in an urban district for twenty years. She started her career with a superintendent who granted teachers considerable autonomy in determining curriculum. With little oversight, direction, or budget, Sonia invested her own money in class sets of books and resources and built units of study that were directly connected to the perspectives and identities of the students in her classes. With high standards and expectations, she developed a level of intellectual curiosity and passion for learning in her students that was unmatched in other classrooms.

Sonia's strong outcomes around student engagement and achievement caught the eye of a new set of administrators, but she consistently felt undermined rather than empowered. She attended professional development sessions where leaders disseminated her ideas and practices without assigning her credit. She was devastated when a grant she wrote and received for student enrichment activities was reallocated to another program. The arrival of a third superintendent came with an edict for all teachers to follow a scripted curriculum with fidelity. Sonia joined the curriculum committee and found herself limited to choosing "classic" white male authors to teach her students of color. She was forced to scrap the multicultural curriculum she had developed and refined over the years. Despite her clear ability to engage and support students, Sonia has had little if any voice in programmatic shifts that have deeply impacted her work. This lack of respect has been reciprocated by her own deep distrust for most administrators who come through the revolving district office door. She continues to stay only because she is one hundred percent committed to her students.

Alienating talented early adopters is a grave misstep in any district. For districts interested in pursuing personalized learning models, it is grossly hypocritical and undermines the entire initiative. All early adopters deserve a level of autonomy, well-resourced classrooms, and a voice in reform efforts. Design teams must determine how to study, document, and make use of the work underway in these classrooms. Our next section explores strategies for recruiting and selecting pilot teachers from your population of early adopters.

RECRUITING PILOT TEACHERS

With approximately 13 percent of any given faculty comprised of early adopters, smaller schools may only have two or three teachers who fit this profile. We recommend that design teams recruit at least two pilot teachers and limit the pilot teacher cohort to a number that can be effectively supported by available coaches or liaisons. Typically, the pilot cohorts we have supported within a school implementation have ranged from four to six teachers per coach, especially during the pilot phase. In larger schools and districts, it is likely you will have more eager candidates than you can effectively support as pilot teachers. Later in the chapter we discuss ways to engage interested early adopter teachers who are not selected to lead pilot implementation.

Best-Fit Considerations

Early adopter teachers are generally the teachers who are taking a class, volunteering to lead after-school activities, and serving on three committees in addition to their classroom responsibilities. Leading a pilot classroom will require serious capacity in terms of additional time and effort, and selecting teachers who are already overcommitted is not recommended. A second consideration is the ability for pilot classroom teachers to communicate and collaborate with each other. A cohort of eight pilot teachers distributed across eight schools does not support informal collaboration and forces teachers to work in isolation. We have found regular opportunities to connect and plan greatly increases the drive and resilience of pilot teachers. While there are no perfect scenarios, we recommend striving for a situation at the top of this hierarchy:

- *Ideal*: A team of grade-level or content-area teachers who share common planning time in a building led by a strong principal who is already getting positive student outcomes.
- *Strong*: A cohort of pilot teachers across grade levels or subject areas in a building led by a strong principal who is willing to revise schedules to support face-to-face collaboration time during the school day.
- *Fair*: A cohort of pilot teachers scattered across grade levels, subjects areas, and numerous buildings. All collaboration efforts will require logistical planning or asynchronous formats.

Pilot teachers are typically great at communicating online or via email to overcome obstacles; however, the value of proximity for co-planning, classroom observations, and informal discussions cannot be overstated.

Finally, design teams should consider pedagogical strengths and philosophies when identifying pilot teachers. Early adopters typically have strong theories, politics, and orientations with regard to instruction. When possible, align the priority practices and classroom experiences the design team identified in chapter 4 to the strengths and interests of your early adopter teacher pool. A teacher who is deeply committed to personalizing through student choice may not be the best fit to implement practices focused on differentiated instruction.

Consider these three best-fit scenarios when selecting pilot teachers, but at the end of the day none of these factors should overshadow the importance of the mindsets, qualities, and competencies as defined. Recruiting a team of teachers who share a similar content area and common planning time is great, but if half the team is reluctant or uninterested in diving into a messy, uncertain experimentation process, then your pilot phase will not result in adequate learning or momentum.

Framing the Initiative

Identifying the right pilot teachers starts by framing the work with humility and transparency. Lead change agents must sell this opportunity as a well-thought-out and critically important next step for the school or district. Savvy early adopters will want to know, "How is this new initiative different from the rest?" Or, "How is it connected to the three other building and district-level initiatives we were told to implement this past summer?" They may ask what freedoms or flexibilities they will be offered in exchange for their time and energy. They may want to know what additional coverage or planning time they will receive. Lastly, they may want to know how this is being communicated to students and families, and how they will be supported if the initiative receives pushback from parents. Early adopter teachers will look for the potential value-add and will want to understand the level of commitment their administrators are investing in this work.

We have learned hard lessons on the importance of clear framing and expectations. The vague process descriptions that accompanied the launch of our Fuse RI fellowship in 2014 paralyzed many pilot teachers and district leaders who did not understand the goals of the project or their responsibilities in achieving them. Our initial consulting touchpoints were confusing and loaded with false assumptions. We quickly revised our model and started year two with diagrams layered on top of timelines, which were supported by memorandums of understanding. Increased attention to planning and logistics took additional prep time but resulted in higher quality consulting work from us and more promising pilot implementations for schools and teachers. Leverage the vision and priority practices to frame your pilots and be specific about your expectations for pilot classrooms.

In our experience, most pilot teacher recruitment efforts fall along two spectrums. First, the design team must determine whether it wants an open recruitment process, where any teacher can apply to be a pilot teacher, or a closed process, where pilot teachers are identified and receive targeted invites from the design team. A hybrid model might include disseminating an interest survey to all teachers—or conducting quick observations in many classrooms before issuing targeted invitations based on results. We have included an example survey on our resources website. While it can add additional time to the recruitment process, we have found that conducting classroom observations is the best strategy for determining best-fit characteristics of a potential pilot teacher. Through observations, design team members can gather evidence on teacher characteristics, mindsets, and competencies;

additionally, the team can identify teachers with a proclivity for implementing the priority practices defined during the initial planning phase. Teachers who are uncomfortable opening their doors for walkthroughs immediately demonstrate a lack of adaptive skills. Within our network, observations have brought clarity to the process for both teachers and team members and have resulted in stronger pilot teacher rosters.

Whether you are inviting pre-selected teachers or opening an application process to all teachers, it is important to clearly communicate the time commitment, classroom-level expectations, and support involved in leading pilot classrooms. Interested teachers will appreciate an opportunity to ask questions and get specific. We recommend drafting a memo of understanding that outlines the responsibilities of both the design team and participating teachers. Include the support and resources that will be offered to pilot teachers, as well as expectations around meetings, data collecting/sharing, and reporting of lessons learned. This informal agreement will set a strong foundation for the next phase of design work and the launch of pilot classrooms. An example memo of understanding that has supported the recruitment of pilot teachers is included in appendix D.

The second spectrum that guides pilot teacher selection defines the degree of freedom and autonomy teachers have in the pilot process. A tight pilot aligned to a research agenda can help test the efficacy of a specific model and will require pilot teachers to strictly adhere to an agreed structure. For example, an emphasis on formative assessment and differentiated instruction implemented through a three-station rotation model, using a specific adaptive math software for a set amount of time each week, is a structured ask for a pilot teacher.

Alternately, loose pilots offer teachers more freedom around implementing stated priority practices. If the design team wants to learn about the multitude of ways teachers connect formative assessment data to differentiated instruction, a loose pilot allows teachers the freedom to explore and creates concurrent experimentation within different contexts. We return to this concept in chapter 6 when design teams and pilot teachers build consensus around launch points. Transparency around design team intentions is helpful when identifying the right teachers to lead the work; expectations should be explicitly stated in all recruitment efforts and materials.

We have found the best pilots fall somewhere in the middle of the tight-loose spectrum. Time and again, efforts sitting at the extremes have faced challenges that have compromised scaling efforts. We suggest avoiding the following scenarios:

1. *Too closed.* We have not had success "volun-telling" (forced participation) teachers to lead pilots. In several cases, forced participation has resulted in teachers dropping out of the pilot or having very little ownership of the work. Even in a closed identification and selection process, teachers should have the ultimate decision in whether or not to participate.

2. *Too open.* We have found that a wide-open recruitment process often results in the participation of teachers who are not true early adopters. While self-selected teachers may have a great deal of interest in exploring blended and personalized models, they will not be equipped to handle the challenges and uncertainties of the process unless they possess the characteristics previously described.

3. *Too tight.* Avoid over-scripting the pilot. Layering mandates around practices, approaches, software, and scheduling limits active experimentation and iteration. The only reason to over-script a pilot is if there is a high need for efficacy data and it is essential to establish a more controlled environment.

4. *Too loose.* Provide enough structure to support pilot teachers as they get started with implementation. In our experience, loose pilots are often connected to weak vision statements and a lack of consensus around priority practices. Teachers in loose pilot environments often flounder and lose steam. Additionally, complete teacher autonomy increases the complexity of validating strategies and determining essential conditions during the formal evaluation.

The best scenarios occur when design teams are highly transparent about vision and priorities, honest about the uncertainties, and committed to supporting pilot teachers through the process. Take the time to discuss the pilot opportunity with strong pilot teacher candidates and allow teacher voices to shape roles, responsibilities, and expectations. Combine adequate guidance with teacher autonomy to elevate the effort.

Once your pilot teacher cohort is confirmed, take some time to acclimate your pilot teachers to the work of the design team. Pilot teachers should be fully briefed on why the team is engaging in a personalized learning initiative, how the vision for the pilot evolved, and the nature of current teacher and student experiences that inspired the selection of priority practices. This is also the time to ensure pilot teachers have enough knowledge and understanding of blended and personalized learning practices to feel confident lending their voices to the process. The design team may choose to orient pilot teachers by reviewing the self-study results, sharing common definitions, building a digital playlist of resources, or conducting classroom visits to schools already implementing this work.

Design teams should also ask pilot teachers to weigh in on the key obstacles uncovered during the self-study. While teams may not have the authority to clear all roadblocks at this stage of the process, it is essential to reduce the impact of as many identified obstacles as possible to support pilot classrooms. Unreliable broadband could be solved by the purchase of classroom hotspots. Strict curriculum pacing guides could be waived or supported by alternate accountability measures. Most importantly, design teams should describe the support pilot teachers will have throughout their implementations. We call this support the pilot "nest."

CREATING THE PILOT "NEST"

We view pilot classrooms as a nested egg; they are precious, fragile, and susceptible to a range of detractors. The design team must build a strong, safe, and supportive environment around these pilots, supplying adequate structure, resources, time, and backing. We have found several critical supports are universal to successful pilots despite the specific obstacles identified and have outlined them in table 5.1. The first is a seat at the design table and a voice in the pilot process. The second is dedicated time for pilot teachers to collaborate within a pilot cohort. This includes time to visit classrooms, co-plan, debrief, and reflect. The third is autonomy to explore different software products as well as approaches for technology integration (unless the pilot is a strict efficacy study). The fourth is enough classroom devices and infrastructure to support the successful implementation of priority practices that would benefit from a blended approach.

The final, fifth support is so important it warrants a separate paragraph. It is the involvement of a coach or design team liaison. Ideally, pilot teachers have access to a coach with expertise in promising blended and personalized learning strategies. However, in situations where schools or districts do not have access to a coach,

TABLE 5.1 **Critical components of pilot "nests"**

1. A voice for pilot teachers in the design process
2. Dedicated time for pilot teachers to collaborate
3. Autonomy to experiment with software and approaches
4. Devices and infrastructure to support online work for at least one-third of pilot students
5. Planning and reflection time with a coach or liaison

this role can be led by an outside consultant, a retired educator, or the reallocated time of a building or district leader. The real value of this liaison is as a facilitator, a sounding board, and a data collector. Despite the level of expertise present, the liaison will regularly co-plan, observe, and reflect with pilot teachers. He or she will talk through pain points, celebrate victories, support ongoing data collection, and document learning to bring back to the design team. The regular presence of this point person is a critical part of the nest that pilot teachers will require to effectively lead the work. We discuss the role of the coach in greater detail when we talk about pilot launch points at the end of chapter 6.

INITIAL COMMUNICATION STRATEGIES/PARALLEL WORK

Lead change agents have used different strategies for communicating the pilot process to school and district stakeholders. We recommend transparent communication, with a special focus on faculty who fall into innovator and early adopter categories. Teachers in these categories who are not leading pilot classrooms still have a lot to offer in terms of identifying and experimenting with personalized approaches, strategies, and tools. This engagement has taken different shapes, depending on the size and culture of a school or district. Some leaders have created school-based subcommittees to support pilot initiatives; others have developed building or grade-level professional learning communities for interested teachers. Some have enlisted early adopters as mentors for less experienced but enthusiastic colleagues; others have asked early adopters to share promising strategies at staff meetings. Early adopters have also been tapped to gather resources in a shared folder and engage in concurrent classroom experimentation efforts. Additional examples include supporting opportunities for interested teachers to convene and explore various practices and resources together (Thursday afternoon "appy" hours, for example), or through more comprehensive readiness assessments that collect the perspectives of a wider group of stakeholders.

● ● ●

Pilot teachers are the bedrock of our Pathway to Personalization Framework. While the design team frames the rationale and defines an initial direction, pilot teachers are the true engine of reform. Together, these two groups collaborate to complete the planning process and launch pilot classrooms, which is the focus of the next chapter.

STRUCTURING THE LEARNING PROCESS

In 2010, Next Generation Learning Challenges (NGLC) established a blended and personalized learning project to support the design and implementation of new school models. (NGLC is a nonprofit initiative that funds and supports personalized learning efforts in schools and districts.) Seven years later, a RAND study was released comparing the rollouts of personalized approaches in NGLC schools to traditional schools across the country in four key implementation areas: learner profiles, personal learning paths, competency-based progressions, and flexible learning environments. As one of the largest and most anticipated studies regarding blended and personalized learning to date, this headline from *Education Week* was particularly apropos: "Personalized Learning: Modest Gains, Big Challenges, RAND Study Finds."[1]

The RAND study outcomes emboldened both advocates and opponents of personalized learning. Both camps leveraged the results to point to either iterative growth and promise or an early obituary for an over-hyped approach. For us, the results were exactly what we expected. The intersection of blended and personalized learning is a fledgling approach working to pivot a centuries-old education system and mindset. Early stage education technology resources are still evolving to build critical efficiencies required for replication and scale. Methods and approaches are still being tested, and, as is the case with any school reform effort, personalization is not a panacea. Reports like this are essential for keeping the conversation rooted in data and research and for supporting evidence-based forward movement.

As we read through the report, this was our biggest takeaway: when schools attempt to implement aspirational practices, they often push too far too fast without building enough structure around the learning process. Personalized learning shifts require an understanding of the relative value of new approaches, the effective communication of *how* to operationalize the work in classrooms, and the creation of *new systems* to support implementation. We had a great deal of empathy for the NGLC teachers and students who reported using technology more often to update personalized learning plans but having no more time to review the data than their peers in the traditional schools. We also felt for the teachers who implemented competency-based progressions, allowing students to move at their own pace online, but then struggled to effectively group them for collaborative work. Teachers implementing new models and strategies require systems to help them understand the rationale behind the changes, address unexpected outcomes, identify persistent challenges, and study whether changes are actually improvements.

At this point in our Pathway to Personalization process, design teams have defined priority practices and recruited a cohort of eager pilot teachers to lead the charge. Now it is time to build an explicit learning process around pilot classrooms that will help identify and validate valuable instructional strategies as they emerge. Creating this infrastructure is essential for moving the initiative beyond isolated classroom exemplars. We have witnessed too many quality examples of personalized learning that have failed to scale beyond pilot classrooms. Across our numerous partnerships, most leaders have mistakenly assumed that creating a model classroom is the mainstay of the effort. In reality, the fulcrum of change is found in the process of validation and documentation that supports replication.

Our pilot process is like a learning expedition in which design teams and pilot teachers set out on an adventure to bring back the holy grail of personalized learning models to the rest of their colleagues. It is modeled after the plan-do-study-act (PDSA) cycle created by Walter Shewhart in 1939 and popularized by W. Edwards Deming in 1950.[2] The PDSA cycle models the scientific method as an approach to developing and testing new ideas. Bryk and colleagues at the Carnegie Foundation have used PDSA cycles to help teams focus on impact when implementing new educational strategies. We find their structure helpful as a standard process for enacting a reform idea so that it can eventually be adopted by educators across diverse contexts and environments.[3]

PDSA cycles start with planning. Design teams have already done significant planning within the plan phase by studying current conditions, agreeing on common definitions, describing the student experience, articulating a vision for pilots, and identifying priority classroom practices. Our pilot phase continues with a bit of additional planning as design teams and pilot teachers work together to define how priority practices will be implemented and what measures will be used to validate these practices. The launch of pilot classrooms corresponds to the do phase of the cycle, which encompasses the experimentation and iteration that occurs throughout pilot work. The collection and review of both formal and informal data throughout the pilot phase—culminating in a formal pilot evaluation—comprises the study piece of PDSA. Codifying validated strategies that support priority practices is the act part of the cycle. Table 6.1 outlines how the PDSA cycles align with essential features of our framework.

This chapter focuses on creating a structured learning process for how teams will learn about the impact of priority practices as they are implemented in pilot classrooms. First, the design team and pilot teachers work together to connect a strong set of initial instructional strategies to each priority practice. Then, the group explores different types of evaluation measures and settles on the instruments it will use to evaluate the pilot process. With a data plan in place, the work shifts to determining how pilot teachers will launch their efforts. To clarify this process, our examples over the next two chapters focus on a single priority practice: *teacher uses data to inform instruction.* This will enable design teams to understand how to structure learning as well as determine how many practices they can concurrently support.

TABLE 6.1 **Anchoring priority practices to learning**

PILOT PHASE			REFINE PHASE
Plan	Do	Study	Act
Identify a set of strategies that will operationalize priority practices; connect strategies to measures	Implement a set of strategies in a pilot classroom; collect measurement data	Analyze measures to determine the impact of various strategies	Attach validated strategies to examples, resources, and curriculum to support replication

IDENTIFYING COMPELLING STRATEGIES

We define the term *strategies* broadly; strategies are essentially the student and teacher behaviors and experiences that improve the learning experience as defined by a set of priority practices. Strategies can be packaged in all shapes and sizes. They can be large classroom models, such as the station rotation or flipped classroom model; substantial approaches, such as daily targeted instruction for small groups based on data; or smaller activities, such as a student-led collaboration routine to support rigorous problem-based work. Strategies support the pilot effort in two central ways regardless of their size. First, they define how priority practices will be carried out in pilot classrooms. Second, they serve as evidence that an instructional shift is present in a pilot classroom. The design team and pilot teachers collaborate to establish a strong menu of initial strategies connected to each priority practice.

Brainstorming

Our process begins with a group discussion of the many ways a priority practice could be realized within a classroom. In preparation for this process, teams can review existing strategies for inspiration. The Highlander Institute priority practices tool includes a sample list of strategies (appendix E) for each of the twenty-eight priority practices listed. Alternately, teams may want to start by looking at elements of teaching and learning that have generated significant effect sizes across meta-analyses of educational research and connect compelling evidence-based strategies to priority practices. Great resources include Hattie's "Index Of Teaching and Learning Strategies" and the National Research Council's book *How People Learn*.[4] Finally, teams can adapt popular personalized learning actions that align with their priority practices. We include a description of six common entry points, including station rotation, project-based learning, choice boards, flipped classroom, learning profiles, and socio-emotional learning in appendix F.

Brainstorming can be done online or through facilitated face-to-face discussions. We like to use a gallery walk protocol that allows the team to actively build on ideas and generate as many strategies as possible. Each priority practice is listed on a large piece of chart paper and posted around a room. The team is divided into smaller groups and assigned a starting point in front of one priority practice. We frame the activity by asking, "If this priority practice was being implemented in a classroom, what kind of teaching and learning experiences would you see?" Armed with pens and sticky notes, participants post as many approaches, routines, models, tasks, and experiences as they can. After five to seven minutes, groups rotate. The next group organizes posts into clusters and spends an additional five minutes adding ideas. Rotations continue until design team members feel like they have an exhaustive lists of strategies aligned to each priority practice.

Let's look at an example that focuses on the practice *teacher uses data to inform instruction*. The expanded design team could begin to brainstorm by thinking about the many ways teachers could leverage data in a classroom. For example, teachers could administer pre-assessments at the beginning of each unit, collect a quick exit ticket after each lesson to determine student mastery, or assign different work based on assessment scores. Then the team can focus on what students may be doing if a teacher is using data. For example, students could use data to set personal goals for the week, find a peer tutor, or determine their next task based on their current proficiency level. Figure 6.1 shows a fuller set of ideas generated for this priority practice.

Selecting Initial Strategies

After completing the brainstorming process, the team organizes and refines the list, selecting three to five strategies that are most relevant, compelling, and manageable. Pilot teachers should weigh in heavily during this selection process. In figure 6.1, a set of four compelling initial strategies are circled, demonstrating consensus among the expanded team that these specific strategies could help pilot teachers operationalize the priority practice of *teacher uses data to inform instruction*. The selection of initial strategies is a key inflection point in the pilot process. Strategy sets define how pilot teachers will approach their classroom implementations and clarify how the design team will understand the degree to which a priority practice is being implemented when they walk through pilot classrooms.

It is common to revise sets of strategies as pilot teachers learn and iterate over the course of the pilot phase. For example, the circled strategies in figure 6.1 are centered on teacher and student data collection, with little emphasis on the ways in which data informs instruction through other strategies such as differentiating content, scaffolding tasks, or collaborating with peers. As teachers and students become comfortable with new data collection and analysis efforts, pilot teachers will expand the scope of their implementation and the design team will add new strategies to the list. Throughout the pilot process, strategies yielding positive outcomes are documented, and less valuable strategies are revised or removed. Updating strategy sets associated with each priority practice takes place during midpoint

FIGURE 6.1   **Generating a set of strategies**

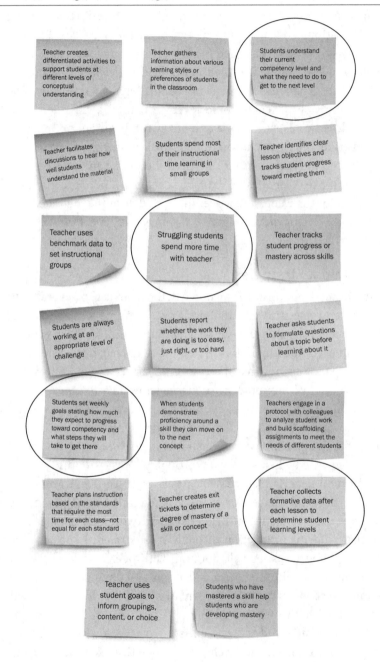

pilot meetings, which we describe in more detail in chapter 7. Defining strategies is critical to establishing a foundation for learning over the course of the pilot and refine phases. The final set of strategies connected to each priority practice at the conclusion of the pilot effort will comprise the personalized learning design that the combined team will seek to scale if promising results are generated within pilot classrooms.

CONNECTING MEASURES TO STRATEGY SETS

Incorporating measures enables the design team to answer three critical questions: What strategies lead to improved outcomes? What conditions support effective implementation? How does implementation vary across pilot classrooms? Taken together, the answers inform replication efforts and establish a knowledge base from which new, implementing teachers can build. (For a review of the critical principles of improvement science, please see table 4.1.) This work begins by considering three distinct types of measures. We recommend selecting process, outcome, and balance measures—adapted from Bryk and colleagues as a component of PDSA cycles—to evaluate implementation efforts.

Process Measures

We define process measures as the changes that can be observed through a twenty-minute observation of a pilot classroom. Process measures allow design teams to quantify the relative presence or absence of the strategies connected to each priority practice and to determine the extent to which key instructional shifts are taking place over time. Process measures also highlight additional strategies or breakthrough moments occurring within a pilot classroom that might prompt a midpoint meeting to discuss strategy tweaks and iterations. We typically recommend using two main process measure tools. One is a strategy rubric that contains the current strategy set connected to each priority practice. An example strategy rubric for the priority practice *teacher uses data to inform instruction* is provided in table 6.2.

Sometimes the most compelling observation points in a pilot classroom are not part of a strategy rubric. For this reason, design teams can elect to use a second, more comprehensive process measure, such as the Highlander Institute priority practices tool (appendix C). Adding an additional tool or establishing a local walk-through protocol helps to capture the comprehensive list of strategies underway

TABLE 6.2   **Sample strategy rubric**

PRIORITY PRACTICE(S): *Teacher uses data to inform instruction*	WALKTHROUGH DATE: _____			
	No evidence	Very little evidence	Some evidence	Significant evidence
Teacher collects formative data after each lesson to determine student learning levels				
Students understand their current competency level and what they need to do to get to the next level				
Students set weekly goals stating how much they expect to progress toward competency and what steps they will take to get there				
Struggling students spend more time with the teacher				

in classrooms at any point in the pilot process. When observed, additional strategies should be recorded and discussed with pilot teachers at midpoint meetings to determine how they are supporting priority practices and whether they should be added to the strategy rubric. We recommend design teams conduct observations at least once every eight weeks using their strategy rubric. One should occur as a baseline measure when pilots are just getting started, and one should occur as a final measure at the conclusion of pilot work. Scheduling one or two additional walkthroughs prior to midpoint meetings will deepen the learning of the design team.

For additional guidance around best practices for conducting walkthroughs, we suggest looking at chapter 3 of *Instructional Rounds in Education: A Network Approach to Improving Teaching and Learning* by City, Elmore, Fiarman, and Teitel. This helpful resource defines a set of protocols for "observing, analyzing, discussing and understanding instruction that can be used to improve learning at scale."[5] This book emphasizes large amounts of anonymous data collection, which is a different approach from our practice-specific process measure, but the note-taking strategies described in the book are applicable under both models.

At the Highlander Institute, we find value in adding two additional features to our classroom walkthroughs. The first involves setting aside a few minutes to ask students questions to verify the presence or absence of certain elements of a strategy rubric. This builds a stronger evidence base than observations alone. Second, we approach observations with an eye toward artifact collection. When observations include a lesson, assessment, resource, tool, protocol, or task that is supporting high quality instruction aligned to the strategy rubric, we encourage pilot teachers to share a copy. The ongoing collection and documentation of artifacts will enable the design team to be more efficient through the refine phase. Training design team members on best practices for describing what they observe and attaching evidence to their descriptions will maximize the value of this process measure. We have found running mock classroom walkthroughs using video of blended and personalized classrooms—prior to conducting observations—helps teams calibrate scoring, collect effective supporting notes, and increase familiarity with best practices for classroom observations.

It is important to distinguish between walkthroughs associated with process measures and teacher evaluations. Process measures evaluate the relative ease of implementation—and the observed benefits—of various strategies, as well as the speed of instructional shifts associated with each priority practice. They are not meant to evaluate teachers. Early adopter teachers lead pilot efforts because they do not require a system of accountability to improve their practice. They continuously improve of their own volition. If the design team has recruited a pilot teacher who does not fit this description, it is better to transition the teacher out of the pilot than use the process measure to attempt to remediate his or her practice.

Outcome Measures

The second type of measure we employ is outcome measures. Outcome measures often refer to traditional, quantifiable education metrics such as attendance rates, behavior referrals, graduation rates, or achievement scores. When considering achievement metrics, state assessments can measure proficiency and allow for comparisons across twelve-month periods but are not great for measuring incremental growth. A validated interim assessment tool can measure progress, proficiency, and growth by comparing beginning, middle, and end-of-year scores for pilot students. These tools also offer comparisons against national averages, previous student cohorts with the same pilot teacher, and peers taught by different teachers. However, these instruments do not always align with the content or pacing within classrooms. Internally designed common assessments administered across subjects or grade levels can quantify academic proficiency and make comparisons across cohorts of peers taught by other teachers. However, these assessments cannot measure growth rates and lack the reliability of nationally normed tools validated by psychometricians. We do not recommend using assessments designed by individual pilot teachers because they lack validity, cannot determine growth rates, and cannot compare achievement across grade level or subject areas. Data dashboards within adaptive education technology can be used to measure progress, but this should not be the sole indicator of achievement. Design teams can start by taking a quick inventory of their existing measurement tools and consider incorporating additional instruments as part of the pilot effort.

A local Rhode Island design team was focused on increasing classroom discourse as a priority practice and was particularly interested in monitoring the impact of associated strategies on ELL students. Rhode Island mandates an annual ELL assessment, but the design team was concerned the instrument would not provide adequate information on how new strategies were supporting growth on a weekly or monthly basis. The team found an additional screening tool with the capacity to track incremental student progress and purchased a limited number of licenses to support pilot efforts.

The growth of personalized models is also pushing the conversation around new outcome measures. Schools play other important roles in addition to supporting academic growth, including teaching empathy and social skills, supporting democracy, fostering creativity, and helping create well-rounded students.[6] There is growing buzz around the connection between socio-emotional competencies, twenty-first century skills (such as collaboration, critical thinking, creativity, and communication), and post-secondary success. There is also growing emphasis on student engagement, motivation, and initiative; we have included several psychometrically validated instruments that measure the development of these skills on our resource website. We encourage design teams to discuss which outcome measures matter most and to secure outcome measures aligned to the student competencies they are trying to cultivate.

Balance Measures

Balance measures formalize the perspectives of teachers and students as new strategies are being implemented. Feedback surveys, interviews, and focus groups are examples of balance measures that articulate the value of a change from the perspective of an "end user." Balance measures often uncover unanticipated outcomes as well as determine the value of specific strategies within a larger set. For these reasons, balance measures provide critical information to the design team when decisions are being made regarding replication. For example, asking students to rate each strategy connected to a priority practice allows the team to consider how well each strategy supported students at different grade levels, within different subject areas, and across different learning profiles. Balance measures are essential for untangling variability between pilot classrooms and pinpointing compelling changes.

Formal balance measures often include student surveys. Some survey questions are repeatedly administered at multiple points in the pilot to compare the perspectives of individual students over time. Other survey questions are tailored to the changes underway in a classroom at a specific point. Regular focus groups are also a great way to leverage student feedback. We have also found that periodic individual teacher interviews are the best way to capture teacher perspectives. Balance measures can be developed internally; the most important consideration is that all pilot classrooms must use the same questions, surveys, and protocols to assess points of variability that arise from implementation iterations or different teacher/student characteristics.

Taken together, process, outcome, and balance measures help present a full picture of the impact of new strategies. According to the Carnegie Foundation, "Measures must be connected to the overall theory of improvement; meaningful and helpful in leading to subsequent changes; accessible and timely; and easy for practitioners to collect, interpret, and use themselves."[7] With an understanding of the three different measures, the team is ready to create a measurement plan.

Building a Measurement Plan

Building a measurement plan involves connecting strategies to measures and scheduling data collection. The initial connection between strategies and measures often reflects the current knowledge and experience of design teams and can evolve to become more sophisticated as teams continue to learn and iterate. Operationalizing process measures is a fairly straightforward procedure as teams can essentially use their strategy rubric and a comprehensive checklist such as Highlander Institute's priority practices tool. In terms of balance measures, creating a series of student surveys or feedback routines connected to strategy sets is also a relatively easy process to manage. For example, when a pilot teacher begins pre-assessing students before a lesson, students can be asked for their feedback on whether the strategy—as currently implemented—adds value for them, as well as their suggestions for improving implementation.

Assigning outcome measures to strategy sets is the most challenging part of this work. Teams can begin by considering the outcomes they hope each priority practice will achieve. Does the design team believe the practice *teacher uses data to inform instruction* will lead to higher student achievement levels? Higher engagement levels? Higher motivation levels? All three? The answers to these questions will determine how teams select outcome measures. Often, teams anticipate that several—if not all—priority practices will generate better achievement outcomes. At a minimum, teams can connect their entire list of priority practices and associated strategies with one outcome measure and rely on teacher and student perspectives to untangle the relative merit of specific strategies. Table 6.3 outlines an example data plan connected to the practice *teacher uses data to inform instruction* and the initial set of strategies defined in table 6.2.

From here, teams think about data collection points across the pilot phase and build an initial collection schedule. Some of the measures can be scheduled flexibly, such as classroom walkthroughs and student surveys. Other measures may need to align with district data collection schedules. Baseline data should be collected before pilot classrooms officially launch. Each measure should have an assigned point person from the design team who is responsible for scheduling data collection and organizing the data for analysis. Under the direction of the lead change agent, team members should assume various roles and responsibilities as directed. Table 6.4 outlines an example data collection schedule based on the plan defined in table 6.3.

TABLE 6.3 **Sample data plan**

PRIORITY PRACTICE(S): *Teacher uses data to inform instruction*		
Process measures	Outcome measures	Balance measures
Strategy rubric defined in table 6.2 Highlander Institute priority practices tool	Achievement: Beginning, middle, and end-of-year data on STAR literacy and math assessment Engagement: Pre/post student survey using the motivation and engagement scale (MES)*	Student surveys providing feedback on each strategy Individual teacher interviews providing feedback on each strategy

*The MES is a practical multi-factor approach to measuring student motivation and engagement. It comprises eleven factors that are grouped under four themes: positive thoughts and behaviors and negative thoughts and behaviors. (https://goo.gl/sbx4dR)

TABLE 6.4   Example data collection schedule

MEASURE	DATA COLLECTION WINDOWS				POINT PERSON
Pilot classroom walkthroughs with strategy rubric (table 6.2)	Baseline: October 1–15	Midyear: December 1–15	Midyear: February 15–28	Final: May 1–15	Assigned, specific design team member
STAR data	Beginning of year: September 15–30	Midyear: January 15–31		End of year: May 15–31	District literacy and math directors or design team member
Motivation and engagement scale (MES) survey	Pre: September 15–30			Post: May 15–31	Assigned, specific design team member
Student surveys	Monthly, with survey questions aligning to the strategies underway in each classroom				Coach
Individual teacher interviews	Monthly, with questions aligning to the strategies underway in each classroom and addressing both successes and challenges				Coach

Thoughts on Project Scope

As design teams define strategies and connect measures, it is important to reconsider the scope of a pilot. During the vision and priority practice selection process, it might have felt like the sky was the limit with regard to the number of practices that could be implemented in pilot classrooms. However, the demands of structuring a learning process around each practice are real. Teams should be honest about their capacity. It is OK to begin with one or two priority practices—particularly when teams are just getting started with the work.

LAUNCHING PILOT CLASSROOMS

Connecting a set of strategies to a set of measures for each priority practice provides pilot teachers with essential guideposts for getting started. This section discusses the work of pilot teachers and design team members from the point of launch. First, we consider how design teams can frame initial entry points with pilot teachers. From there, we discuss the critical role of the coach or liaison throughout the course of the pilot phase and wrap up with a brief introduction to the curriculum challenge that teams will most likely wrestle with throughout the implementation process.

Determining Pilot Launch Points

With a menu of priority practices and associated strategies in hand, design teams and pilot teachers should be intentional about how the work gets started in pilot classrooms. Similar to the "tight-loose" spectrum we introduced in chapter 5 during the recruitment of pilot teachers, it is now time to consider the level of consistency or autonomy that will frame initial pilot efforts. Would your team like to study the implementation of the same strategies across all pilot classrooms at the same time? Or, would your team prefer to grant pilot teachers the autonomy to select a practice and strategy that most resonates with them? There are several possible hybrid approaches. Working together, pilot teachers and design teams can identify a lead priority practice and allow teachers to choose an associated strategy and a specific course, topic, or subject area as entry points. Or, the team can focus on one subject area and allow teachers choice around practices and strategies; or, the team can build consensus around a more prescriptive approach and identify subject areas, priorities, and strategies that all pilot teachers will use as launch points. In an effort to clarify the various possibilities, we offer the launch points of three different pilot teachers.

Yarissa is a fifth-grade ELA and math teacher in a small urban district that supports five thousand students across twelve schools. Over 80 percent of students qualify for free or reduced lunch, 23 percent receive special education services, and 26 percent are identified English language learners. Yarissa's design team was focused on differentiation to support the large numbers of students who were working below grade level across multiple subject areas. Priority practices included using data to inform instruction, differentiating tasks based on student needs, providing students the opportunity to offer feedback on their learning experiences, and offering students choice. Yarissa's team gave her complete discretion around where to begin, and she decided to focus on her reading block and integrate four strategies across the three priority practices simultaneously: She collected daily formative data on reading skills using an online formative assessment tool; she connected student results to specific learning objectives and used this information to prepare more targeted small-group lessons; she set up differentiated activities within the independent and collaborative stations instead of having all students engage in the same activity; and she carved some class time each week to discuss these changes with her students and solicit their feedback.

Maya is a high school history teacher in a large urban district that supports twenty-five thousand students across forty-one schools. Within her building, over

86 percent of students qualify for free or reduced lunch, 12 percent receive special education services, and 46 percent are identified English language learners. Maya's school-based design team identified student engagement as a key challenge and selected four priority practices that focused on project-based learning, creating connections between subject matter and student identities, engaging in work that is authentic, and differentiating tasks based on student needs. The design team secured administrative consent to update course titles and content and directed pilot teachers to begin with a project-based focus. Maya's World History course was changed to Civics, covering similar standards with content pulled from current events. Maya started her year with an identity project that engaged students in self-reflection around their cultures, families, histories, and experiences. Students took part in discussions and created projects based on stereotypes and micro-aggressions they had experienced, with the goal of raising awareness and encouraging a deeper understanding of the different identities that exist in the diverse school community.

Val is a first-grade teacher in a small suburban district that supports 2,500 students across four schools. Fourteen percent of students qualify for free or reduced lunch and 15 percent receive special education services. Val's design team identified the need to increase academic growth for all students, with a focus on students at the extreme ends of the academic spectrum—those who are either struggling or high-achieving. The four priority practices selected included a focus on differentiated instruction, using data to inform instruction, offering students choice, and making lessons relevant through real-world connections. The design team asked pilot teachers to begin by focusing on the practice of differentiated instruction. Val decided to start by differentiating her thirty-minute phonics lesson and leveraged four strategies across two priority practices (differentiation and using data to inform instruction). Breaking from her traditional routine of delivering a whole-group phonics lesson on the rug each morning, Val pre-assessed students on the skill she was planning to teach the following day and grouped students based on their level of mastery. The students with the greatest needs spent the majority of the subsequent phonics lesson at the small group table with Val. Students who had already mastered the concept applied and extended their knowledge at the collaborative center, and students who were almost there spent ten minutes with Val at the start of the lesson and then practiced the skill using an online software program for the remaining twenty minutes.

Supporting Pilot Teachers

As we referenced at the end of chapter 5, the most critical predictor of successful pilot phases has been a dedicated coach. The person in this role is typically the glue keeping the pilot moving forward and all participants engaged and accountable. If coaches are not part of the design team, they need to be oriented to the vision, priority practices, strategy sets, and launch points established. It is important for design teams to bring coaches into the larger redesign conversation prior to connecting them with pilot teachers to avoid false starts and to keep pilot implementations connected to the strategy rubric. Pilot teachers often begin their work with coaches by co-planning initial blended and personalized lessons and attaching resources, tools, curriculum, and lesson plans to strategies. While many pilot teachers are able to create their first blended lessons with relatively little support, they often appreciate having another adult in the room when they try something for the first time.

Whether design teams choose a dedicated coach or a liaison, there are several key tasks associated with this role:

1. *Support pilot teachers as a thought partner*: Coaches and liaisons support brainstorming, co-planning, and research, but pilot teachers often report their role as a sounding board is most appreciated. In ideal scenarios, coaches schedule weekly or bi-weekly touchpoints with pilot teachers. Liaisons who are able to spend time in pilot classrooms increase their value as collaborative partners and often accelerate experimentation simply by listening and offering suggestions.

2. *Coordinate logistics*: All pilot teachers need a point person to document their reflections and develop a process for communicating this information back to the design team. This includes immediately sharing identified obstacles with the lead change agent and following up to report on how these obstacles are being reduced. This also includes sharing breakthrough moments and early promising strategies with the design team, as well as other teachers in the pilot cohort, and collecting artifacts, lessons, and resources connected to these breakthroughs. The liaison connects the dots between individual pilot classrooms and brings cohesiveness to the effort.

3. *Support data collection efforts*: Liaisons gather test scores, surveys, and checklists; they lead focus groups; they schedule design team walkthroughs. They reinforce the importance of continually collecting evidence and ensure data collection efforts evolve to align with iterations in pilot classrooms.

Whether these responsibilities are handled by a seasoned blended and personalized learning coach, a set of mentor teachers, a building leader, a district administrator, or a formalized professional learning community, pilot teachers should be able to identify the liaison who is supporting their work. The school year is a busy, demanding time for educators at all levels of the system. It is easy to lose track of the learning underway in pilot classrooms; without support, pilot teachers are unlikely to reach their potential, which significantly undermines the success of the whole initiative. We discuss professional learning and ongoing embedded coaching in more detail in chapter 11.

Considering the Current State of Curriculum

As design teams and pilot teachers select entry points and prepare for pilots, it is important to consider the degree to which existing platforms and curriculum will either support or hinder pilot efforts. The efficiencies offered by education technology software, such as learning management systems, are significant for streamlining teacher workflow demands associated with blended and personalized instruction. Similarly, we have witnessed many pilot efforts that have been stymied by a lack of curriculum resources or adaptive software. Even though they may be up for the challenge at first, pilot teachers should not be responsible for creating personalized curriculum on top of implementing new practices and strategies. Design teams anticipating that existing platforms and curriculum are insufficient to support pilot teachers should research and consider products that would best support their selected set of strategies and test these tools as part of the pilot process. Often, software companies are willing to provide a few free, short-term licenses to support pilot efforts. Understanding the benefits and outcomes associated with various tools is an important part of a blended and personalized pilot process.

Ultimately, priority practices and related strategies will need to be attached to resources, tools, routines, lessons, and activities in order to successfully impact teaching and learning and be replicated by other teachers. Pilot teachers might be able to connect all the dots, but many of their colleagues will require more structured support. Design teams should prepare for the fact that promising pilot efforts will not scale without adequate and aligned curriculum and software resources. This challenge is so critical we dedicate an entire chapter to the current status of curriculum and software (chapter 10) and discuss how a local network of districts are collaborating to develop a curriculum solution in Rhode Island (chapter 12).

Communicating with Families

Pilots are a learning opportunity for schools and districts interested in creating a more personalized learning experience for students. When design teams run their self-study with due diligence, create a connected vision statement, and structure pilots around priority practices and strategies, pilot implementation will launch from a strong foundation. Teams should feel confident that pilot classrooms will create better learning environments for students than traditional classrooms around the district. However, despite the level of design team confidence, it is important to communicate with the parents of students who will be part of these classrooms. Be clear about the changes that will take place in pilot classrooms and the rationale behind the effort. Full disclosure will alleviate the negative connotation associated with experimenting with other people's children without their consent. Generally, parents will be excited that their children will experience a more personalized learning environment under the direction of a talented teacher. However, they should always have the option to decline participation.

● ● ●

Facilitating effective pilot classrooms requires a clear commitment from the design team to structure pilot work with a focus on learning. Framing the pilot process through strategy sets connected to data measures positions teams to learn quickly and use evidence to assess the value of classroom changes. In chapter 7, we continue to emphasize how data and learning play a central role during ongoing pilot efforts, as well as the formal pilot evaluation. Pilot classrooms may last for six months or thirty-six months; the work continues until the design team can confidently extract strategies that are improving student outcomes and learning experiences.

EVALUATING THE PILOT

As teams officially launch pilot classrooms, let's take a closer look at the pilot experience of Yarissa, our fifth-grade ELA and math teacher from a small urban district. To review, Yarissa and her pilot cohort of six teachers were anchored by the priority practices of using data to inform instruction, differentiating tasks based on student needs, providing students the opportunity to offer feedback on their learning experiences, and offering students choice.

Yarissa focused her initial work within her daily reading block and decided to address three priority practices simultaneously. She collected daily data on reading skills using online formative assessment tools. She connected student results to specific learning objectives and used this information to prepare more targeted small-group lessons. She set up differentiated activities within the independent and collaborative stations instead of having all students engage in the same activity. And, she carved some class time each week to discuss these changes with her students and solicit their feedback.

Right away, Yarissa noticed that her new data collection routines were improving her instruction. She realized that the quality and amount of data she was collecting every few days was enabling her to reframe her approach to instruction by identifying learning objectives rather than focusing on a lesson as a whole. Breaking down instruction this way helped Yarissa identify specific student misconceptions

and understand when mastery was attained. Over time, her small-group instruction and ongoing formative assessments became much more targeted, and she
began organizing all her literacy instruction around learning objectives. Students
began moving out of her intensive intervention groups at significantly faster rates.

Once Yarissa upgraded her small-group instruction, she began to focus on
expanding student choice. Rather than asking all students to present information
the same way at centers, she allowed students to decide which format would allow
them to best communicate their learning—a written response, an audio response,
an image and caption, a video, a story, or a hybrid of several. This led to the creation of digital choice boards, which expanded choice to more activities. Through
trial and error, she learned that students greatly preferred collaborative activities
to quiet, independent work. In response, Yarissa built scaffolded choices that promoted student discussion and collaboration.

With successes came challenges. The most obvious emerging obstacle was
the amount of time it took to plan daily differentiated content for all her centers.
Yarissa pitched her evolving classroom model and early positive results to her fifth-
grade teaching partners and enlisted them as collaborators to share the planning
burden. Another obstacle centered around Yarissa's limited knowledge of edtech
tools. Again, she responded creatively. When she heard about a great new tool,
she added it as a choice to her digital choice board, encouraging students to learn
the tool and create a prototype example. The students who engaged in this choice
were then responsible for teaching the tool to the whole class; Yarissa learned with
her students. As Yarissa paused to reflect on the impact of her classroom changes,
she recognized how critical student input was to her progress. She began collecting student feedback through whole-group and small-group discussions as well as
through quick surveys. Her questions began to probe deeper, moving from feedback on various choices and activities to questions about student interests—what
students wondered about, what they valued, and what they wanted to learn.

Another breakthrough occurred when Yarissa started providing students with
more individual and actionable feedback on their work. She implemented tools
that allowed her to communicate asynchronously with students and then moved
toward more formal student conferencing and weekly goal setting every Friday. She
noticed increased growth rates on skill development when students understood
how close they were to mastering a learning objective. As student engagement
and motivation increased, achievement scores followed. Higher averages on her
weekly and quarterly assessments paved the way for significant growth in interim

benchmark assessment scores between the beginning and end of the year. When Yarissa expanded the scope of her pilot to include math, her center time was more flexible and her direct instruction table resembled more of a help desk. Students determined when to seek support and reinforcement directly from Yarissa, when to collaborate on problems, when to find a peer tutor, and when to go after more challenging applications.

At the end of the pilot period, Yarissa and her colleagues polled students and asked them to rank their favorite ways to learn. Assuming that tech-based center work would win in a landslide, they were astonished to find that the overwhelming favorite was teacher-led small-group instruction. Their least favorite? Teacher-led whole-group instruction. Yarissa articulated her rationale for these results: "Meeting students where they are builds much stronger relationships with individual kids. I have always enjoyed great relationships with students, but there was something much deeper about the connections I made during the pilot. Students could feel that I really knew them, cared about them, and was committed to moving them forward."

By all accounts, Yarissa led an incredibly successful pilot classroom. Her story is not uncommon, epitomizing what is possible when a talented early adopter teacher is empowered. But her story comes with a word of caution. We have seen many design teams trust their pilot teachers to unequivocally lead their own process. They grant pilot teachers full autonomy to create amazing classrooms with little to no oversight or accountability. Leaders assume pilot classrooms are progressing and do not walk through classrooms or check in with any degree of rigor or consistency. This is where the process breaks down in many districts. For teams interested in replicating priority practices beyond pilot classrooms, an overreliance on pilot teachers is not sustainable. Our framework requires a hands-on approach from the design team while pilot classrooms are running. Design teams must stay accountable to the structures they have built for pilot classrooms; there is an incredible amount of learning to capture, organize, discuss, and consider. A dedicated commitment to disciplined inquiry and improvement science is required.

Pilot teachers are well into their implementation efforts in this chapter, and we spend the first section discussing activities that support a process of continuous improvement during the pilot period. This includes supporting pilot teachers as they collect classroom data, developing a process for organizing cohort data, and facilitating midpoint meetings to review progress to date. The second section marks the end of active piloting and orients pilot teachers and design teams toward a formal pilot evaluation. We discuss how to prepare and summarize data stories and leverage a final decision-making protocol that will position teams to determine next steps.

ACTIVE DATA COLLECTION AND ANALYSIS

While we are well aware of the demands involved in active data collection, we want to reinforce the importance of leveraging at least one common instrument for collecting each type of data measure (process, outcome, and balance) across a pilot cohort. Without evidence, the work of pilot teachers will not generate a collective knowledge base, which is the goal behind integrating elements of improvement science into the effort. As the design team observes, analyzes, and meets to discuss iteration with pilot teachers, data collection processes will evolve and improve over time. Design teams can elect to increase the rigor of their data collection and analysis at any point.

Cohort versus Classroom Data Collection

Cohort data collected during the pilot period enables a design team to compare the impact of new strategies across varied pilot classrooms. This facilitates the study of overarching policies, infrastructure, and conditions that support or hinder a strategy. It also pushes on issues of variability by shining a light on strategies that are successfully implemented across different grade levels and subject areas by teachers with different strengths. In contrast, data collected by pilot teachers within their own classrooms defines individual breakthroughs and iteration points. While pilot teachers are generally relieved of cohort data collection duties, they are actively and continuously collecting and analyzing classroom data to assign value to specific strategies, uncover obstacles, and push their own practice.

As early adopters, pilot teachers are typically familiar with making evidence-based decisions. They can gauge their commitment level to a practice by how often they implement it over the course of a week. They tend to note how changes in practice impact weekly assessments, quick formative check-ins, student engagement, or participation levels. And, they are typically comfortable asking for student feedback and making improvements based on suggestions. Pilot teachers may feel confident collecting process, outcome, and balance measures during their pilot implementations; at minimum, we advocate for a focus on balance measures. Classrooms where students have actively co-designed and iterated on new practices in partnership with their teachers—in first grade through twelfth grade—have vastly accelerated shifts to more personalized learning models. Our three featured pilot teachers leveraged multiple data measures to support iteration and validation.

Yarissa adeptly leveraged classroom data during her pilot. She noticed how her formative data efforts became more targeted and deeply rooted into her classroom routines over time. She observed how student engagement shifted across different stations and activities and monitored how quickly students moved out of intensive intervention groups. She tracked student averages on her interim and summative assessments, and she invested significant time into honing systems for student feedback that led to targeted iterations. Based on her data collection efforts, she was able to identify specific strategies that she felt were most responsible for student academic gains.

Val, the first grade pilot teacher we introduced in chapter 6, was interested in improving achievement outcomes on the STAR interim assessment tool for both her struggling students and the large proportion of students with beginning-of-year (BOY) scores at the ninety-ninth percentile. In previous years, Val had noticed that her strongest students lost ground over time, ending the school year squarely in the proficient range but averaging closer to the ninetieth percentile. At the end of her pilot year, Val found that the additional challenge she continuously offered her highest students throughout the year enabled them to remain at the ninety-ninth percentile, while greater numbers of her struggling students ended the year at benchmark. As she iterated during her pilot, Val noticed that her students at all levels were more willing to persist through challenging work when they were able to publish using a creativity app for an audience beyond the classroom. She attributed her strong STAR results to the new culture of rigor that she was able to build during her pilot.

Maya, the high school pilot teacher we introduced in chapter 6, leveraged culturally responsive instruction to build student engagement and achievement in her pilot classroom. Maya was interested in collecting evidence to support the decision to transition her world history course into a more relevant civics course. Using her own summative assessments Maya found that, on average, her civics students outperformed her history students in writing skills, reading skills, and technology skills by almost 30 percent. While both sets of students were learning the same standards, she noticed greater student effort, investment, and skill development in her civics students. Although the student cohorts in both courses were different, Maya was able to quantify the value of her instructional and curricular shifts.

For Yarissa, Val, and Maya, collecting their own classroom data built an evidence base that supported their new pedagogy and allowed them to pinpoint valuable changes. For pilot teachers who struggle with managing data collection, a coach or liaison is best positioned to support these efforts. While classroom data can be extremely compelling, disparate data sets are not sufficient for understanding the impact of pilot efforts across varied classroom environments. Over time, we have realized the importance of establishing cohort measures that collect the same data from each pilot classroom, supporting direct comparisons. The power of both classroom and cohort data resides in the ability of the design team to uncover the stories behind the numbers during midpoint meetings.

Midpoint Meetings

In addition to informal updates, design teams should schedule at least one midpoint meeting to review progress and learning made to date. We recommend teams consult their data collection schedules to determine logical reflection points. Based on the schedule outlined in table 6.4, it would make sense to schedule a midpoint meeting on December 17 after the first round of classroom walkthroughs has been conducted, and a second midpoint meeting on March 1 to review two sources of cohort data: midyear benchmark assessment scores as well as information from the second round of pilot classroom walkthroughs.

Agendas for the midpoint meetings should begin with time for pilot teacher reflection. Each pilot teacher should have the opportunity to share his or her experiences, including implementation challenges and breakthroughs and any classroom data he or she has been collecting. As teachers discuss how they are operationalizing strategies, key insights and implementation tweaks will emerge. If new challenges are identified, the team should discuss how to reduce both real and perceived barriers. It is important for design team members to set a meeting tone that does not pit one pilot experience against another. The goal is to build a foundation of knowledge about common levers and pressure points that support change.

After pilot teachers have concluded their share-outs, the conversation should shift to the analysis of any cohort data collected. Summarized walkthrough data, graphs aligning student balance data with specific strategies, and spreadsheets comparing student achievement data across cohorts will spark questions and uncover trends. Data protocols, such as the ATLAS protocol we reference in chapter 3, will come in handy as design teams wrestle with subgroup data as well as potentially sensitive classroom observation data. Be mindful of the fact that pilot teachers are making themselves vulnerable through this process. They should be applauded for their efforts regardless of immediate behavior changes or outcomes.

Next, conversations should focus on the relative strength of current strategy rubrics, and teams should discuss possible revisions and additions. Often, new strategies will be identified and some original strategies may be difficult to implement or may show little impact. After discussing the rationale behind potential iterations, the team should adjust the strategy rubric to reflect these insights. It is important to note that it often takes pilot teachers six weeks to find their footing with a new practice. Some strategies may generate insignificant academic outcomes by midyear but lead to stronger scores by year end; and some strategies may predominantly impact nonacademic outcomes. Try not to rush to conclusions unless the evidence suggests new practices are doing more harm than good.

Let's return to Yarissa and her implementation of the practice *teachers use data to inform instruction*. Her pilot cohort of six teachers (a teacher at second grade, third grade, fifth grade—Yarissa, sixth grade, and two ninth-grade ELA teachers) started the work in different places, and they all had a lot to share during their first midpoint meeting. While the high school teachers began their pilots by focusing on student choice, the elementary and middle school teachers all began their pilots with a focus on leveraging data and reported on their experiences implementing the four main strategies connected to this practice. During Yarissa's turn to share, she described her process for daily formative assessment as well as the tools and resources she was finding most successful. She shared her schedule for small-group instruction, which showed how she was able to spend more time with struggling students each week. She also discussed her breakthrough of attaching learning objectives to each lesson in her curriculum, including the process she used and the initial classroom outcomes that were generated.

After the share-outs, the team reflected on the cohort walkthrough data recently collected, discussing the implementation patterns as well as challenges behind the data. Ensuing conversations about using data returned to Yarissa's new strategy of attaching learning objectives to each lesson; teachers across grade levels found this concept compelling and were interested in adopting it in their classrooms. In response, the design team revised the strategy rubric, adding a fifth strategy centered on the use of learning objectives and revising the fourth strategy to align with this new process.

These updates are reflected in in table 7.1.

TABLE 7.1 Updated strategy rubric

PRIORITY PRACTICE: TEACHER USES DATA TO INFORM INSTRUCTION
Original strategies
Teacher collects formative data after each lesson to determine student learning levels
Students set weekly goals stating how much they expect to progress toward competency and what steps they will take to get there
Struggling students spend more time with teacher
Revised 12/17: Students can articulate their current understanding of specific learning objectives
New common strategies
Added 12/17: Teacher identifies learning objectives connected to each lesson
Added 3/1: Students leverage posted data to find a peer tutor
Added 3/1: Students form collaborative groups based on interests

During the second midpoint meeting there was a lot more to discuss. Yarissa shared how her data practices were evolving in her math block. Her elementary colleagues shared a breakthrough strategy of leveraging data to pair peers for tutoring support. When students achieved proficiency on a certain skill, they were deemed masters and awarded a sticker on a poster of learning objectives that hung in the classroom. When students were struggling with a skill, they had the opportunity to identify and work with a master to help address confusion or misconceptions. All pilot teachers were excited to adapt this strategy to fit their unique classrooms, and it was added to the strategy rubric.

Yarissa's middle school colleague shared her discomfort about the fact that the majority of students receiving intensive intervention in her classroom—including increased teacher time at the expense of self-directed learning—were boys of color. She felt like her grouping practices were sending an implicit message to the class about who is smart and who is not smart in our society, and she was concerned that her personalization practice was supporting unintentional segregation. The team was reflective and supportive. They knew that this complicated issue deserved further study and decided to undergo a second set of student shadow days and establish a student cogen to gather more information. Discussion generated ideas across priority practices as well as across current mentoring and parent engagement initiatives. Within the *using data* practice, the coach brought up a strategy of using data to convene collaborative groups around interests to allow different groups of students a chance to work together. The team felt this would reframe groups as flexible in the eyes of students, sometimes built on proficiency and sometimes built on interest. Pilot teachers agreed that this would be a valuable addition to all classrooms and added this strategy to the rubric as well.

After Yarissa and her colleagues shared their reflections, the team compared interim assessment data from the beginning and middle of the year. They identified higher patterns of growth in reading scores across elementary and middle school classrooms, which correlated to the fact that these teachers had launched pilot efforts in their literacy blocks. In middle school pilot classrooms, it was noted that English language learners made particularly large reading gains when compared to their classmates and peers in other classrooms. Math scores across pilot classrooms were generally similar to growth rates in non-pilot classrooms. The group discussed results and established hypotheses for various trends.

The team also reviewed walkthrough data during the midpoint meeting and were pleased with the evidence they saw in the elementary and middle school classrooms; all but one of the cohort teachers was making progress on three identified strategies for the priority practice *teacher uses data to inform instruction*. The walkthrough data for this priority practice was less positive in the high school classrooms as these teachers were focused on increasing choice and, while they had explored these strategies, had not been able to establish much traction around leveraging data in their classrooms. This led to an interesting design team conversation regarding barriers and challenges unique to the high school structure. The high school teachers definitely expressed a higher level of frustration than their pilot colleagues around this practice; the design team agreed to free them up so they could visit nearby high school classrooms where early adopter teachers were making strides in data use within ELA courses. By the end of the second midpoint meeting, the design team had a significant amount of data collected and strong documentation that aligned strategies and challenges to both classroom and cohort data sets. They were also purposeful about updating strategy rubrics (see table 7.1).

Despite the amount of data collected or the number of midpoint meetings facilitated over the course of a pilot period, it is important for design teams to determine a hard stopping point for pilots in order to formally reflect, analyze data, and determine strategic next steps.

COLLECTING AND ORGANIZING COHORT DATA

While pilot teachers and design teams have been continuously studying pilot efforts through ongoing classroom data collection and periodic midpoint meetings, the formal pilot evaluation is a more comprehensive effort that considers all cohort level data collected. The design team will require some organization and direction, with respect to generating user-friendly templates to analyze data sets. As discussed earlier, ideally there is at least one data-savvy administrator on the design team who has access to all student data and can take the lead. With clear templates and expectations established, assigning a specific team member to organize data across each type of data measure (process, outcome, balance) will help distribute the work.

There are several points to consider during the pilot evaluation. The first is an inventory of all strategies implemented in pilot classrooms. The second is the extent to which the combination of process, outcome, and balance measures validates these strategies. The third is an initial understanding of essential conditions and the variability involved in implementation across the range of pilot classroom environments. From there, teams determine whether practices are ready for replication, whether an additional pilot period is necessary, or whether the path forward includes some combination of both.

Preparing Process Measure Data

In order to capture all the strategies being implemented in pilot classrooms at the end of the pilot period, we recommend that design teams conduct final pilot classroom observations by leveraging strategy rubrics as well as the full Highlander Institute priority practices tool (appendix C). Final walkthroughs should document the degree to which practices and strategies are present within classrooms and continue to identify related teacher actions, student behaviors, routines, lessons, and experiences the team would like to organize in greater detail. Teams can accomplish this by taking detailed notes on what they see happening in classrooms during these final observations, asking extensive questions of students during and after observations, and having follow-up conversations with pilot teachers. If possible, design team members should film as many successful classroom practices as possible. Classroom video clips serve as rich artifacts for scaling purposes during the refine phase.

Table 7.2 demonstrates the level of implementation observed during final walkthroughs of Yarissa's pilot cohort of six teachers. The results can be compared

TABLE 7.2   Final walkthrough data from pilot cohort

PRIORITY PRACTICE: Teacher uses data to inform instruction	EVIDENCE ACROSS SIX PILOT CLASSROOMS			
Original strategies	No evidence	Very little evidence	Some evidence	Significant evidence
Teacher collects formative data after each lesson to determine student learning levels	2 out of 6 classrooms		1 out of 6 classrooms	3 out of 6 classrooms
Students set weekly goals stating how much they expect to progress toward competency and what steps they will take daily to get there	2 out of 6 classrooms		1 out of 6 classrooms	3 out of 6 classrooms
Struggling students spend more time with teacher	2 out of 6 classrooms			4 out of 6 classrooms
Revised 12/17: Students can articulate their current understanding of specific learning objectives			2 out of 6 classrooms	4 out of 6 classrooms
New Strategies				
Added 12/17: Teacher identifies learning objectives connected to each lesson				6 out of 6 classrooms
Added 3/1: Students leverage posted data to find a peer tutor			1 out of 6 classrooms	5 out of 6 classrooms
Added 3/1: Students form collaborative groups based on interests	1 out of 6 classrooms		1 out of 6 classrooms	4 out of 6 classrooms

to data collected during baseline and midpoint walkthroughs to determine how quickly various strategies were implemented in different classrooms and the degree to which each classroom shifted in relation to each priority practice over time. As table 7.2 indicates, there was significant variability in implementation across strategies within this practice. Ideally, data summaries include the specific grade levels within each evidence category to help the design team connect strategies with particular grade levels or subject areas. The varied results are used to discuss the conditions that were present in classrooms with the most significant shifts.

Despite the inherent limitations of this data set, the design team can leverage it to generate more sophisticated questions and uncover key information. To what degree did this priority practice shift instruction in pilot classrooms? How similar was the implementation of teachers across a single strategy? What is the story behind classrooms with little or no evidence? Did teachers with more incremental shifts experience different obstacles? If so, what barriers would they consider most important to mitigate before attempting to replicate this work? Many teachers showed an impressive spread of strategies over time; what strategies did they find most valuable or easiest to implement? What strategies would pilot teachers recommend as effective entry points for their colleagues?

Once process measures have been examined, it is often helpful to conduct individual pilot teacher interviews to cull additional insight and begin to collect and link artifacts to support replication. Table 7.3 summarizes the information collected during Yarissa's interview. Column one lists the priority practices that were most instrumental in her classroom. Column two links key strategies with the resources and tools that supported implementation. Yarissa's reflections are recorded in column three.

Preparing Outcome Measure Data

It is critical to review cohort outcome measures in order to demonstrate whether student learning, confidence, engagement, attendance, and/or behavior outcomes improved across pilot classrooms. Data reports should compare baseline data for students in participating classrooms (beginning of the year) as well as data collected during the middle and end of the year. Even if a design team is solely focused on academic outcomes, it might be worthwhile to investigate additional student-level data to add depth to the story. For example, did attendance surge during your pilot implementation in comparison to prior years or peer classrooms? Were behavior incidents lower when compared to other classrooms or prior history of individual students? Did homework completion spike or plunge in pilot classrooms? Additional data can help build a stronger evidence base.

Yarissa's pilot cohort compiled STAR data from the beginning, middle, and end of the year and then discussed their perspectives on what was behind specific classroom trends and overall patterns of improvement. Aggregated class summaries of STAR reading data is included in table 7.4. While all pilot classrooms exceeded district averages, some gains were more significant and the data table provides an interesting foundation for a conversation about implementation variability. While looking at aggregated data is valuable for understanding general trends, data should also be disaggregated to determine the impact on individual students and various student subgroups. While the data in table 7.4 does not offer this kind of depth, actual STAR reports uncover disaggregated trends and show student growth rates in addition to proficiency levels. Outcome measures allow us to address the following questions: What are the characteristics of the students who benefited most from

TABLE 7.3 **Information collected from Yarissa's interview**

PRIORITY PRACTICE	RESOURCES/STRATEGIES LINKED TO DETAILED INFORMATION	REFLECTIONS
Students have the opportunity to provide input and feedback on learning experiences	*Template* for daily feedback *Survey* at the end of class Quick lesson *debrief routine* after last station rotation Reflection journals (*protocol*)	"Immediately saw an impact here. Students truly appreciated having their voices heard and enjoyed being brought into the process as partners."
Tasks are differentiated based on students' needs	Different *playlists* and varied *collaborative station activities* with interventions/extensions as needed (across two centers)	"I had always differentiated the direct instruction center, but I effectively reached more students by differentiating tasks and group activities too."
Teacher uses data to inform instruction	*Exit tickets*—Google forms *Quizizz* *Study Island* *Weekly goal-setting template* *Learning progression scope and sequence* *Mastery assessments* *Data posters* for peer tutors	"Developing a learning progression with objectives for each lesson was a game changer. I was able to really target instruction using this data and enable students to understand exactly where they were with regards to mastery."
Feedback process is kind, specific, and helpful	Observed online feedback in *shared docs* "*1 Glow 1 Grow*" method *1:1 conferencing protocol*	"This was key to increasing rigor and kept me focused on mastery. Great to have a feedback cycle throughout the learning process rather than just during the final product."
Students set goals for their learning tasks	*Weekly goal-setting template* Process for goal setting—*info doc* *Student reflections on goal setting*	"Goal setting kept kids accountable to me but more importantly to themselves. They could not coast—they became more self-directed and independent."
Students have choices in how they demonstrate their understanding	*Playlist template* *Digital choice board template* Choice tools: *Padlet, SeeSaw, Adobe Spark, Google Slides, Storyboard*	"Choice vastly improved student engagement and quality of work." "Planning burden was a significant challenge."

Note: Italicized text is linked to additional, more detailed information.

TABLE 7.4 Reading data from the pilot cohort

STAR ASSESSMENT DATA FOR READING			
Teacher	Percent of students reaching grade-level benchmarks		
	Fall	Winter	Spring
Pilot Classroom A	22%	50%	73%
Pilot Classroom B	33%	43%	76%
Pilot Classroom C	35%	45%	53%
Pilot Classroom D	30%	45%	63%
Pilot Classroom E	42%	54%	59%
Pilot Classroom F	35%	54%	70%
Average scores across all district classrooms	27%	38%	50%

the instructional shifts? Struggling students? High achievers? English learners? Special education students? Further, how do the outcomes of pilot student cohorts compare with their grade-level peers in non-pilot classrooms, or when compared to similar students during previous years, under a different model, prior to pilot implementation? Was it easier to move the data in elementary classrooms? How many students finished the year significantly below grade level? Analyzing outcome measures against multiple strategies—and potentially multiple practices—relies on the perspectives of pilot teachers to determine relative impact.

Preparing Balance Measure Data

A review of balance measures in connection with process and outcome measures helps clarify the value of specific strategies. While isolating variables through the analysis of process and outcome measures is often difficult, conversations with pilot teachers, students, and parents are generally straightforward and transparent. Balance measures can uncover powerful stories about how particular strategies are impacting students.

At the end of the pilot period, Yarissa and her pilot cohort asked for student feedback on each of the strategies that they implemented over the course of the year. A summary of resulting data can be found in table 7.5. Across various grade

TABLE 7.5 Student cohort balance measures

	PRIORITY PRACTICE: Teacher uses data to inform instruction					
Abbreviated strategy set	Percent of students who agreed or strongly agreed to enjoying each strategy					
	2nd	3rd	5th	6th	9th	9th
Collection of formative data	85%	78%	90%	82%	N/A	N/A
Struggling students spend more time with the teacher	95%	88%	96%	62%	22%	32%
Students set weekly goals	75%	78%	96%	94%	N/A	N/A
Students understand their current level of mastery on learning objectives	95%	89%	90%	94%	87%	84%
Students use data to find a peer tutor	95%	96%	96%	94%	90%	92%
Collaborative groups are formed around interests	90%	88%	90%	88%	N/A	84%

levels, there was uniform student approval for strategies that centered on finding a peer tutor, engaging in collaborative groups and tasks, and understanding their level of mastery of a skill. The design team assembled student focus groups to dive deeper into the reasons why students were generally enthusiastic about these three strategies.

In contrast, there was significant disparity in student perspectives on the practice that required struggling students to spend more time working in small groups with the teacher. In second-, third-, and fifth-grade pilot classrooms, struggling students enjoyed spending more time with the teacher, and this additional instructional time yielded positive achievement results. In sixth- and ninth-grade classrooms, the sentiment was less positive. When the design team investigated this discrepancy, they learned that the older struggling students felt frustrated and punished by the long and intense daily interactions with their teachers. They watched their peers making choices and working together and craved this flexibility and self-direction, even when their current proficiency level prevented them from independently completing the work. The design team discussed how variation in grade levels greatly impacted student response to this strategy and how iterations on this strategy at the middle and high school levels—such as earned autonomy, heterogeneous grouping, asynchronous video support, or more scaffolded independent activities—could lead to stronger outcomes and more satisfied students. Data from balance measures is particularly valuable when design team members can connect feedback to specific practices, teachers, and students.

Identifying High-Impact Practices: The Fruit Salad Effect

In our framework, pilot classrooms are learning laboratories where multiple methods, tools, and resources are tested simultaneously. Hypothetically, promising strategies should rise to the top as less impactful strategies are tested and abandoned. In reality, pilot classrooms simultaneously generate strong and weak results in scenarios where it is often difficult to isolate variables. Within our framework, this variability is expected and supports rapid iteration within our pilot classrooms. Design teams generally connect a set—or multiple sets—of strategies to the same outcome measures and then encourage pilot teachers to experiment creatively and broadly. Because we adopt this approach, our pilots become a metaphorical fruit salad, featuring different combinations of teacher strategies, edtech software, flexible learning conditions, hardware, curriculum, coaching, teacher strengths, and more. As teams make decisions about what priority practices and associated strategies to replicate, it is helpful to have deeper insight into exactly which components of the fruit salad had the greatest impact.

We have found that high-value strategies bubble up through teacher and student feedback. Whether through the cohort balance measures that are layered on top of outcome and process measures or the ongoing classroom data and student feedback collected, pilot teachers can generally report, with a high level of accuracy, the relative value of different strategies. Consulting pilot teachers to tease out valuable elements prevents teams from discarding an entire bowl of fruit salad because of one spoiled ingredient. When this is not the case, an additional, more targeted pilot phase is suggested.

Preparing Information on the Presence of Barriers

Pilot teachers working to identify promising blended and personalized practices inevitably bump against the system. Attention must be paid to systems theory—how "the behavior of a single autonomous element is different from its behavior when the element interacts with other elements."[1] Systems theory is a framework for untangling complex elements working together to produce a result. It underscores that pilot classroom successes will not seamlessly translate into the larger system. To better understand how variation and roadblocks impact pilot classrooms, design teams need to identify and address friction points that could become deal-breakers during the process of replication. The team must consider how system-level impediments, individual acts of heroism, or unexpected one-time circumstances influenced pilots.

In their book *Innovation and Scaling for Impact*, Seelos and Mair offer a process for helping social endeavors maximize their scaling impact. They discuss the importance of evaluating "problem spaces" and define four dimensions of problem spaces for social enterprises to study before considering scale.[2] These challenges are directly applicable to education systems: Cognitive barriers involve gaps in knowledge and learning; economic barriers encompass resource deficits; political barriers involve relationships and policies; and normative barriers reflect challenges caused by the traditional system. Pilot teachers have been sharing challenges throughout the pilot period; we recommend design team members also weigh in on barriers based on the pilot evaluation results. In table 7.6, Yarissa's design team summarized reflections by category and tagged identified barriers to elementary, middle, and high school pilot classrooms.

Within the education sphere, cognitive barriers comprise the knowledge and skills teachers and principals require to effectively support replication and scale. Design teams must get a handle on the magnitude of professional learning and support required for teachers to implement priority practices. For Yarissa's team, cognitive barriers will require direct messaging and scaffolding for teachers to help them learn to let go of control. The additional barriers identified may require significant thought, planning, and ongoing support, such as how to actively involve students in instructional redesign efforts.

In terms of economic or resource barriers, design teams need to begin to unearth the budgetary implications of the hardware, software, curriculum, coaching, and other resources required to effectively replicate the successful practices of the pilot phase. There are several resource barriers to consider in table 7.6. Yarissa's team discussed the possibility of allocating funding for devices while still dedicating resources to ensure ongoing coaching support. While design teams may identify potential strategies for addressing these challenges, these barriers are tied to the budget. We acknowledge the complexities and imperfect timeframes constraining budgetary decisions; ideally, these decisions are made in partnership with the district leadership team.

While the challenges of economic and cognitive barriers are real, Seelos and Mair believe that these technical problems are relatively easy to overcome. New

TABLE 7.6 **Summary of barriers identified by pilot teachers**

Cognitive	Pilot teachers struggled with the need to directly instruct students on every skill versus recognizing that some students could learn with minimal support. We need to scaffold processes for helping teachers let go of control. (ES, MS, HS)
	Students need to be actively involved in the change process. This requires strong classroom culture and positive teacher-to-student relationships. (ES, MS, HS)
Economic	Initially, we thought that increasing common planning time would be the most important factor for successful implementation, but it was actually one-to-one embedded coaching. This is a must for new teachers. (ES, MS, HS)
	Supporting first graders with multiple, complicated sign-on processes was untenable. (ES)
	Planning for daily differentiated instruction across centers is unsustainable. (ES, MS)
Political	Common planning time at the middle school was often monopolized by student discipline issues, preventing teachers from progressing on their macrodifferentiation model. (MS)
	The rigidity of intervention prevented students from being supported by the specialist most aligned with their needs; this was also wasted time for students at or above level. (ES, MS)
	Even with explicit support from the administration, there was a great deal of discomfort around abandoning the scripted curriculum and daily pacing guide. We kept coming back to this as a cohort and it slowed our progress. (ES, MS)
	YouTube was blocked in the classroom. The suggested "download-and-play" workaround was not easy to leverage and not always successful. (ES, MS, HS).
Normative	The high school bell schedule (forty-two-minute class periods) prevented pilot teachers from trying center-based work or setting goals. Limited time made many personalized practices extremely hard to manage. (HS)
	High school students were unable to leave the building to explore their interests in real-world settings due to liability issues at the district level. (HS)

Key: Elementary school (ES), middle school (MS), high school (HS)

ideas and solutions can be rapidly tested and tweaked, and positive results can typically be directly observed and expanded. Conversely, political and normative challenges have more complex implications with regard to scale. Within education, political barrier plays out across two domains. The first is relational and involves the nature of power dynamics within schools and districts. This is often characterized by the concepts of "culture and climate." Generally, relational issues are downplayed in the pilot phase due to the ownership and autonomy granted to the design team and pilot teachers; when school culture issues present themselves, the team must plan to address these challenges before attempting to scale practices within a building. The second theme centers on the flexibility of current policies.

Referencing table 7.6, the middle school will require a new policy for handling student discipline to allow departments to focus common planning time on co-planning. Similarly, a revised policy on fidelity to the scripted curriculum and pacing guides will be critical to communicate to teachers. Policy barriers are termed political because they are often wrapped up in legacy decision making or threaten the stakeholder group or individual responsible for developing them. Understanding why these political barriers exist and identifying root causes will help the team cultivate the right individuals to support solutions.

Finally, normative barriers refer to the structural forces at play that support the status quo within school systems. In table 7.6, both challenges in this category are related to the high school. The high school bell schedule is a deeply entrenched legacy construct that limited the expansion and success of station rotations in the ninth-grade ELA pilot classrooms. Further, policies forbidding flexible entry and exit from school were a barrier to pilot teachers attempting to operationalize student choice through career shadowing activities. Resolving normative problems requires significant consensus building and a true commitment from all district stakeholders to take risks, explore options, and fail forward. Like political barriers, normative barriers may require backward mapping to identify the people and levers impeding proposed solutions. Identifying the evolution behind these barriers and the individuals who control potential changes is the first step in generating solutions. Do not attempt to unravel legacy constructs without considering the voices of all stakeholders as well as the reverberations redesign efforts may have across an education ecosystem.

We have watched system challenges cripple the expansion of early pilot successes. An accurate and comprehensive list of barriers identified within pilot classrooms is an important stepping stone for exploring future scaling strategies. Design teams should determine which barriers are easy fixes and what challenges will require the involvement of additional leaders. In order for personalized learning to thrive beyond pilot classrooms, the design team will need to routinely consider how to resolve the frustrations and challenges encountered throughout the implementation process.

PILOT ANALYSIS AND DECISION MAKING

At this point, design teams should have enough information to connect the dots through a formal analysis. Like a war room before a strategic invasion, your design team meeting table may be strewn with observation data, outcomes data, survey data, pilot classroom artifacts, and perceived barriers. Once data has been summarized and discussed, we recommend centering the analysis conversation around two key questions:

- Does the evidence collected across measures validate the practices and strategies implemented during the pilot period?
- What special conditions, barriers, or variability have impacted the implementation of strategies?

The data analysis template depicted in table 7.7 shows how Yarissa's design team summarized and analyzed data collected around the priority practice *teachers use data to inform instruction.*

TABLE 7.7   Data analysis template

Validated	Teachers articulate learning objectives connected to lessons; measure mastery of learning objectives	This was a breakthrough strategy for all pilot teachers and led to more targeted instruction and assessment, as well as to greater student ownership. Teachers universally agreed that this strategy led to stronger achievement, which was supported by scores.
	Teachers collect formative data on student progress after lessons	Five out of six teachers leveraged this strategy multiple times per week and deepened their understanding of student competency levels.
	Teachers use data to find a peer tutor	Students loved this strategy across grade levels and subject areas, and it led to significant increases in achievement, according to teachers.
Promising	Struggling students spend more time with the teacher	This strategy was most effective for elementary and lower middle school students who most enjoyed the extra teacher time. Achievement data associated with this strategy was highest for elementary teachers. High school students considered this to be punitive and the practice was stopped quickly.
	Students engage in weekly goal setting	Half of the teachers regularly leveraged this strategy and one found it extremely compelling. It is worth codifying Yarissa's approach and continuing to study impact.
	Students form collaborative groups based on interests	This strategy was leveraged toward the end of the pilot period in all but one classroom. Students responded positively to the strategy; evidence showed that it increased engagement, particularly for boys; more study needed.
Inconclusive	Teachers collect formative data (HS)	Data practices were generally inconclusive at the high school level.

The design team was pleased with evidence collected around this priority practice at the elementary and middle school levels and felt confident that the practice was leading to positive student outcomes and more personalized instruction. They also felt that they had enough resources, artifacts, classroom video clips, and teacher and student reflections to support a new wave of implementing teachers.

Then the team pivoted to a focus on identified barriers (table 7.6). They realized that the planning burden was a significant common challenge and needed to be addressed before moving forward with a replication plan. They also realized that coaching support would be critical for new, implementing teachers. The team reflected on the stakeholders that would need to be involved to revise policy barriers. Based on the extent of barriers at the high school level, the team determined that an additional pilot period was necessary to study how new policies and systems could create better conditions for their personalized model.

Their final consensus at the end of the formal pilot evaluation included several parts. The first was that further implementation would depend on how effectively they could address challenges and put support in place for teachers. The second was that validated strategies would have the best chance of effective replication in classrooms that reflected the same grade levels as the elementary and middle school pilot teachers: second, third, fifth, and sixth. Leveraging the resources developed in pilot classrooms that directly connected strategies to scaffolded curriculum would vastly decrease the planning burden for new teachers and provide them with a strong foundation of knowledge on which to build.

In most cases, formal pilot evaluations uncover strategies that are ready to move forward and strategies or conditions that require additional study. Second pilot periods could involve the recruitment of new teachers or more structure and support for existing pilots. If the data is inconclusive, then pilot teachers may need more time, more coaching, and/or additional resource support, usually in the form of curriculum or software. We have successfully supported a second pilot phase in several schools, when pilot teachers found the priority practices effective, but struggled to keep up with content and assessment creation. Failing forward is a common experience in blended and personalized learning trials; leverage lessons learned to refine strategy sets and craft a more effective pilot process. When a set of validated strategies is defined, teams are ready to move these strategies into the refine phase.

Structuring a learning cycle requires a heavy time commitment from both the design team and pilot teachers. Our example focusing on the practice of *teachers use data to inform instruction* shows the extent of the work required to study a single practice; the addition of multiple practices and strategies complicates implementation, data collection, and data analysis. However, the deep learning that took place around this practice for Yarissa and her team is evident. We encourage teams to persevere through the process, build on successes, and learn from challenges.

DEFINING THE CHASM

Once a design team has decided to move forward with particular strategies, they begin to consider the needs of the next wave of implementing teachers. Returning to Rogers's diffusion of innovation theory introduced in chapter 3 (figure 3.1), the design team considers the qualities of teachers who are part of each category: innovators, early adopters, early majority, late majority, and laggards. Geoffrey Moore, author of *Crossing the Chasm: Marketing and Selling Disruptive Products to Mainstream Customers,* pioneered the concept of the chasm in the adoption curve—the critical gap between early adopters who are visionaries capable of quickly integrating innovations into their routines and lifestyles, and the early majority who are pragmatists and will not buy new products until they are established value-adds.[3] Moore posits that once a product crosses the chasm and is embraced by the early majority, large-scale adoption is feasible. Figure 7.1 demonstrates the placement of the chasm.

We find the chasm concept plays a compelling role in complex educational change. The characteristics of early majority teachers, as well as their colleagues

FIGURE 7.1   **Defining the chasm**

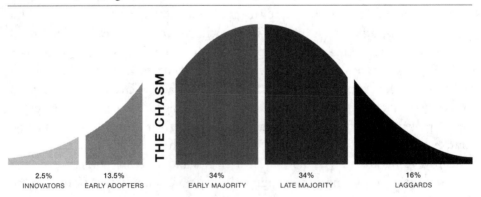

| 2.5% | 13.5% | 34% | 34% | 16% |
| INNOVATORS | EARLY ADOPTERS | EARLY MAJORITY | LATE MAJORITY | LAGGARDS |

Source: Moore, Geoffrey A. 1991. *Crossing the Chasm: Marketing and Selling High-Tech Products to Mainstream Customers*. Oxford, UK: Capstone Publishing.

further down the adoption curve, suggest that they possess a different mindset, capacity, and approach to change—not different in a negative or antagonistic way, different in terms of the information and support they require to be successful implementers. Just because new priority practices have been connected to promising evidence and embraced by pilot teachers does not mean they will directly translate into the classrooms of the larger faculty. This realization is often disregarded in school reform efforts; many leaders in our partner districts assume pilot classrooms can simply be replicated as whole units once a set of strategies is validated. Time and again, this hypothesis has proven false.

In order to identify the varied needs of different adopters, we created an adoption matrix (figure 7.2), which maps adopter categories along a continuum. We believe the most critical adopter needs are associated with the level of structure that accompany validated strategies as they cross the chasm. In our matrix, there are

FIGURE 7.2   **Adoption matrix**

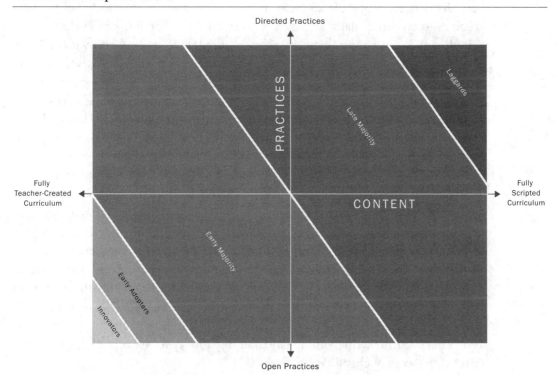

two main sources of structure: the availability of quality curriculum materials runs along the *x* axis, and the level of guidance and direction attached to validated practices and strategies runs along the *y* axis. Innovators sit in the bottom left quadrant of the matrix and require very little existing curriculum, as well as very little guidance around practice, to implement new ideas. Early adopters thrive in conditions where they can leverage a few curriculum resources and general guidance to build their own approach to integrating practices and curricula. Early majority teachers require a larger baseline of existing curricular resources and more guidance around practices. Late majority teachers need to have about 75 percent of curricula and practices scripted for them, and laggards require fully scripted curriculum resources attached to highly directed practices. We define the explicit integration of practices and curriculum as a *bounded solution*.

The adoption matrix provides some important insights into managing personalization initiatives. First, innovators and early adopters will not be able to effectively innovate in environments that require strict fidelity to scripted curriculum. Second, in order to scale personalized learning efforts beyond early adopter teachers, districts must provide 25 to 50 percent of the curriculum resources teachers require to construct daily lessons. Teachers on the other side of the chasm simply do not have the same capacity as early adopters to build their own curricula. We define curriculum as a robust set of prepared lessons, activities, resources, and assessments that are scaffolded to meet the needs of different learners in a classroom. We do not consider a scope and sequence of standards to be curriculum. Finally, scaffolded levels of guidance around the integration of practices and content—from fully flexible to fully scripted—must be prepared to engage teachers at various points on the adoption curve.

When the design team performs a curriculum audit, it will most likely uncover a significant curriculum challenge, which will impact the pace and progress of scaling efforts. While the design team will participate in developing a strategic solution to curriculum (which we untangle in chapter 10), building a curriculum is not the work of the team. Instead, members focus on defining levels of guidance and support that will help more teachers implement priority practices. This includes creating implementation pathways to organize validated strategies and attaching them to detailed examples and resources. The goal is to provide teachers along the adoption curve with adequate choice and support to successfully join the implementation effort. Constructing an implementation pathway for each priority practice is part of the work of chapter 8.

• • •

The conclusion of the pilot phase is cause for design team celebration. Whether or not strategies were validated, your school or district hopefully captured and documented significant learning through the process and can build on this foundation. Most likely you still have strategies or conditions that require more study. If you have validated strategies that are worthy of replication, you are ready to begin the refine phase.

In their 2017 white paper "All That We've Learned: Five Years Working on Personalized Learning," Wright, Greenberg, and Schwartz caution readers: "We must move with urgency but not rush our efforts to reach scale. . . . There is a danger in trying to scale too quickly because if we do not have the right conditions, we run the risk of worse outcomes, thus killing the innovation before it has time to mature."[4] The work ahead continues the methodical process of establishing the right conditions for scale.

The refine phase marks a critical shift in our pathway framework, from a focus on the roughly 15 percent of early adopters and pilot classrooms to the 85 percent of teachers on the other side of the chasm. Through documentation and communication efforts, design teams create a bridge across the chasm to enable more teachers to engage in the work and increase the impact on students.

REFINE

Pathway to Personalization Framework

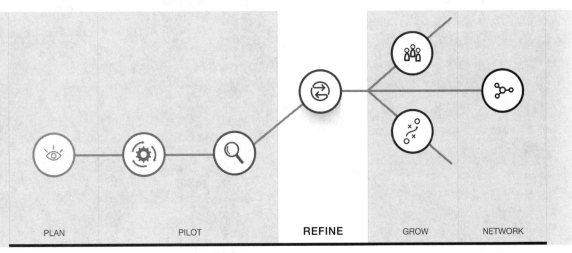

PLAN PILOT **REFINE** GROW NETWORK

Create pathways

CREATING
PATHWAYS

One of our most unforgettable district collaborations involved a large urban district committed to becoming a personalized learning district. Leaders limited design team membership to district level administrators and hired the Highlander Institute team to work directly with a cohort of pilot teachers. Priority practices embodied flexible learning environments, data-driven decision making, and differentiated instruction. At the end of the year, the district administration was pleased with the shifts they noticed across pilot classrooms, including an increase in student collaboration and discussion and higher engagement levels in class.

Without consulting pilot classroom teachers, district leaders distilled one model from the pilot experience to scale across the district. The following year an administrative directive mandated that all district teachers leverage the station rotation model for both math and ELA instruction in every classroom, every day. While the station rotation model was the most easily observable aspect of the pilot classroom design, administrators disregarded the other strategies that were supporting the priority practices. For example, ELA teachers at the high school were integrating full-class Socratic seminars that were resulting in higher levels of student discussion and engagement.

The decision to replicate a model rather than a set of practices and supporting strategies left teachers struggling to understand how a center-based instructional approach would add value to their classrooms. The district was thoughtful about providing professional development and ongoing support to teachers. However, the model was an extremely challenging shift for the majority of teachers and the nature of the mandate caused reluctant teachers to resist. Meanwhile, enthusiastic teachers went underground as they tweaked the model, thinking the district would consider their iterations non-compliant. Most educators in the district ignored the mandate, developing distrust for the district vision and maligning the whole concept of personalized learning. Building principals were left having to defend the initiative while fielding constant complaints from teachers about fidelity to the model. Predictably, this well-intentioned attempt to simplify the scaling process led to an incredibly problematic rollout and much goodwill lost.

There is a natural tendency on the part of leaders to want instruction across their district to have a sense of consistency and uniformity. This instinct is efficient from a leadership standpoint. It facilitates coherence across internal messaging, professional learning, and communication with parents and students. It simplifies classroom observation protocols. It makes curriculum decisions and purchasing easier, and it is appreciated by parents who can rely on consistent approaches across grade levels. There are definite positives to mandating a singular approach; however, when attempting to replicate promising personalized learning practices, levels of iteration and autonomy are necessary to move practices across the chasm. By narrowing the scope of a personalized learning implementation to one highly defined option, leaders are communicating that they know exactly what is best for each of their teachers. Fidelity to a rigorous, research-based model is a time-honored approach in education, but as an organization we do not believe blended and personalized learning can be treated like a boxed curriculum rollout. In our example district, the teachers responded predictably to the ultimatum.

In their book *Innovation and Scaling for Impact*, Christian Seelos and Johanna Mair explore the intersection between investments in novel ideas (innovation) and the replication of high-value ideas based on existing strengths (scaling). They are very clear about the relationship between innovation, scaling, and impact: "Innovation per se does not create impact. Innovation generates the *potential* for impact creation. Scaling creates impact from innovation. If you don't know how to scale, don't innovate!"[1] The effective replication of blended and personalized approaches requires a new way of thinking about scale. Our model encourages design teams to empower new implementing teachers by creating pathways that offer guidance and structure while allowing for teacher voice and input with regard to adoption.

With a clear understanding of the direction and promise of the initiative, teachers have autonomy to choose a validated strategy that aligns to their classroom needs and select from detailed pilot examples, resources, and curriculum connections to support their implementation. More than experimentation that happens within the pilot phase, this work is the true innovation behind successful school and district efforts.

When a formal pilot analysis validates a set of strategies connected to a priority practice, teams enter the refine phase to create a bridge across the adoption chasm. There are four components to this work. One is the creation of a pilot story that broadly captures pilot learning in order to consistently message the work and generate excitement. The second is the creation of implementation pathways, connecting validated strategies with resources and examples to support the next wave of implementing teachers. Third is a plan for establishing bounded solutions that connect successful strategies with curriculum. And fourth is the formalization of the pilot teacher cohort as a research and development engine to grow the evidence base, test new assumptions, and study key questions that continue to emerge as districts move to scale. Through the description of each element we offer guidance, essential questions, and examples to help design teams effectively translate the work of pilot teachers.

CAPTURING THE PILOT STORY

The data, artifacts, and conversations from the formal pilot analysis have likely generated significant learning and insights. It is now time to pull the most important pieces into a story to share with district stakeholders. This is an important step that, in our experience, is often overlooked by district partners. In addition to providing new teachers with important foundational information about the initiative and sharing the power of priority practices, communicating the pilot process is an important way to initiate two-way conversations and solicit feedback from stakeholders with various perspectives. There are several elements that help make the pilot story presentation particularly compelling for all audiences.

The first is a clear, updated vision statement that reflects the lessons and epiphanies of the pilot phase. It is common to find the work has strayed or pivoted from the original vision and priority practices. A strong, relevant, and specific vision statement should answer the question, "Why are we pursuing blended and personalized approaches?" This will bring clarity to the overall effort. The second is a refined definition of what blended and personalized learning means within the local context. This can include core elements distilled from the pilot phase, clarification of shifting roles for teachers and students, or a vivid description of the ideal student experience. The definition should help stakeholders visualize important instructional shifts.

Leaders from Loudoun County public schools in Virginia have crafted a strong example of a vision and definition that is meaningful to stakeholders and clearly communicates what the school district values:

> The [vision] of Loudoun County Public Schools is to empower all students to make meaningful contributions to the world. Personalized Learning is dynamically tailoring learning experiences to students' strengths, needs and/or interests. A PL approach supports [our existing focus on project-based learning] by encouraging the following: (1) Access to significant content for students who may have learning gaps, (2) Challenges for students who have shown basic mastery, and (3) Relevance for all students as their interests help shape the direction of "meaningful contributions to the world."[2]

When the vision and definition reflect voice and input from pilot teachers, is clear enough for a non-educator to understand, offers a compelling picture of how shifts can benefit students, then the design team is ready to capture the pilot story. This is best accomplished through the stories of pilot teachers and students. Document breakthrough classroom moments, teacher reflections, and student outcomes through videos, quotes, and work samples to engage and inspire various stakeholder audiences. Support key pilot lessons and learning with data and evidence. Devote equal attention to how the team learned from both successes and failures. Discuss how the expanded design team worked together to solve problems and reduce obstacles. Finally, explicitly connect pilots to the vision and priority practices and set the stage for ongoing discussions enabling all stakeholders to have a voice in the process of replication and scale.

Introducing the pilot story can take several forms. Presentations can leverage a stand-and-deliver format, with pilot teachers and students sharing alongside design team members. Pilot information can be captured in a playlist, with audience members reviewing the information asynchronously and sharing their thoughts and ideas through small- or whole-group conversations during a meeting. Content can be separated into various stations or centers, with audience members making choices about the information they are most interested in learning. When possible, compelling presentation formats should model the priority practices deemed valuable during the pilot process, allowing audiences to experience the new approaches as learners.

IMPLEMENTATION PATHWAYS

The pilot story anchors a personalized learning initiative to positive outcomes and lessons learned for a broad audience, with the dual goals of clarifying the rationale for the work and generating broad enthusiasm for the effort. *Implementation pathways* define—in specific detail—how new implementing teachers can access and build on the work of pilot teachers. The artifacts, platforms, routines, lessons, projects, and tasks created in pilot classrooms are an incredibly precious resource for teachers joining the initiative. Hopefully, design teams have continuously collected and organized these artifacts, aligning them to the specific strategy and priority practice they support. Implementation pathways serve as a user-friendly repository for all this information.

Ideally, each implementation pathway should focus on a single priority practice; however, they can be combined if priority practices are similar and aligned. Implementation pathways should be clearly organized and widely accessible. Based on funding and capacity constraints, design teams can assemble resources as a simple table of links in a shared document; develop a more detailed website; or create a robust, searchable online database that leverages existing platforms and systems.

The Rationale for Creating Implementation Pathways

Our concept of an implementation pathway was inspired by observations of several schools and districts that struggled with early scaling efforts. We recognized that when new implementing teachers did not benefit from the specific knowledge and experience gleaned by pilot teachers, their replication efforts often floundered.

In one partner district, a set of strategies connected to the priority practice of *students are collaborating* was validated across pilot classrooms. One strategy that was implemented by every pilot teacher was a protocol that guided students as they worked in groups. The protocol prompted students to give thoughtful feedback, respect group members, stay on task, use soft voices, and actively participate. One pilot teacher in particular, Carmen, established an incredible classroom culture of collaboration. It was magical observing her fourth graders in action. Small heterogeneous groups of students—many requiring additional support for learning disabilities, behavior, speech, and reading—were effectively and respectfully working together in multiple ways to accomplish tasks and solve problems. Excited by the affirmation, the design team immediately began bringing more teachers through her classroom to observe her impressive models of student collaboration. The principal featured Carmen during a staff meeting and advocated for all teachers to leverage the collaboration protocol.

However, the design team and principal failed to study the deep scaffolding Carmen established with her fourth-grade students and how it was ultimately responsible for her classroom culture. Over the course of two months, she had carefully walked her students through elements of the protocol so they clearly understood the expectations. She captured video of various student groups during collaboration time and reviewed clips with the whole class, discussing both good examples as well as inappropriate behaviors. She ran fishbowls where students watched their peers engage in collaborative work and then reflected on how well they had followed the protocol. She identified students with particular acumen in aspects of the protocol and ran an exemplary collaboration group for the class to observe. It was time-consuming and rigorous, requiring incredible commitment to the priority practice.

Neither the snapshot received during a walkthrough of Carmen's classroom nor the general overview presented during the staff meeting provided enough guidance for teachers to replicate the strategy. There was simply not enough information shared to enable teachers to cross the adoption chasm. Consequently, failed efforts were blamed on the students, and teachers quickly reverted to their traditional instructional models. Implementation pathways seek to prevent this scenario by explicitly defining and documenting how teachers can replicate and iterate on validated strategies.

Key Features of Implementation Pathways

Each strategy within an implementation pathway is linked to a detailed set of resources. In addition to providing instructional support, these materials enable the next set of teachers to fully understand the goals and intentions behind each strategy, as well as the kind of outcomes they can expect from implementation.

As we have experimented with the concept of implementation pathways, several features have become particularly important. It is helpful to include access to the results of the pilot phase so new, implementing teachers can review the evidence behind the strategies presented. It is also beneficial to organize strategies in a way that helps new, implementing teachers identify an appropriate entry point. Returning to our collaboration example, the implementation pathway for this priority practice could feature resources attached to three targeted strategies: training students on collaboration protocols, leveraging collaboration to practice and build basic skills, and leveraging collaboration to support higher depth of knowledge (DOK), as exemplified in tables 8.1–8.3.

Another helpful feature is the addition of a tagging structure that clarifies the implementation level of each resource. The templates in tables 8.1–8.3 use the

TABLE 8.1   **Implementation pathway strand #1**

PRIORITY PRACTICE
Students are collaborating
STRATEGY
Train students on collaboration protocols
(E = entry-level, M = midlevel, C = complex)

Resource	Details
Introduce *GROUPS Protocol*	*Video*: Students introducing protocol (E) *Video*: Teacher reflections on using protocol (E) *Teacher reflections*: Lessons learned (E) *Fishbowl activity*: Identifying strong collaboration (M) *Self-evaluation activity*: Developing collaboration skills (M)
Grade level: Second to eighth *Teacher to visit*: Carmen (fourth grade)	

Resource	Details
Group *role cards*	Each member of the group selects a role to play and is assessed on his or her performance by group members and the teacher (M)
Grade level: Third to tenth *Teacher to visit*: All fourth-grade classrooms	

Resource	Details
Seven norms of collaboration	Developing and sustaining productive group work (E)
Grade level: All *Teacher to visit*: All fourth-grade classrooms	

Note: Italicized text is linked to additional, more detailed information.

TABLE 8.2   **Implementation pathway strand #2**

PRIORITY PRACTICE	
Students are collaborating	
STRATEGY	
Leverage collaboration to build basic skills	

(E = entry-level, M = midlevel, C = complex)

Resource	Details
Routines to support this goal	*Routine*: Establish peer experts (E)
	Routine: Identify a peer partner and schedule a meeting during collaboration time (M)
	Video: Student reflection on peer support during creation green screen activity (M)
	Tutorial: Video explaining how to set up and coach students around green screen usage in classrooms (C)
Grade level: Second to eighth *Teacher to visit*: Carmen (fourth grade)	

Resource	Details
Peer-assisted learning strategies (PALS)	Build reading skills through partner reading, paragraph shrinking, and a prediction relay (M)
Grade level: K–6 *Teacher to visit*: Sandra (third grade)	

Resource	Details
Reciprocal peer tutoring	Students alternate between the role of tutor and tutee using a protocol to practice a skill (E)
Grade level: Second to eighth *Teacher to visit*: Carmen (fourth grade)	

Note: Italicized text is linked to additional, more detailed information.

coding structure of E = entry level, M = midlevel, and C = complex. Further, attaching grade-level ranges to resources enables teachers to pinpoint best-fit options. Finally, including specific pilot classrooms where each strategy can be observed offers an additional layer of support to teachers.

TABLE 8.3 Implementation pathway strand #3

PRIORITY PRACTICE
Students are collaborating
STRATEGY
Leverage collaboration for higher depth of knowledge (DOK)

(E = entry-level, M = midlevel, C = complex)

Resource	Details
Creation apps on Google Chrome to demonstrate knowledge	Students choose a way to demonstrate their learning by selecting an app as a group and supporting each other in the creation of individual prototypes (C)
Grade level: Third through twelfth *Teacher to visit*: Carmen (fourth grade)	

Resource	Details
Performance tasks	Students choose a task and partner up around similar choices to develop solutions (C)
Grade level: Second through twelfth *Teacher to visit*: Sandra (third grade)	

Resource	Details
Design Thinking toolkit	Protocol for developing solutions or prototypes in small groups (C)
Grade level: Third through twelfth *Teacher to visit*: Ed (sixth grade)	

Note: Italicized text is linked to additional, more detailed information.

A final feature worth contemplating is the level of guidance attached to each strategy. Returning to the adoption matrix we introduced in chapter 7 (figure 7.2), the vertical axis is defined by the amount of direction attached to a practice. Open practices have less guidance; directed practices are more scripted. For example, the peer-assisted learning strategies (PALS) method listed in table 8.2 provides a highly structured protocol for students to use as they build specific skills. This thirty-five-minute literacy protocol includes partner reading, paragraph shrinking, and a prediction relay. This would be considered a highly directed strategy. Conversely, leveraging creation apps on Google Chrome to demonstrate knowledge, a strategy documented in table 8.3, is highly open. Teachers using this strategy have flexibility to select specific apps and determine the assignment connected to the software; with this flexibility comes an additional planning burden. Some implementation pathways are color coded to identify strategies that are more or less directed.

It is important to note none of these strategies is attached to curriculum. The PALS strategy requires teachers to provide appropriate reading material, and leveraging Google Chrome apps requires teachers to integrate content and provide instructions, templates, and/or rubrics to support the strategy. Attaching explicit curriculum to strategies results in the creation of bounded solutions, discussed later in greater detail.

When pilot teachers and design teams sit down to assemble an implementation pathway, they start with a review of the artifacts collected during the pilot phase. If additional artifacts are needed, requests can be made of pilot teachers who were successful with these strategies. In addition, it is helpful to collect supplementary information, such as classroom video demonstrations of how strategies are implemented, as well as student and teacher reflections on the value of a strategy. The goal is to build a small but credible set of high quality examples to get the next wave of teachers up and running. As new methods and associated resources are implemented successfully across more classrooms, they should be added to implementation pathways.

While important for replication efforts, implementation pathways are a short-term strategy for bridging the chasm. They represent a strategic way for teachers to build on the efforts of pilot teachers. However, pilot teachers represent a small sample size; not all grade levels or subject areas are represented in the pilot phase. As a diverse range of teachers implement validated strategies, the number of effective resources will multiply, overwhelming a shared document or template. At this point, design teams must determine more sustainable systems for connecting a growing knowledge base around strategies with grade-level and content-area curriculum. Embedding validated strategies within curriculum is the long-term goal. This will require integration with learning management systems or localized digital curriculum platforms.

BOUNDED SOLUTIONS

Bryk and colleagues emphasize the importance of reducing the complexity of a new approach through the creation of stronger systems: "Improving productivity is . . .

about designing better processes for carrying out common work problems and creating more agile mechanisms for sensing and reacting to novel situations."[3] In our model, creating better processes involves two elements: implementation pathways and bounded solutions. An implementation pathway organizes validated strategies and associated resources linked to a priority practice. Bounded solutions go a step further and explicitly connect strategies to curriculum and standards. If implementation pathways are a rope bridge across the chasm, bounded solutions are a well-engineered concrete bridge reinforced with steel bars that can safely support chasm crossing for much larger groups.

The adoption matrix (figure 7.2) was created to show the scaling limitations of personalized learning initiatives that do not include bounded solutions. Without them, we believe design teams will be unsuccessful in scaling their personalized learning initiatives beyond early majority teachers. Returning to our collaboration example, the creation of an implementation pathway with video examples and teacher testimony from Carmen helped some teachers implement collaborative activities with greater effectiveness and frequency. However, other teachers struggled, not because of the protocol, but because they were unable to find or create engaging, rigorous tasks to anchor student collaboration activities. Carmen and several of her colleagues enjoyed the autonomy of building their own tasks for student collaboration; however, teachers on the other side of the chasm struggled to vet appropriate tasks and did not have the capacity to create their own. These teachers require bounded solutions to implement this priority practice.

Developing bounded solutions for all grade levels and content areas requires long-term planning. In addition to being linked to implementation pathways, bounded solutions are intimately connected to how a design team is approaching their curriculum challenge (a topic we explore in chapter 10) and how design teams and district leadership teams are thinking about scaling tactics (a topic we explore in chapter 9). We see two main paths through this odyssey. One involves a focus on early majority teachers, and the other involves the identification of existing quality curriculum resources that are already connected to priority practices.

Plan for the Early Majority

Without the presence of strong personalized learning curriculum resources, we recommend focusing initial replication efforts on early adopter and early majority teachers. Early majority teachers are practical, and they will not hesitate to leverage a valuable strategy. Geoffrey Moore offers a great definition of individuals in this category:

> . . . [the] early majority want to buy a productivity improvement for existing oper-
> ations. They are looking to minimize the discontinuity with the old ways. They
> want evolution, not revolution. They want technology to enhance, not overthrow,
> the established ways of doing business. And above all, they do not want to debug
> somebody else's product. By the time they adopt it, they want it to work properly
> and to integrate appropriately with their existing technology base.[4]

Translating these concepts to education, early majority teachers want high
quality, easy-to-implement, reliable strategies with low risk and moderate support.
Leveraging the adoption matrix, early majority teachers can thrive when highly
directed practices are paired with lower amounts of existing curriculum or when
more open practices are connected to more scripted curriculum options.

Returning to our implementation pathway for the priority practice of *students
are collaborating,* early majority teachers could find success with just a small degree
of curricular guidance and a well-designed implementation pathway. These teachers do not necessarily need access to bounded solutions because pilot teachers,
like Carmen, have validated a strategy and eliminated initial uncertainties around
implementation. A detailed implementation pathway, combined with a repository
of high quality tasks (such as the Performance Assessment Resource Bank or the
Buck Institute Project Search), and a moderate degree of coaching support, would
adequately enable most early majority teachers to cross the chasm.[5]

As they gain experience, early majority teachers can join early adopters to build
bounded solutions, generating a curriculum work group that comprises approximately 50 percent of a faculty (see figure 3.1). With framing and support from a
district- or building-level curriculum team, teachers can attach validated strategies
to specific lessons, tasks, and projects, tag them to specific learning standards, and
share them with their colleagues. As these resources grow in number and complexity, an organized and accessible digital system will be needed for sharing and
expanding solutions.

Plan for a Focused Effort

Alternately, the design team can drill down on a single grade level or content area
where pockets of strong personalized curriculum already exist. In one of our local
elementary schools, the curriculum team developed fully scripted maker-space
units integrating art and fourth-grade STEM standards. The units included performance tasks, content, activity templates, and rubrics—all necessary materials and

resources—for fall, winter, and spring modules lasting four to six weeks. Connecting this curriculum to the strategies defined on implementation pathways establishes a bounded solution for all fourth-grade teachers to leverage. Each member of this teaching cohort can determine how to adapt or iterate on the solution based on his or her comfort and capacity.

Integrating implementation pathways with curriculum to establish bounded solutions is the key to scaling personalized learning models. Yet, when we consider the scope of standards, subjects, and grade levels that we aspire to align with priority practices, we acknowledge this must be an incremental process. A second-grade late majority teacher may receive access to an incredible bounded solution for phonics but still need to wait for resources to support his or her six additional content areas. As we constantly reiterate to administrators, principals, teachers, and students, generating the curriculum and software necessary to support scale is a slowly evolving process.

When considering the degree of change that is comfortable and manageable for new, implementing teachers, a gradual approach makes sense. In the journal article "Four Teacher-Friendly Postulates for Thriving in a Sea of Change" (originally printed in 1994 and reprinted in 2007), math teacher Steven Leinwand puts the concept of gradual change into perspective: "It is unreasonable to ask a professional to change much more than 10 percent a year, but it is unprofessional to change by much less than 10 percent a year."[6]

Creating bounded solutions is not a linear process and there are no perfect workflow systems. The work will happen in starts and stops and run parallel to curriculum design and strategic scaling efforts. Design teams can opt to kick the notion of bounded solutions down the road until further decisions regarding strategy and barriers have been clarified. However, the concept should always be somewhere in mind; a disregard for bounded solutions will jeopardize replication and scaling efforts.

FORMALIZING AN R&D ENGINE

The final piece of the refine phase centers on a process for transforming the pilot classroom concept into a formal research and development (R&D) mechanism for continuous learning. While pilot teachers have helped to identify scalable strategies, they are just getting started on their own personalized learning journeys. By continuing to experiment with promising approaches—as well as testing the value of specific resources, policies, and ideas generated by the design team—they will ultimately serve as a highly valuable, ongoing school or district resource.

As the design team shifts attention toward building pathways for replication, pilot teachers are well positioned to accelerate their learning and experimentation. In their 2017 white paper, "All That We've Learned: Five Years Working on Personalized Learning," Wright, Greenberg, and Schwartz describe the importance of continuous learning and ongoing testing: "Great schools build the system to formalize continuous improvement, devote enough resources, and make their schools true learning organizations."[7]

Establishing a formal R&D engine within a school or district will require some forethought and planning around several components. The first is valuing and compensating R&D teachers for any additional work they are managing on top of their regular teaching loads. This can include additional planning and/or collaboration time, as well as possible stipends. Alternately, R&D teachers can be offered a reduced teaching schedule with specific time directed toward coaching, mentoring, or planning.

From a professional development lens, it is important to structure ongoing opportunities for R&D teachers to visit the classrooms of advanced practitioners across the district and state, as well as attend and present at conferences. We have found a large percentage of amazing pilot teachers—and early adopters—are quickly recruited out of the classroom to fill coaching positions. We strongly advise design teams to consider how these teachers can remain in the classroom for at least part of the day to accelerate experimentation and learning. Finally, the R&D engine will need a point person or small advisory team to coordinate communication, collect and analyze ongoing data, and share findings.

We recommend teams draft a proposal to the school or district leadership team describing how a formal R&D engine will strategically support the ongoing personalized learning initiative, as well as the roles, additional resources, and capacity it will require. Here are a few options to consider:

1. *Professional learning*: Lab classrooms led by former pilot teachers can support professional learning for school or district stakeholders. Lab classrooms demonstrate what the vision and rationale look like in reality, and lab teachers have the expertise to work individually with their colleagues or lead professional development activities based on teacher needs. In our experience, a twenty-minute observation of a lab classroom, followed by a twenty-minute debrief

and coaching session, is the most powerful catalyst for bringing more teachers into the work.

2. *Creating infrastructure*: R&D teachers can focus on continually strengthening implementation pathways and/or developing bounded solutions. By exploring curriculum options and testing software, they can increase options while easing the burden of implementation for their colleagues. Simultaneously, their ongoing discoveries and breakthroughs will support continuous learning and iteration, ensuring scaling efforts are as efficient, relevant, and effective as possible. Creating a user-friendly process for sharing new strategies, resources, and tools is an important element of this role.

3. *Formal evaluation of solutions*: As challenges emerge from scaling efforts, R&D teachers can help identify, create, and test new policies, professional learning modules, etc. Further, as the design team considers new directions or additional layers of personalization, R&D teachers will be critical in determining alignment and assessing value. As education innovation continues to move at a dizzying pace, formalizing a process for testing new concepts is invaluable and keeps the focus on how promising ideas can be effectively adapted into the unique conditions found within every school.

4. *Ongoing data collection*: Finally, R&D teachers can support ongoing research by continuing to collect data across process, outcome, and balance measures in their own classrooms. Lab teachers can connect iterations to evidence before new practices are introduced to the larger faculty. Furthermore, by developing and testing new evaluation instruments, lab teachers can help shape how a district measures what they value the most. Once ready, new measures and processes can cross the chasm, with R&D teachers supporting planning and rollout efforts.

The field of education will never stop iterating. As we continue to reinvent research-based strategies within twenty-first-century learning contexts, the time and resources invested in supporting a well-oiled R&D engine will ensure continuous reforms underway are relevant, aligned, and valuable.

● ● ●

The refine phase is an opportunity for pilot teachers and the design team to carefully act on pilot data and leverage results to set the stage for forward movement. Creating resources such as pilot stories, implementation pathways, and bounded solutions takes time, but these materials form the backbone of scaling efforts.

The design team is now ready to transition to the grow phase, which starts with the vetting of pilot information with both teachers and leaders. From there, the design team and district leadership team collaborate to determine appropriate scaling strategies. Through each process, the focus remains on flexibility, relevance, continuous learning, and iteration.

GROW

Pathway to Personalization Framework

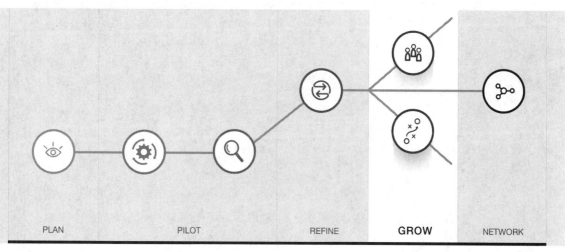

PLAN · PILOT · REFINE · **GROW** · NETWORK

Align communication
and strategic scaling

Contemplate the
curriculum challenge

Personalize the
professional learning

ALIGNING COMMUNICATION AND STRATEGIC SCALING

We have learned valuable lessons about scaling tactics from an excellent principal named Kristen who leads an elementary school in Rhode Island. As the principal and lead change agent for her personalized learning initiative, Kristen supported a pilot teacher cohort of four teachers over the course of one academic year and worked with her pilot teachers to develop a strategic approach to scale. Leveraging an extraordinarily strong school culture, adequate resources, and effective routines for teacher collaboration and sharing, Kristen shared lessons learned from the pilot phase with the full staff and collected some additional information from her faculty before solidifying her plan. Using the personalized learning progression (figure 2.2), she asked her teachers to self-assess their classrooms along the progression and identify one manageable step they could take to start to move to the next level. Then, pilot teachers led several professional learning simulations where they modeled a new practice for colleagues based on their classroom self-assessments. Further, all staff were scheduled to conduct learning walks through pilot classrooms and reflect on their observations. Afterward, Kristen facilitated a fishbowl debrief, allowing pilot teachers to share successes, failures, concerns, strategies, and student reflections with the whole staff. Finally, she fielded questions, asked for feedback on possible scaling directions, and created shared implementation folders for the faculty with artifacts from pilot classrooms. The faculty responded with enthusiasm, prompting Kristen to establish two simultaneous scaling strategies.

The first involved all teachers, who were asked to focus on two priority practices: *differentiating instruction* and *grouping students based on data*. Kristen developed bounded solutions for her staff by offering explicit guidance and connecting the work to existing resources. At a minimum, teachers were asked to support two instructional groups each day during math and reading. Students who were not working directly with their teachers could access adaptive software programs and work on skills at their own pace. Most teachers felt comfortable leveraging their existing center-based structure and were eager to experiment with different activities across multiple centers. Some teachers were ready to leverage playlists and a more flexible classroom model, combining independent, collaborative, and teacher-directed work in response to student needs. As long as teachers could describe how they were specifically implementing the two priority practices, they had freedom to pursue strategies aligned to their strengths and classroom contexts. As teachers dabbled with choice and pushed their practices, Kristen added video of model classrooms and new strategies, updated resources to implementation pathways, and led frequent learning walks to showcase different strategies. Committed to providing coaching, feedback, and support to new, implementing teachers, Kristen shared this responsibility with her pilot teachers. The team of five met once a month to co-plan, brainstorm new ideas, address challenges, and reflect on their work. During whole-staff professional development and learning walks, the pilot teachers worked with their colleagues by co-teaching, modeling practices, observing (in person and with videos), and debriefing as requested.

The second scaling strategy invited a second cohort of teachers to implement additional priority practices deemed valuable in the pilot: leveraging technology to support student collaboration and authentic project work. Kristen attached additional resources to this opportunity, including bi-weekly embedded coaching support and supplementary devices. The entire faculty responded positively to her recruitment efforts, and she created an application process to help her identify six teachers to participate. These teachers leveraged the foundational resources initiated during the pilot phase and were encouraged to pursue other strategies. In addition to offering embedded coaching, Kristen provided them with time to collaborate and observe each other.

Based on the enthusiasm and interest of her full staff, Kristen made plans to include remaining teachers in a third cohort the following year. On reflection,

Kristen credits customization and iteration as the main strengths of her scaling efforts. She continuously adapted her plan to respond to the needs and interests of her faculty while meeting the needs of teachers at various stages of implementation. She also attributes her success to the expertise and flexibility of her faculty. Her ability to leverage a talented special education teacher as a behavior interventionist, for example, enabled her to provide 70 percent of coaching support in the first two years. As the one administrator within her small school, distributed leadership practices created both the infrastructure and the strong culture to support scaling efforts. Kristen's scaling tactics were successful because of her deep commitment to providing the right levels of information, support, and agency to her teachers. Transformational education shifts will not happen unless initiatives value the perspectives of teachers as a hallmark of scaling efforts. Simultaneously, administrators must be involved to help align, frame, and support the initiative.

With the pilot and refine phases complete, the design team should revisit the human capital assessment (appendix B) they took during their initial self-study (chapter 3) and reflect on the status of buy-in across the system. Once the data is summarized and formatted, the team should identify both strengths and needs across the assessment to guide immediate efforts. Teams should identify relationship-building and communication work that requires prompt attention across school board members, the superintendent, district leadership teams, principals, early adopters, full faculty, students, parents, and the community. Who is standing in the way of potential scaling efforts and what information or messaging do they need to get on board and support the effort? Ideally, scores across stakeholder groups have increased to the two-to-three range for strongly positioning replication efforts. Until this point, administrators could have various levels of engagement with the design team. When considering how to cross the chasm, the design team must engage decision makers at the highest levels of the system. As Eric Ries states, "After an entrepreneur has incubated a product in the innovation sandbox, it has to be reintegrated into the parent organization. A larger team eventually will be needed to grow it, commercialize it and scale it."[1] Design teams need to engage the right leaders at this point to determine priorities, identify challenges, and establish the appropriate scope of scaling efforts.

In this chapter, we discuss the importance of engaging stakeholders at all levels to vet materials developed during the refine phase and to share their perspectives on scale. We start by focusing on bottom-up coalition building and feedback. We then discuss essential collaboration with top-down leadership. After considering several readiness indicators, we explore a continuum of scaling strategies and present two additional case studies. We end the chapter with a renewed focus on strategic communication, examining tactics for building relationships as well as suggesting a portfolio of documents and activities to ensure transparency and consistent messaging.

ESTABLISHING BOTTOM-UP VIABILITY

The main goals of vetting pilot materials with teachers is to gauge the amount of enthusiasm for the work and to understand how well initial implementation pathways will position teachers for success. We recommend two sets of activities to reach these goals; the first is sharing the pilot story broadly with all stakeholders, and the second is deeply vetting implementation pathways with early majority teachers. We are mindful that local context will play a role in the order of operations described in this section. When district leaders drive all decision making, teachers will want to understand the degree of leadership commitment in place before investing their time in vetting materials. However, some leaders will not commit to the process without the clear excitement and endorsement of teachers. In some cases, it makes sense to frame the opportunity with both groups simultaneously so that they can consider the details of the initiative together and hear each other's initial questions and concerns.

Sharing the Pilot Story

Disseminating the pilot story helps stakeholders understand, contemplate, and ultimately operationalize newly constructed instructional shifts and enables the design team to collect feedback and address concerns. Whether disseminated as a presentation, panel, blended lesson, or discussion, meeting with teachers, administrators, parents, and community members builds relationships and uncovers concerns and misconceptions. Delivering information through the simulation of priority practices is particularly powerful, and offering audiences time to reflect, discuss, question, and provide feedback is essential. Most humbling, do not expect stakeholders to appreciate the incredible time and energy that has been devoted to this work. Be magnanimous and allow their perspectives to refine your thinking.

In the school-based scaling story at the beginning of the chapter, as well as in the district-based and charter network stories that follow, disseminating the pilot story required more than a single meeting, and key messages were included in a variety of follow-up communications. As John Kotter notes in his book *Leading Change*, effective leaders "use all existing communication channels to broadcast the vision. . . . Without credible communication, and a lot of it, the hearts and minds of the troops are never captured."[2] We have watched lead change agents generate incredible momentum for implementation by conducting a variety of follow-up activities after an initial presentation. Some created weekly emails centered on a story of success, an upcoming professional learning opportunity, or a call to action. Some organized periodic breakfast meetings for teachers to learn more about the work underway and for parents to provide feedback on the efforts. Some established regular opportunities for teachers to share breakthrough moments with colleagues at staff meetings or through asynchronous formats. Some established professional learning communities and invited staff to participate in face-to-face conversations and Twitter chats. One dynamic principal shared clips from inspirational TED Talks or videos each week to motivate nervous teachers to try new things. The common features of these follow-up efforts include consistent messaging, multimodal communication, and continuous feedback loops. The common purpose includes reinforcing the vision and demonstrating an enduring commitment to the work.

Change agents can gauge the current level of teacher interest in the pilot initiative by noting participation in follow-up activities and collecting additional feedback through one-on-one hallway conversations, focus groups, or surveys. There is a dual purpose to understanding the level of teacher enthusiasm. Design teams need to consider interest levels as they contemplate scaling strategies with the leadership team; simultaneously, they need to plan ongoing communication efforts to continue to build momentum and address concerns.

Vetting Implementation Pathways

Once the larger faculty is familiar with the pilot story, design teams have the opportunity to assess the value of implementation pathways. Generally, this process generates feedback from a self-selected group of teachers who are optimistic about the pilot story. Design teams can create an open call for feedback by asking interested teachers to complete an exit ticket after participating in a pilot story share-out, generate a post-meeting survey, or handpick teacher representatives from certain grade levels or content areas. As a first step, we recommend teachers walk through pilot classrooms with a design team member to give them a better sense of how the priority practices were operationalized during the pilot phase. Then, they should be granted access to the draft implementation pathways to explore at their convenience, with specific questions to consider, such as the following:

- What are you most excited about?
- What strategies seem relevant to your classroom?
- What would you like to try first?
- What information is missing that would help you with implementation?
- What kind of support is required for you to be successful?
- What are you worried or nervous about?

Teachers can share their feedback individually through interviews or surveys, or in small focus groups with design team members and pilot teachers. Feedback should give the design team enough information to determine next steps. In the best-case scenario, implementation pathways provide enough of a foundation to engage and support a new set of teachers. Alternately, the design team will need to reconvene with pilot teachers to make revisions and then engage teachers for a second wave of feedback. Collecting quantitative (How many teachers are excited?) as well as qualitative (Biggest fears include . . .) data from participating teachers helps focus the design team around necessary revisions. Sample rating categories can be found in table 9.1; the ratios in the right-hand column depict the number of teachers (out of twelve) who agreed with each statement. Implementation pathways will always be a living resource and drafting pathways is just the beginning of a long-term process of documenting instructional shifts that are capable of moving personalized learning into the mainstream.

ESTABLISHING TOP-DOWN VIABILITY

Ideally, the design team has been engaging with leadership and governance throughout the pilot process in some capacity. However, if these leaders have limited knowledge of the pilot story, sharing lessons learned as well as pilot teacher and student perspectives is a great starting point. Often, leaders immediately appreciate that the initiative incorporated multiple data measures and was built on a rigorous process. Once leadership groups understand the rationale and results, it is valuable to facilitate pilot classroom observations for them to see the practices in action. Once leaders have confidence in the pilot process, the leadership team and

TABLE 9.1   **Soliciting feedback on implementation pathways**

QUESTIONS ASKED TO EARLY MAJORITY TEACHERS	TEACHERS WHO RESPONDED POSITIVELY
Do you find the identified priority practices relevant and compelling?	11 out of 12
Can you identify an entry point that would add value to your classroom?	10 out of 12
Could you implement relevant strategies with minimal support?	6 out of 12
Are you interested in implementing any strategies described in the coming months?	9 out of 12
Would you like to help strengthen the draft pathways?	9 out of 12

the design team begin to work together. Determining an organizational structure that supports lean and efficient communication is important. Since conversations will be ongoing through scaling and replication efforts, we recommend forming a committee with representatives from both groups and designating a lead facilitator. The committee can launch through a series of meetings but will need to evolve into an ongoing management structure if the district is serious about scaling efforts. Whether your group decides to form a committee or include the full design team and leadership team in ongoing conversations, we will use the term *combined team* to indicate when discussions or decisions require the involvement of both groups.

The combined team begins with the goal of establishing two essential leadership assurances:

1. *Alignment*: After studying alignment between the personalized learning initiative and other existing priorities, leaders should be willing to either prioritize the personalized learning initiative or communicate how the personalized learning model will complement other initiatives.
2. *Conditions*: After studying current barriers, leaders should be willing to create the right conditions for replication, including an investment of time and money and an examination of current systems and policies.

With these two goals in mind, the combined team maps the larger school or district problem space across five categories: competing initiatives, economic barriers, cognitive barriers, political barriers, and normative barriers (conceived by Seelos and Mair and introduced in chapter 7).

Competing Initiatives

The first activity helps combined teams articulate how replication efforts could complicate or contradict current priorities within their various initiatives, roles, and areas of expertise. Teams must identify and prioritize all current initiatives, assess the degree of alignment between the personalized learning initiative and each effort, and clarify where teachers should focus their time. Typically, something will need to be compromised, eliminated, or put on the back burner to make room for the new work. This is a challenging task. Most initiatives are attached to leaders who fought to make them priorities. If personalized learning is indeed a priority, then tough decisions will need to be made and communicated across all levels of leadership.

Yarissa, our pilot teacher from chapters 6 and 7, was caught in the middle of competing initiatives when her district leadership team began to study alignment. While leaders had high confidence in the work, some of the practices collided with the pacing requirements and instructional practices mandated by the recently purchased reading curriculum. A massive district investment, the curriculum was rolled out to elementary and middle school teachers with strict fidelity directives. This tension paralyzed the initiative until the leadership and design teams could come to consensus. Leaders decided to sit on the fence, offering curriculum autonomy to anyone who joined the personalized learning cohort while continuing to mandate fidelity for the rest of the staff. This offered Yarissa and her team the flexibility to draft bounded solutions while her colleagues further down the adoption curve continued to benefit from a highly structured curriculum. While straddling competing initiatives works as new methods are being codified, eventually leaders need to commit to a direction and clearly communicate their priorities.

Economic Barriers

In the Greeley-Evans case study discussed later in this chapter, limited resources resulted in some key decision points at the district leadership level. The team decided to initially hold off on purchasing additional devices and focus on priority practices that did not require the heavy integration of technology, such as student collaboration. They leveraged available resources to fund coaching positions to support new, implementing teachers and build on the implementation pathways already developed. The team concurrently drafted a budget that expanded coaching positions as more schools joined the initiative and ultimately supported the purchasing of hardware for all participating classrooms.

If the personalized learning initiative is highly valued and the leadership team is ready to make a long-term commitment to the effort, it is time to start thinking about the resources required to support effective replication. The lead change agent should start this conversation by sharing the pain points uncovered during the formal pilot analysis, possible solutions for reducing these challenges, and a sense of the costs attached to each solution. Ensuing conversations should focus on identifying levers that lead to the greatest impact for students and teachers. Limited resources will require decisions around the magnitude and focus of initial scaling efforts. Common resource demands of scaling efforts include hardware, software, digital content/curriculum, and infrastructure (broadband, technical support, etc.). Human resources include the costs associated with coaching and professional development. Both sets of investments should be carefully considered to craft scaling efforts with high potential for impact. In most cases, new investments require the reallocation of existing funds; savvy design teams come to the table with a list of line items they are willing to relinquish.

Cognitive Barriers

The conversation around cognitive barriers can begin with teacher reflections on the initial implementation pathways and the degree to which current teacher expertise aligns with priority practices. If elementary teachers are already working on differentiated, small-group instruction within a response-to-intervention model, the training and support required to increase targeted differentiation will be manageable. However, if the majority of high school teachers primarily leverage lectures and note-taking strategies to deliver content, this shift will require significantly more time and support to realize.

To a large extent, cognitive barriers overlap with resource limitations. Design teams and pilot teachers have built considerable expertise as they have navigated our framework. Think creatively about how to leverage this growing resource to support new, implementing teachers. Professional learning opportunities should be aligned to the level of support new teachers will need as they begin implementation. Ideally, all teachers involved in replication efforts will have access to coaching or embedded support, collaborative planning time with colleagues, opportunities to learn from other practitioners and experts, and content and delivery methods that are personalized to meet their needs. At this point, any external organizations or consultants enlisted to support the effort should explicitly align their services with the development and execution of implementation pathways.

The initial mapping of cognitive barriers will help teams determine the comprehensive needs of teachers and establish a timeline for meeting these needs. Crafting a comprehensive professional learning plan requires significant thought in addition to resources. We discuss this further in chapter 11.

Political Barriers

Political barriers represent both the policy implications of expanded efforts as well as the status of culture and climate across a school or district. In addition to the policy issues uncovered in the pilot evaluation, there are often significant policy ramifications to the prioritization of competing initiatives. Combined teams need to contemplate the relative complexity of a variety of policy shifts and a timeline for moving forward. Without a clear direction for navigating the demands of competing initiatives, replication efforts should be scaled back. Trial policy revisions or waivers can be explored in R&D lab classrooms or with a small cohort of early adopters. Policy revisions in support of implementation pathways position schools or districts well for more comprehensive scaling efforts.

Universally, we have found it is extremely difficult to support effective scaling efforts—or pilot efforts—in schools with poor culture and climate. Seelos and Mair caution us to be thoughtful about the degree of relational barriers present in a problem space, noting that "social enterprises need to engage much more deeply, much more directly, and over much longer time" to address relational challenges.[3] As we discuss in chapter 11, strong leadership and a positive, empowering culture are crucial to successful scaling efforts. In our experience, scaling the work to teachers without these conditions is a waste of time and resources. In our West Belden case study presented later in this chapter, school leaders assessed their readiness for blended and personalized approaches and found culture was a significant barrier. In response, they significantly slowed implementation timelines and focused on developing and empowering teacher voice. In general, culture must always be addressed first.

Normative Barriers

No matter how personalized learning priorities take shape within a school or district, new approaches will likely put a strain on various legacy systems and will ultimately require some pretty radical restructuring at the systems level. We have previously alluded to "the system" as a huge challenge to the successful implementation of blended and personalized practices. Design teams need to understand the extent to which priority practices bump against system constraints and the degree to which legacy constructs will impede replication efforts. Again, the lead change agent can start the discussion by sharing normative constraints identified by pilot teachers.

When normative barriers pose a critical threat to successful replication, we recommend engaging R&D teachers in a second pilot process to help identify breakthroughs to these challenges. This could lead to the creation of an autonomous "school-within-a-school" or "school-within-a-district" model, vastly increasing flexibility and experimentation for a specific set of students. Alternately, this could lead to more incremental exploration. Either way, comprehensive replication efforts are not recommended when teachers immediately face normative barriers as they begin implementation.

Identifying and mapping the problem space within a district or school is an important starting point for considering scaling tactics. Design teams can create a heat map to identify the presence of barriers across the whole district, individual schools, grade-level bands, and content bands. From there, teams can develop a realistic understanding of the relative complexity and potential impact of different scaling efforts.

CONTEMPLATING SCALING STRATEGIES

In the 1987 cult classic movie *Princess Bride*, self-proclaimed genius Vizzini continuously uses the word "inconceivable" to describe events he does not expect.[4] After several uses, revenge-seeking swordsman Inigo Montoya turns to Vizzini and says, "You keep using that word. I do not think it means what you think it means."[5] What does scale mean within your local context? Defining the concept is harder than it sounds. Any leader can make broad-stroke statements such as, "We want these best practices in every classroom, in every school, across every district in the country," but such declarations are typically met with skepticism. When stakeholders at all levels have offered feedback on the pilot initiative, implementation pathways have been vetted, and barriers have been mapped, then the combined team is ready to articulate a timeline and framework for scaling efforts.

Common Scaling Scenarios

Across our many partnerships, several scaling scenarios have emerged as the most popular next steps for combined teams to consider.

1. *Second pilot phase*: Sometimes in our haste to move through a framework, we bounce to the next step too quickly. Lackluster levels of buy-in from stakeholders from the top or bottom suggest forward movement will be challenging. The best option forward in this case is to enlist concerned stakeholders in the development of a second pilot phase that considers a new vision and priority practices.

2. *R&D study*: When initial feedback from teachers and leadership is enthusiastic but the personalization effort is plagued with barriers, the initiative is not ready to cross the chasm. In this case, the vision and priority practices endure and R&D classrooms explore potential solutions. Learning cycles could explore strategy adaptations, policy shifts, systems changes—whatever the combined team determines as a strategic focus. Running multiple layers of concurrent learning cycles is possible but demanding; design teams should determine a manageable number of classrooms to study and support.

3. *Cohort model*: If buy-in at both levels seems high and barriers will not be an initial deal-breaker, design teams can engage interested teachers on the other side of the chasm. A popular incremental approach involves a cohort model where a subset of teachers or schools self-select to be included in project expansion work. This model works particularly well when design teams clarify participation expectations as well as outline specific support. Often, pilot teachers are leveraged as mentors and participating teachers have access to embedded coaching, additional planning time, and hardware or software resources. The design team may need to expand to keep close tabs on cohort classrooms. Implementing teachers will require midpoint meetings as well as the data collection support offered to pilot teachers. It is preferable to add cohorts slowly to ensure that adequate support, study, and reflection are part of the process. Scaling through a cohort model offers additional time to expose early and late majority teachers to the work—and create more structured resources—prior to inviting them into subsequent cohorts.

4. *Full implementation*: With extremely high buy-in and minimal barriers, full implementation is an option. Moving from the pilot phase to full implementation can be risky without exceptional alignment, strong leadership, a quality set of bounded solutions, thoughtfully planned professional learning and coaching support, and the ability to attend to the needs of early majority, late majority, and reluctant teachers simultaneously. In our experience, full implementation

efforts are most successful when focused on one or two practices strongly aligned to existing initiatives and comprehensive curriculum.

Figure 9.1 maps these four common strategies against issues of buy-in and barriers.

Many teams move forward using a hybrid strategy. Kristen's story at the beginning of the chapter is an example of a hybrid approach to full implementation. Based on the enthusiasm of the full faculty, Kristen identified two priority practices she wanted to see in every classroom. She also leveraged a cohort model to identify a set of teachers who were interested in exploring some of the more challenging

FIGURE 9.1   **Mapping scaling strategies**

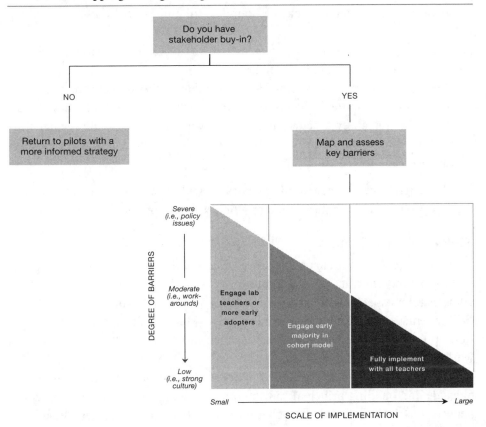

priority practices from the pilot phase. Districts could potentially divide priority practices across scenarios by identifying a focus for all teachers, organizing a cohort approach to pursue more challenging practices *and* tasking R&D teachers with exploring solutions to current barriers attached to additional practices.

As design teams grapple with various options, we have a few reflections to share:

- We find merit in the concept of scaling slowly and learning quickly.
- We suggest focusing on teachers or schools who are most interested in and best positioned to tackle the work. Participating schools should boast strong leadership and school culture.
- We recommend clear communication surrounding non-negotiables as well as where teachers have choice and flexibility.
- New artifacts and strategies should be continuously added to implementation pathways. The establishment of bounded solutions should also be ongoing work.
- We strongly recommend working closely with the R&D engine to explore solutions to new and ongoing challenges.
- We emphasize continued data collection and analysis as successful pilot practices move into more diverse contexts and are implemented under new conditions. More than ever before, the design teams should dedicate regular time to midpoint meetings and respond to successes, failures, unintended consequences, and false assumptions.

As design teams consider scaling tactics aligned with their problem space, they are ready to put stakes in the ground around the details of initial scaling efforts.

Staking Rocky Ground

While the focus of this chapter has been on action-oriented tasks that support replication and scale, it is also important to acknowledge that most teachers and administrators operate within the debilitating constraints of our traditional education system, which is highly resistant to change. Months of planning and preparation up to this point do not alter the fact that most public education employees work mainly in isolation and are consistently caught between a rock and a hard place. Superintendents are positioned between mayors and school committees on one side and building principals on the other. Building principals must navigate between district directives and teacher pushback. Teachers must translate building mandates into instructional practices they can sell to their students. Students must deal with teacher expectations as well as pressures from parents and the community in which they live. Change efforts must successfully maneuver through the push and pull at each level.

That is a tough order. It is possible that a set of validated strategies might need to survive the politics of a school board, a district administrative team, a teachers' union, a parent association, and a school community before finding their way into the hands of a cautiously optimistic teacher. And, after spending countless hours redesigning lesson plans to operationalize new practices, a high school teacher still must determine how to communicate these changes to a classroom of students who have spent every school day for the past nine years within a traditional model. Consider the conversation that might ensue:

> *"Good morning students. Today, instead of listening to me lecture and then completing a test on Friday, you are going to learn independently and in small collaborative groups. Your assignments will be multi-step and build in complexity over the course of the week. If you do not complete your assignment to a level '3' on this rubric, I will ask you to resubmit the assignment. You may have to do this multiple times, but I will be here to support you in a one-on-one setting as you work to demonstrate mastery."*

After a few moments of silent consideration one brave student speaks up:

> *"Come on Mister! Don't be lazy. Just teach us what you want us to know and let me take my test like I do in all my other classes."*

We have developed a great deal of empathy for leaders and educators who consistently face multiple bureaucratic constraints across their job descriptions. Our efforts to prioritize relationships and communication were borne from our observations of the current dysfunction within the system. However, building relationships is not a panacea. We are mindful that there will be rocks of various sizes and hard places that are complicated to rectify. As teams stake their plans for scale into the ground, messaging requires a level of finesse, and plans benefit from ongoing flexibility.

The first stake establishes the "what" of the initiative: what specific priority practices, strategies, and implementation pathways will be the focus of initial replication efforts? This can range from centering on one practice to creating a menu of options that may appeal to various subject and grade-level educators. The second stake targets "who" will be involved in initial scaling efforts. Combined teams can target a set of grade levels, a particular content area, a school-based effort in buildings with strong leaders, a self-selected teacher cohort, all teachers across a district, or a hybrid of these options.

The third stake involves the "how" of initial scaling efforts. Will teams scale with an initial implementation pathway and bi-weekly coaching? Will all participating teachers be part of a professional learning community? Will midpoint meetings occur regularly? Will pilot teachers be mentors? Will participating teachers be part of creating bounded solutions? As impediments and politics become apparent, tactics may need to be shifted, revised, or reframed to align with the realities of current systems and conditions.

To support combined teams through the process of staking initial scaling efforts, we have included three stories of scale. The school-based approach to scale is Kristen's story, which started the chapter. A district as well as a charter network example are included at the end of the chapter. With a scaling strategy drafted, the design team is ready to return to a focus on developing communications strategies.

ELEMENTS OF A COMPREHENSIVE COMMUNICATIONS PLAN

As design teams reflect on current levels of knowledge, concern, and buy-in around the initiative and contemplate communication options, it is important to clarify goals around a public relations effort. In March 2017, the Learning Accelerator and Education Elements partnered on a guide entitled "Communications Planning for Innovation in Education."[6] This document is a must-read for design teams and their expanding coalitions as they develop a communications plan to support the replication and scale of their blended and personalized learning model. Information presented describes the process of creating a culture of communication, understanding the messaging needs of various audiences, and measuring communication efforts. The document includes many district examples of communications plans, artifacts, and activities. In the sections that follow, we outline some strategies to consider, activities that have been successful in other districts, and deliverables that should be crafted for wider dissemination.

Strategies to Consider

We have found that it is useful for design teams to identify the various stakeholder audiences that will require messaging around the personalized learning initiative in progress. Based on previous efforts to share the pilot story and vet implementation pathway drafts, the design team should have a sense of how stakeholders are responding to the work and what additional information or opportunities they will need as the initiative proceeds. We have adapted a table from Ed Elements and the Learning Accelerator to create a stakeholder messaging template (table 9.2). This template can be leveraged to help craft messaging, offer clarity, ease concerns, and identify teachers and principals who are particularly ready to engage in communication efforts.[7]

TABLE 9.2 **Stakeholder messaging template**

TARGET AUDIENCE	WHAT THEY VALUE	INFORMATION THEY NEED	KEY MESSENGERS	DESIRED ACTIONS FROM THE TARGET AUDIENCE
All		• Vision, rationale, and priorities • How to define, message, and support the work		• Active support for the initiative
District leaders	• Efficiency • Outcomes • Alignment	• How this initiative will align with or impact other initiatives • How their roles and responsibilities will shift • Expectations	• Superintendent	• Support for policy revisions • Collaboration to support effort and reduce obstacles • Effective communication with schools, parents, and community
School leaders	• Clear vision/messaging • Balanced autonomy • Support • Alignment • Resources	• Clarity around expectations, clear plan • Talking points for teachers, students, and parents • Culture-building activities	• District leaders • Design team • Students • Pilot teachers	• Focus on instructional leadership/culture building • Promotion of teacher collaboration and sharing • Effective communication with teachers, students, and parents
Teachers (particularly early majority)	• Relevance • Proven strategies • Reliability • Efficiency • Support • Autonomy	• Alignment • Validation/evidence • How this addresses a meaningful problem of practice • Clarity around expectations • Talking points for parents	• Pilot teachers • Principals • Superintendent	• Interest in implementation pathways • Feedback on the plan • Students as partners in future planning and implementation efforts

(continued)

TABLE 9.2 **Stakeholder messaging template,** *continued*

TARGET AUDIENCE	WHAT THEY VALUE	INFORMATION THEY NEED	KEY MESSENGERS	DESIRED ACTIONS FROM THE TARGET AUDIENCE
Parents	• Engagement • Achievement • Happiness of their child(ren)	• What this means for their child(ren) • Timeline for change • Opportunities for feedback	• Superintendent • Principal • Teachers • Students	• Increased engagement with school community • Becoming active partners and advocates
Students	• Engaging, relevant academics • Agency and ownership of learning • Pride in achievements	• Clarity around potential changes • Opportunities to provide feedback	• Principal • Design team • Teachers	• Becoming partners in the reform effort • Increased agency and ownership of their learning
Community members	• Innovation • Collaboration	• How they can support the effort	• Superintendent • Principals • District leaders • Students	• Becoming active partners, advocates, and/or funders
School boards	• Strong outcomes • Fiscal responsibility • Clear and standardized policies • Student privacy	• Clarity around purpose • Alignment • Policy implications • Understanding of myths vs. realities connected to BPL/ screen time • Funding structures	• Superintendent • Students • Pilot teachers • Respected community leaders	• Pilot classroom visits • Interaction with pilot students • Updated policies and funding structures to support initiative • Positive messaging to the community

An important consideration across all audiences is how to strengthen and expand mechanisms for two-way communication and ongoing feedback. This often involves concurrent strategies ranging from personal conversations to surveys after meetings or presentations, to asynchronous discussion boards, to ongoing focus groups. This is a time-consuming effort, but ongoing input from willing teachers, principals, and parents is essential. Your initiative will stall during the grow phase if your design team does not find a way to promote continuous discussion. Design teams must work to simultaneously increase the number of stakeholders with deep knowledge of the initiative while leveraging new voices to support productive iteration.

Critical Communication Artifacts

As design teams continue to consider audiences and build relationships, it is useful to create specific public relations collateral to share with various stakeholders. While teams should construct the artifacts most aligned to their situations, we recommend considering a few different options.

We have found creating an infographic that clarifies the main components of an initiative is a helpful exercise for design teams and can be beneficial to a variety of stakeholders. Leaders in Greeley-Evans School District 6 developed the graphic featured in figure 9.2 to succinctly present their priority practices to a district-wide audience. Creating a visual representation helps develop a brand for the work that can be added to letters, posters, flyers, and websites. The graphic is easy to

FIGURE 9.2   Creating a graphic to facilitate messaging

What Are the Key Elements of Blended Learning?

TIGHT FEEDBACK LOOPS

Students receive immediate feedback using digital tools and direct teacher feedback

QUALITY STUDENT-TO-STUDENT INTERACTION

Students engage in sustained academic conversations with their peers

STUDENT OWNERSHIP

Students are clear about where they are in their learning progression and become the drivers pushing to meet their learning needs

TARGETED SMALL-GROUP INSTRUCTION

Students receive small group and individual support tailored to their learning needs

Source: Greeley-Evans School District 6

recognize and clearly communicates the purpose and core elements of the personalized initiative.

Generally, the next step is developing sets of talking points directed toward each stakeholder audience. Common messaging features include the updated school or district vision, as well as the working definition of blended and personalized learning. Subsequently, teams can create a series of one-pagers tailored to different audiences. After reviewing the information, all audiences will want to know where to go for more details and how they can provide feedback to leaders.

District leaders from Loudoun County, Virginia went a step further, creating communication planning toolkits for their principals. As outlined in the TLA/Ed Elements communication guide previously referenced, leaders created a set of information for school leaders that included the vision and definition of personalized learning, talking points that directly addressed school concerns, detailed alignment between the personalized learning effort and two complementary initiatives, and a communications template for effectively messaging the initiative to school stakeholders.[8] The toolkit also included exemplary artifacts from initial efforts around the district and a variety of communication suggestions. Each principal was asked to leverage the information provided to create a "Why PL?" story to present to staff, including personal stories about the value of personalized learning.

As teams begin to build communications materials, establishing a personalized learning landing page within a school or district website is a great next step. Informational documents can be housed on the site, as well as materials from the pilot phase. Pilot classroom videos, success stories, and resources can help a variety of stakeholders visualize proposed instructional shifts. Pilot teachers can be invited to blog about their experiences; a Twitter feed can highlight posts with your initiative hashtag. Design teams can also leverage the landing page to provide access to feedback forms, research connections, ways to get involved, and examples of success from other districts in the country. Additionally, access to continuously updated FAQ documents enables design teams and leaders to address questions and concerns in multiple venues. A good district website to explore is the Personalized Learning page created by Fulton County Schools.[9]

• • •

This chapter emphasizes the importance of establishing intentional communication strategies as design teams plan for scale. This is often complex, time consuming, and arduous work, yet it is critical to the future success of the initiative. Any plan for scaling a personalized learning initiative must consist of equal parts compassion, clarity, and persistence.

As we have alluded to over the past three chapters, two essential challenges have required ongoing attention from design teams and district leadership as they consider how to grow initiatives: curriculum and professional development. We explore curriculum and the role of personalized learning platforms in chapter 10 and explore personalized professional learning more deeply in chapter 11, defining these challenges from new angles, discussing the current limitations of the field, and emphasizing the roles and responsibilities of leaders in this new space.

Case Study: Scaling in Greeley-Evans, a Districtwide Approach

Greeley-Evans School District serves more than twenty-two thousand students in the communities of Greeley and Evans, Colorado. The district includes twenty-five district-operated schools, plus six charter schools, and an online academy. Over the past five years Deagan Andrews, director of instructional technology, and Jon Cooney, principal of the Bella Romero Academy of Applied Technology, collaborated with other district leaders to spearhead personalized learning efforts across the district. The work was incubated at Bella Romero when the school was launched to consolidate two under-performing district schools. An initial focus on small-group instruction and tight student feedback loops paved the way for the exploration of personalized approaches, quickly generating stunning student achievement growth. Studying the critical practices underway at Bella Romero and in early adopter classrooms across the district, Deagan and Jon refined lessons learned and landed on four key practices that could be implemented in any classroom despite the amount of technology present: tight feedback loops (data-driven decisions), quality student-to-student interactions, student ownership, and targeted small-group instruction.

From there, the team took their show on the road, conducting a listening tour with stakeholders across the district. At ten different stops along the tour, the team presented a short set of talking points on their vision and rationale behind blended learning, early lessons learned across the district, and their current thinking around replication efforts. The remainder of the meeting was spent listening to stakeholders and soliciting their feedback. The team was extremely interested in how teachers and administrators would respond to their concept, asking them for their overall impressions, as well as how this initiative could help them solve a current problem of practice. Conversations across tour stops were inspiring and engaging. Deagan followed up by establishing a district-wide community of practice on personalized learning, drawing interested stakeholders to a high school gymnasium on an early-release Monday to engage in deeper discussions with colleagues. Face-to-face discussions were scheduled every two months, with continuing opportunities for teachers and leaders to discuss, share, and think together through an online community of practice housed on a district platform.

Next, the team drafted an innovation configuration—a comprehensive rubric designed to define, support, monitor, and measure the growth of the four key practices initially identified. Each practice was broken down into behaviors and strategies that reflected implementation across four levels: beginning, emerging, stabilizing, and systematizing. Practitioners at both the classroom and school level could leverage the rubric to identify both current and aspirational implementation of key strategies. Considerations such as frequency of use, consistency of practice, differentiation, personalization of efforts, and evidence of impact separated various implementation levels. The rubric was created as a living document that could grow and adapt to the realities of the scaling effort.

Examining available funding, the team initially allocated resources to establishing quality, tailored professional learning support for teachers rather than to purchasing more devices. They created a plan to support embedded coaching. They created a process for peer or mentor teachers to observe and provide feedback to new, implementing teachers. They vetted various online courses connected to the four priority practices and developed templates for how individual or small-group professional development might be crafted to meet teacher needs across the four instructional priorities. They also relaxed highly restrictive district policies around curriculum and pacing for participating schools.

Based on the human and financial resources available, an implementation timeline was created to organize the roll-out of the four priority practices. The preliminary plan scaffolded scaling efforts over four years and focused initially on schools that demonstrated a high level of readiness for the work. The design team aspired to learn, refine, and adapt throughout the process to improve both the experience and the impact of the initiative as more schools engaged in the work. They developed a competitive application process that included classroom walkthroughs and readiness assessments. They looked for evidence of strong infrastructure, leadership, culture, and a high level of enthusiasm for the work. In the first year, nine schools applied and the team could afford to support four.

Teachers in participating schools started by self-assessing on the innovation configuration and selecting one practice to focus on for the quarter. They developed individual professional learning plans, identifying steps to move their practice forward along the progression and choosing their preferred method(s) of professional learning. The team provided support around coaching, collaboration, and collecting evidence of impact. Meanwhile, Bella Romero continued to iterate and explore practices, systems, and tools, playing the role of a district R&D engine. New schools were added each year through a similar process, with the team making adjustments and revisions as necessary. Initial iterations helped clarify directives and highlight where teachers had the opportunity to explore and create best-fit strategies. Noticing the growing, unsustainable burden that accompanied a wide-open approach to curriculum, the team began to define digital content and streamline processes for the next cohort of schools. They continued to study a variety of measures and learned that instructional shifts were producing great gains for high- and middle-performing students, but struggling students were continuing to struggle. Considering feedback from a variety of stakeholders, the team began to approach practices that supported student agency and ownership from a new lens.

Over five years, the district has integrated seventeen of twenty-five schools into the scaling effort, falling short of their planned full district implementation in year five because of a resource shortage that would have compromised the support systems. As teachers, principals, and administrators continue to refine and study the results of personalization efforts, experimentation and iteration are ongoing features of the work. A copy of the Greeley-Evans innovation configuration can be found on our resource website.

Case Study: Scaling in a Charter Network

The Chicago International Charter School (CICS) network coordinates a portfolio of fourteen schools managed by diverse operators with the goal of offering varied and high-quality school options to Chicago families. In 2011, the Distinctive Schools Network was launched to make deep regional impact in the Midwest through instructional innovation and assumed control of four CICS schools. Leaders at distinctive schools were interested in leveraging personalized learning models to transform their four initial schools into student-centered, twenty-first-century learning environments. They identified four core practices to be the focus of initial reform efforts: students would have learner profiles, learning would be competency-based, students would learn in flexible learning environments, and learning plans would guide student progression through units. As a K–8 school previously challenged by a very compliant, teacher-centered instructional model as well as low morale, CICS West Belden welcomed the change.

Principal Scott Frauenheim and Assistant Principal Colleen Collins were responsible for leading transformation efforts at CICS West Belden. Recognizing the faculty would not respond well to jumping from one scripted instructional model to another, they began by focusing on improving the school culture and designing the implementation process in partnership with teachers. For the first time, teachers had a voice in reform efforts. The process of building collaborative, trusting relationships with faculty members was an ongoing transition worth every hour of the extra time it required. They began by defining personalized learning within their context and settled on a definition that emphasized strong teacher/student relationships as the foundation for providing tailored instruction. They conducted a self-study and developed a rationale for why change was necessary at West Belden. Teachers identified stagnant growth, disengaged students, and the strict behavioral code as pain points and examined the core practices articulated by distinctive leaders for potential solutions. Scott and Colleen tapped five early adopter classroom teachers—approximately 25 percent of their faculty—to lead pilot classrooms and reached consensus around an initial entry point: flexible learning environments. They established a replication timeline with the expectation that all teachers would begin implementation within sixteen months and asked faculty members to reflect on the resources and support they would need to work within this time frame. Scott and Colleen empowered all teachers by supporting classroom visits to other schools, funding participation in national conferences, and facilitating the creation of various communities of practice outside the school. They emphasized the importance of continuous learning, trying new things, and adopting a mindset for change. They established an environment where all teachers were committed to dedicating positive energy to this work yet were comfortable proceeding without a set script to follow.

Pilot teachers defined flexible learning environments to include three components: a physical space that provided room for different learning experiences, a staffing model that connected students with the right teacher to meet their needs, and a schedule that allowed for larger, more flexible blocks of time. They took the doors off the hinges in pilot classrooms and established two pilot learning cohorts. The first- through third-grade "space" included three pilot teachers and eighty-four students, and the fourth- through fifth-grade "space" included two pilot teachers and fifty-six students. This dramatic shift was initially uncomfortable and required Scott and Colleen to invest heavily in policies, systems, and resources to support pilot teachers. They reconfigured the schedule to provide cohort teachers with 120 minutes of uninterrupted collaborative planning time each day and freed up special education and ELL teachers to participate during these meetings as well. As pilot teachers found their groove, they selected additional practices to explore, developing student learning profiles and then tackling competency-based learning progressions and student learning plans. Throughout the process, Colleen acted as the liaison, convening pilot teachers every Friday for lunch to reflect and document their learning.

Meanwhile, Scott and Colleen engaged the full faculty in pilot efforts by encouraging teachers to visit pilot classrooms and by empowering pilot teachers to share promising strategies across the four practices during professional learning time. At the end of the school year, pilot teachers assembled everything they had learned across all four practices into templates for their colleagues to access. However, over-scripting replication efforts received strong pushback from teachers who wanted to iterate or approach a practice from a different angle. Teachers preferred clear guidance that enabled them to design systems and processes for their own classroom or grade-level needs. Teachers with demonstrated competency in curriculum, technology, and policy helped craft the non-negotiables that provided guideposts for flexible implementation.

Over the course of four years, CICS West Belden has become a national model for school transformation. Yet, as Scott has transitioned to assume the position of president/COO of the Distinctive Schools Network and Colleen has become the principal of CICS West Belden, both feel what makes their model successful is that they have never emerged from the pilot mentality. West Belden teachers feel like they will never be at the point where they will be completely satisfied with their instructional model and continue to test, refine, and iterate as they learn more each year. Scott and Colleen's efforts to prioritize relationships and work in partnership with teachers on transformation has resulted in an exceptional, empowering school culture. The scaling approach developed at West Belden has been a model for other distinctive schools that have joined the growing network; the process is always adapted to meet student needs across schools. Their story demonstrates how schools within a larger district can leverage an accelerated plan-pilot-refine process at the school level to personalize the replication of a vision and set of priority practices established by a district design team.

While each of our three case studies offers a different lens on the concept of scale, there are common elements that positioned each for success. Leaders within each example supported teacher voice and choice, combining top-down guidance with bottom-up decisions to increase the relevance and impact of implementation activities. In each example, teachers were able to take ownership of the work while adding to a growing knowledge base around priority practices. Further, each story demonstrates a willingness from the lead change agent to adapt or iterate on the scaling plan based on the responses of teachers and principals; continuous communication, transparency and ongoing learning are the important hallmarks of strong scaling strategies.

CONTEMPLATING THE CURRICULUM CHALLENGE

At a recent middle school site visit, we had the pleasure of walking into an exceptionally crafted lesson focused on landmark Supreme Court cases over the past five decades. Eighth-grade students were tasked with researching a historic case, contemplating the conditions that enabled passage, tracing democratic principles defined in the decision back to the Constitution, and evaluating the decision from the perspective of a specific family. The activity allowed students to choose from four cases and decide how they were going to present their learning and analysis. Playlists attached to each case included readings tagged to Lexile levels, high-interest video clips, and human interest articles from various perspectives. Graphic organizers provided additional scaffolding for students who required more structure and support, and rubrics clarified expectations. As students formed groups around a case of interest, the teacher met with individual students to review their data from a recent formative assessment. Meanwhile, students in groups engaged in productive conversations and discussed creative options for demonstrating their learning.

Our quick debrief with the teacher after class uncovered some interesting facts. The department had no budget for curriculum materials but prioritized common planning time and encouraged teachers to create their own units of study aligned to the state social studies framework. When the school launched personalized learning reforms, the curriculum burden had moved beyond what even early adopter teachers could handle, forcing teachers to rethink how they used their allocated planning time. Led by a particularly talented teacher, this group of social studies teachers had aligned their planning efforts and began collaborating on the creation of playlists and resources. Following templates and guidelines developed by the lead teacher, the group divided lessons into segments and were each responsible for creating one-sixth of the work. The lesson we had just observed had taken a total of twenty-five hours to build—just over four hours per teacher. "Building lessons around personalized practices is incredibly time-consuming," the teacher remarked. "We are really struggling to rebuild the curriculum. It is slow going, and there is absolutely no way we could do this individually."

In our experience, the practice of delegating curriculum responsibilities to teachers continues to be the norm, and the subsequent creation of consistently superb lessons, like the one described, continues to be difficult to achieve across an ever-widening range of content and courses. Tasking teachers with the creation of their own personalized learning lessons may seem like an empowering opportunity for teacher autonomy and creativity but is actually an unsustainable and insurmountable burden, particularly when personalized practices are first introduced into classrooms.

Over the course of the past nine chapters, we have been very intentional about connecting blended and personalized learning models to strategies and actions rather than devices and software. While we remain steadfast in this position, we also acknowledge the important role technology has to play in sustaining new practices within a personalized curriculum. We have seen numerous schools and districts struggle to scale personalized learning practices without utilizing technology to support implementation. To be clear, we are not implying technology is the sole missing component capable of bringing personalized practices to scale, but as Dr. Beth Rabbitt, CEO of the Learning Accelerator states,

> Technology is one of several mechanisms educators can use to personalize a student's experience in school. It is entirely possible to personalize instruction without it; indeed, practitioners have done so for centuries. But seeking to increase personalization simply by trying harder using the same tools as we have in the past, particularly when seeking to do so at a greater scale than we have before, is not a reasonable strategy for systems change.[1]

The need for bounded solutions that connect personalized learning strategies to curricular resources is tantamount for attempting to scale pilot successes;

equally important is infrastructure that supports teacher workflow and efficiency, which we believe is tied to the purposeful integration of technology in classrooms. In this chapter, we explore both the problems and potential of current curriculum and technology features. The first section takes stock of current curriculum products and defines emerging needs within personalized models. We encourage teams to define curricular non-negotiables and consider how a combination of buying, borrowing, and building resources can increase levels of personalization within a school or district's current curriculum products. The second section explores the intersection of curriculum and technology, with a focus on how technology is supporting the delivery of content, empowering student creativity, and promoting authentic learning environments. We discuss limitations and emerging directions and conclude with a case study of how Fraser public schools in Fraser, Michigan, have approached their curriculum challenge.

As the market works to catch up to the newly defined demands of the field, temper your expectations and leverage your creativity. The space is evolving quickly and we are eager to see what the future holds for teachers, students, and families.

THE CURRICULUM CHALLENGE

In this section, we navigate the sticky challenge of establishing a comprehensive, personalized curriculum aligned to the vision and priority practices articulated by design teams. There is no clear roadmap forward within a curriculum market that does not yet understand the instructional shifts underway within personalized models or how to create products that support student-centered classrooms. However, the outlook is slowly improving,

Defining the Challenge

Research clearly points to the need for a rigorous, aligned curriculum to ensure all students fully develop their understanding of key topics and elements. Studies like the one led by Thomas Kane at the Center for Education Policy Research at Harvard University found high-quality instructional materials had a substantial effect on student achievement, especially in math.[2] A highly scripted and well-sequenced curriculum aligns with a research-based view of learning, according to the National Research Council, as "new knowledge must be constructed from existing knowledge."[3] Proponents of comprehensive curriculum products also point to resources such as the What Works Clearinghouse or EdReports, which review existing research on various products and are often at the center of purchasing decisions for schools and districts.[4]

We do not deny the critical importance of providing teachers with high quality curriculum materials. We believe we can be personalized learning advocates without being traditional curriculum deniers. Yet, we also acknowledge a central tension around this concept. In his rebuff of personalized learning titled "Three Versions of Personalized Learning, Three Challenges," professor Daniel Willingham points out the complexity that personalization brings to lesson planning: "With more decision points, the pathway through the lesson gets 'bushier' and 'bushier' and we greatly multiply the amount of high-quality instructional content we need. That's a formidable challenge."[5] Willingham is spot-on with this contention. There is widespread agreement that high quality personalized curricula is the cornerstone of strong personalized learning implementation efforts and that the field has not evolved to the point where these materials are widely available. While it would be wonderful to establish a research base supporting the impact of personalized curriculum, traditional education research methodology is not capable of studying a theory of action that vastly increases the number of variables at play. Consequently, educators must weigh the relative value of moving in this direction. Willingham goes on to say that *if* we are able to solve this curriculum problem, then he is "ready to believe that there could be a benefit to student motivation, and that for some, that benefit could be significant."[6] For those who believe that this benefit has great value and is worth pursuing, upgrading curriculum resources poses both a formidable and urgent challenge.

Diving deeper, two central problems emerge with regard to current curriculum products. First, most standards-aligned traditional curriculum is packaged for whole-class delivery using a one-lesson-per day model. This assumes that all students are ready to build the same skills and competencies together and require the same amount of time to build proficiency. Most curricula in this format come with a teacher script, a specific instructional timeline, and an expectation of fidelity to the program. Some offer a tier of differentiation or accelerated problems, but the emphasis is on maintaining consistent, standardized core instruction. The second critical challenge is the lack of diverse viewpoints and cultural relevance within most standards-based curriculum options. Put simply, our curricula must move beyond a white, male, Christian, English-speaking, heterosexual, upper-middle-class perspective if we are serious about engaging the growing number of children who do not see the world through that lens. As a starting point, majority and minority perspectives within any classroom should see their voices appropriately represented within curriculum, and current materials fall woefully short of this experience.

For teachers committed to increasing personalization in their classrooms, the current state of curriculum requires them to spend planning periods, evenings, and weekends unbundling, repackaging, and supplementing lessons to align with the needs, interests, and identities of their students. Over a school year of 180 days, teachers must identify and manage tasks in the form of lessons, activities, demonstrations, investigations, labs, projects, and more—covering almost sixty-five thousand minutes of class time. As we demonstrate in our adoption matrix (figure 7.2), this planning burden is beyond the capacity of 75 percent of a teaching faculty. Consequently, the curriculum challenge is one of the most paralyzing issues for schools and districts looking to scale personalized learning.

In short, traditional curriculum has a personalization problem and personalized learning has a curriculum problem. The reality is that a "both/and" approach to curriculum is needed. Regardless of the details within a unique personalized learning vision, educators need sets of high quality, digitally accessible tasks that are scaffolded, standards aligned, and appropriately sequenced to build on prior skills and knowledge. For personalized learning visions emphasizing student agency, tasks may offer students choice in how they develop a competency or how they demonstrate mastery, as well as allow students to set goals and progress at their own pace. For initiatives emphasizing deeper learning competencies, tasks may support multidisciplinary study, project-based work, and collaborative activities. Further, in order to move beyond the rigid structure of standardized assessment, teachers require a menu of varied and rigorous performance assessments tied to specific competencies.

Articulating Curriculum Non-negotiables

While the process of securing and aligning curriculum within the current market of options will be imperfect, aligning priority practices to existing curricula and internal expertise is a good place to start. In her book, *Go Blended!*, Liz Arney launches the selection process by asking readers to first make "a list of your non negotiables, as doing so will help you greatly narrow the field of . . . offerings."[7] This process will also help teams understand the extent of the gaps between what they have and what they need. For example, in a classroom where student collaboration and ongoing student discourse are priority practices, a curriculum relying on teachers delivering thirty-minute daily lessons and providing students thirty minutes of practice on adaptive software will not fit the bill. The limitations of this curriculum require teachers to find or create high quality group tasks and carve out time for students to engage in these tasks. When priority practices are not supported by the curriculum, the creation of bounded solutions—explicitly connecting practices to curriculum—is necessary. In addition to understanding your non-negotiables and current gaps, clarifying the level of resources available to purchase, borrow, or build curriculum will greatly impact your decision-making process.

Buying Curriculum

Expanding a curriculum to align with priority practices is generally achieved through one of the three B's: buying, borrowing, or building. Buying typically refers to the purchase of digital resources or software licenses, which is the most efficient way to address curriculum gaps when money is not an obstacle. There are several sources for directing teams to high quality options, which we describe on our resources website. The Fordham Institute offers several great options, including the report "Finding the Right Tool for the Job: Improving Reading and Writing in the Classroom," which provides in-depth reviews of promising ELA edtech tools.[8] The report is a particularly valuable resource because it transparently names the reviewers of each edtech product, includes perspectives on standards alignment, and offers opinions on the curricular value associated with upgrading from free to premium services. It is our hope that Fordham and other nonprofit curriculum research organizations will launch similar reviews of education tools and platforms across additional content areas and instructional design models. We highly recommend considering these third-party reviews as well as your own internal pilot data when making purchasing decisions. In her book, Arney cautions against trusting "the research from the vendor until you've validated it."[9] This is where pilot classrooms and ongoing R&D engines can be especially valuable.

Borrowing Curriculum

Borrowing curriculum is basically a euphemism for finding something free on the web. According to a RAND study revised in April 2017, 98 percent of secondary school ELA teachers and 99 percent of elementary school ELA teachers draw on "materials [they] developed and/or selected [themselves]," and those materials are most often pulled from Google (96 percent) and Pinterest (74.5 percent).[10] These results were similar for math. Opponents of personalized learning often point to this evidence as proof that this approach is academically harmful to students, and they have a point. We do not support haphazard searching for free curriculum resources, but when teachers are left without guidance or options, they are forced to leverage whatever they can. Our approach to implementation pathways and bounded solutions begins to address this problem by providing teachers with increasing levels of direction and structure to prevent them from turning to the open web. We envision a collaborative, incremental approach to identifying high quality free resources, where pilot teachers and their early adopter colleagues vet sites and share materials with their early majority colleagues. Together, early adopter and early majority teachers curate more detailed content for their late majority colleagues. Establishing a connected, viable, personalized curriculum using this process takes time but has several advantages, including leveraging teacher talent, promoting collaboration and ownership, and decreasing the need for random searching.

Alternatively, there is growing promise for free, comprehensive curricula thanks in part to a national initiative called #GoOpen. This movement is shining a light on well-constructed, open educational resource (OER) libraries and repositories. The launch of EngageNY.org in 2011 is a particularly strong example of the power and reach of quality open instructional materials. The site is developed and maintained by the New York State Education Department (NYSED) and was established to provide New York teachers with curriculum, assessments, and professional learning related to the implementation of Common Core learning standards. Available resources include video demonstrations of instructional shifts, relevant and scaffolded lessons presented in a logical sequence, and assessments—all covering a K–12 scope for both ELA and math. In 2017, Julia Kaufman and colleagues studied EngageNY adoption. Over an eighteen-month study, the EngageNY.org website had approximately 12.11 million page views, with approximately 55 percent of views occurring in one of forty-six states outside of New York.[11] The report concluded, "[I]f online (OER) materials are provided in progressions that are well-aligned with state standards, teachers may be more apt to use those materials on an ongoing basis for their instruction, and districts could be more apt to recommend and require use of those materials."[12]

The advent of EngageNY.org has signaled a future for comprehensive, highly vetted OER curriculum, and we hope to see many more on the open market in the coming years. These full scope and sequence curricula are even more exciting when paired with supplemental curriculum repositories that offer additional content areas, deeper tasks, and increased blended learning functionality. Websites such as Khan Academy offer courses, lessons, and practices that enable "anyone to learn anything."[13] The Buck Institute's resource bank of performance tasks and project-based learning materials are aligned to the Common Core state standards.[14] Teaching Tolerance's website has a database of culturally relevant lesson plans as well as a personalized learning lesson plan builder to support culturally responsive instruction.[15] PhET's interactive simulations engage students in science and math explorations.[16] OER (open educational resources) Commons offers a vast library of supplemental curricular materials that can be curated and adapted by teachers.[17]

There is a growing body of quality open materials; however, there are still significant challenges to leveraging the borrow approach. First, many OER materials are limited to PDF formats that are not ideal for blended learning classrooms and are not particularly engaging for students. Second, OER generally requires a local investment of human resources to support the curation of materials aligned to a particular set of competencies and priority practices. Third, unless OER materials are vetted and integrated into a local learning management system, leveraging curated OER requires significant professional development support. Teachers must be trained to decipher common OER patterns and make sense of the resources in various libraries, as well as become familiar with different lesson formats. Finally, OER do not often include best practices for special education populations or English language learners, and few consider cultural relevance. Typical materials are often traditional in design, Eurocentric in orientation, and built without many differentiated options. Essentially, integrating OER into a curriculum solution requires a significant human capital investment.

Building Curriculum

The final option for securing curriculum is to build it internally. Leveraging staff expertise to design tailored curriculum resources increases district and teacher control but also increases the time frame required for development. When existing options do not align with your priority practices, building curriculum from scratch may be a worthwhile option. Some districts have leveraged grade-level or subject-area teams of content experts and early adopters to fill curriculum gaps; other districts have asked teachers to upload specific elements of their curricula into a shared drive or learning management system, essentially creating an internal OER repository. When developed along a K–12 continuum, curated resources are particularly valuable to teachers supporting students who are multiple years above or below grade level on certain competencies. A major challenge involved in internally designing curriculum is defining a standard for high quality materials and ensuring all elements meet this standard. In some cases, consortiums of districts have collaborated to assemble teacher- and student-facing resources. In chapter 12, we discuss an effort underway in Rhode Island to support collaborative curriculum building combined with OER vetting and tagging through a statewide networked improvement community.

Often, design teams leverage all three B's to cull together a curriculum aligned to priority practices and local context. The critical work of the design team is providing leadership around how the paid, free, or built resources can best be integrated and organized to support teachers. Teachers should clearly understand the goals of various resources and how they fit with other curriculum mandates or expectations. Teachers also require explicit guidance regarding the process or circumstances for replacing or supplementing a resource. Developing a comprehensive, rigorous curriculum that supports teachers as they implement priority practices is a central challenge faced by all design teams. Once materials and resources have been gathered, a parallel issue is how teachers access the curriculum in a way that promotes efficient workflow. Combined teams that are committed to effective replication will need technical infrastructure, which is the subject of our next section.

THE INTERSECTION OF CURRICULUM AND TECHNOLOGY

While there are a variety of personalized practices that do not require technology integration, we have found that technology has played a growing role in helping educators implement priority practices by supporting workflow efficiencies. At the classroom level, Yarissa (our pilot teacher from chapters 6 and 7) alleviated the burden of planning differentiated reading instruction across more than six grade levels by leveraging a reading software that was able to translate a Common Core-aligned task into six different Lexile levels. This edtech innovation helped empower all students to build the same depth of text analysis skills, despite their current reading levels. At the organizational level, a nonprofit in Tucson, Arizona, wanted to connect teachers and students with community experts who had similar academic interests. Through the integration of a mentor database—and an aligned tagging system—teachers were able to search an online repository for local mentors with targeted expertise who were willing to support classrooms working on various projects.

If we are thoughtful and conscientious consumers, then there is no end to the problems technology can help solve within our education system. Conversely, if we are careless sheep flocking to the products with the biggest buzz, then there is no end to the problems that technology can cause. A burgeoning edtech market, quantified at 855 companies in 2015, has enabled us to operationalize previously unimaginable levels of personalization.[18] However, finding the right software to support your personalized model is one of the most challenging aspects of building a sustainable initiative. In the sections that follow we discuss three main supporting roles for technology that have emerged from the blended and personalized classrooms we have encountered. We purposely present both the potential promise and the current issues surrounding each. We then discuss our hopes for game-changing breakthroughs in the near future and present a few points for consideration as we make do with the scenarios before us. All of our insights are grounded in the perspectives of early adopter teachers, principals, and district administrators who are leading the charge and uncovering the possibilities and pitfalls of this truly nascent space.

edtech to Support Content

The advent of learning management systems (LMS) has greatly improved efficiencies associated with disseminating lessons, collecting student work, organizing grades, and managing communication between students, teachers, families, and school leaders. Infrastructure supporting the digital organization of activities has enabled students to access curriculum and assignments anytime and anywhere, expanding the reach of teaching and learning. Simultaneously, LMS software has eliminated the need for time-consuming and tedious teacher tasks, including photocopying and organizing student information. At Highlander Institute, we sometimes describe the function of an LMS by using a plumbing metaphor. Just as the plumbing system in our homes ports water from city reservoirs to our taps on demand, teachers now have an efficient way to deliver content to students. However, this investment is only valuable if high quality content is flowing through the pipes. When teachers must create and upload all of their own lessons or link to outside software programs and websites within an LMS, the quality of materials can vary.

As the concept of an LMS has matured, districts have had the opportunity to purchase curriculum and LMS components together. Many edtech products combine quality curriculum materials with full-featured LMS infrastructure, including data analytics, student rostering, and multi-grade activities across all content areas. Some programs enable teachers to upload their own content to complement the embedded curriculum while others are built on machine algorithms that can adapt to student needs based on success or failure within the system. While these functional improvements have increased the presence of good, clean water in the pipes, there are still several challenges facing combined teams as they cull together a personalized curriculum.

First, whether or not curriculum is part of an LMS, computers do not have the analytic power to distinguish high quality from low quality curriculum. Vetting the built, bought, and borrowed curriculum within any LMS is still the responsibility of curriculum directors. Further, vendors are not always transparent when making claims about the alignment between their product and the priority practices of a unique personalized learning model. This must also be vetted and confirmed by design team members, pilot teachers, or curriculum experts.

The second challenge is the workflow inefficiencies that have emerged as teachers implement multiple, discrete software systems. Most LMS and curriculum software programs are essentially built like a walled garden, making it difficult for teachers to integrate their favorite apps into the system or combine assessment information from multiple sources into a single, user-friendly report. If various tools and systems are not compatible with an LMS, teachers must organize and manage a variety of student sign-on passwords, data reports, and assignments in different places. The lack of interoperability within current LMS options has been a significant challenge for combined teams to navigate. A high quality plumbing system with pure water is difficult to use when the pipes in a building only connect to one of the many faucets people expect to use. If design teams build implementation pathways that incorporate multiple software apps, they should also attempt to find a platform that can accommodate the integration of these different tools and websites to simplify access and logistics.

edtech to Support Creation

There is a popular notion surrounding twenty-first-century education models that learning new knowledge is no longer the goal. With an accessible and robust Internet, the ability to learn new knowledge is instant. Rather than memorizing and regurgitating information, students should be creating new knowledge, and technology is expanding the opportunities for student creation at a rapid pace. This requires a shift in how we think about the utility of technology in schools. An exclusive focus on content and curriculum has often resulted in layering adaptive software programs on top of antiquated pedagogy and traditional, teacher-centered learning environments. In a 2016 EdSurge article entitled "The Overselling of Education Technology," Alfie Kohn questions what kind of learning should be taking place in school: "If we favor an approach by which students actively construct meaning, an interactive process that involves a deep understanding of ideas and emerges from the interests and questions of the learners themselves, well, then we'd be open to the kinds of technology that truly support this kind of inquiry. Show me something that helps kids create, design, produce, construct—and I'm on board."[18] When priority practices emphasize choice, creation, collaboration, or deeper learning projects, technology can and should be used as an open-ended resource for a range of media creation. We have watched students demonstrate their learning by using green screen technology, stop-motion animation, podcasting, screencasting, and website development—as well as represent new knowledge by creating a cartoon, an advertisement, a blog post, an avatar, a game, or a reenactment. The possibilities and opportunities are endless. While we would love to see technology being used equally to support content delivery and creativity, most classrooms still err on the side of content.

This is particularly noticeable when we compare the use of technology among students at schools within different socioeconomic levels. Another 2016 EdSurge article called "What a Decade of Education Research Tells Us About Technology in the Hands of Underserved Students" describes a digital divide where technology is used primarily for remediation in low-income neighborhood schools and also used for simulations, creation, and authentic applications in higher-income neighborhood schools. According to professor Mark Warschauer from the University of California, Irvine, "Using digital tools solely for drill-and-practice activities and remediation can and often does negatively affect student achievement, not to mention engagement, motivation, and self-esteem."[19] In response, we encourage all teachers, but particularly teachers of underserved student populations, to establish students as content creators rather than content consumers by empowering them to design and build original digital content through a process of inquiry.

The challenge involved in this call to action is the current lack of well-designed instructional tasks, projects, and rubrics that support rigorous student creation opportunities. While it is easy to find a list of creation apps on the Internet, related lessons and curriculum extensions are not easy to find. Many teachers understand the power and potential of cameras and screen annotation for achieving higher levels of student ownership and agency but may not have the skills or knowledge to build a quality project outline or guiding rubric. The field would benefit from an organized repository of creation apps with a tagging system to help teachers easily connect creation opportunities with quality lessons, content, and assessment. Once again, the need for bounded solutions to support high quality, sustainable implementation is clear.

edtech for Authentic Learning

In classrooms around Rhode Island, we have noticed that students are craving a more authentic learning experience. They often struggle to see the point and purpose of school because the curriculum does not connect to their reality. Increasingly, technology is allowing students to ground learning in relevant contexts through open-ended inquiry, critical thinking skills, and metacognition. In some situations, students study and develop solutions to real problems in their neighborhoods, communities, and world. In others, they engage in work that mimics the world of professionals using industry-standard technology and processes. For combined teams prioritizing student ownership, self-direction, agency, interests, project-based learning and/or identity, it is beneficial to connect students with the community and world outside the classrooms walls.

A variety of communication and collaboration tools support authentic learning opportunities. Video chats bring experts from around the globe into classrooms while flexible reference materials, such as Google maps, support creative global research opportunities. Software is emerging to support the organization and management of student internships and mentor programs that enable students to connect with caring adults who share a common interest or passion. With the job market evolving at lightning speed, it is heartening to see students learning skills in work environments, earning job certifications, and connecting to the workforce in growing numbers. According to Julia Freeland Fisher of the Clayton Christensen Institute, "Mounting evidence suggests that whom students know can shape their aspirations and access to opportunity. Access to relationships can buffer risk, increase grades, bolster well-being, and support students to and through college."[20]

New movements are also underway to support teachers in offering students the opportunity to share their learning beyond a classroom audience. Shareyourlearning.org provides a variety of teacher toolkits to help students develop learning presentations, exhibitions, and student-led conferences with the goal of increasing student engagement by making learning public. These materials are a great starting point for considering how preK–12 students can become experts on a topic and find a platform for teaching, informing, debating, or persuading other people to take action. Edtech has only begun to scratch the surface with platforms and software to support these efforts. The challenge continues to be how to effectively integrate these tools into a comprehensive, efficient, user-friendly system so that any tool or software can be seamlessly integrated into any personalized learning system.

The Next Level of edtech

As the blended and personalized field has evolved, practitioners and policy makers have begun to realize that, until relatively recently, edtech products were being developed to support traditional classroom and course models. This is to be expected of entrepreneurs who have learned primarily in traditional environments and hope to appeal to large markets, many of which are still in the very initial phases of a personalized learning shift. While entrepreneurial educators and parents have created software to address personalized learning needs, most products are not built to be used flexibly or aligned with priority practices. The relative adaptability of software versus traditional textbooks suggests that companies could be more creative and flexible in how they build products to support multifaceted implementation. This will happen when more districts can articulate a demand for this functionality and entrepreneurs have a deeper understanding of the major instructional shifts within personalized learning models.

Liz Glowa and Jim Goodell conducted a deep investigation of the current limitations of edtech products in their 2016 paper titled "Student-Centered Learning: Functional Requirements for Integrated Systems to Optimize Learning." The authors frame the challenge this way: "The processes of student-centered learning and the data that prove most critical to support student-centered learning are different from the processes and data used to support traditional classroom models and school operations. Many of the current information and data systems were designed with a course-centric/teacher-centric approach needed for basic accountability compliance and to support a 'factory model' of school organization."[21] Glowa and Goodell argue learning platforms and management systems require a modular architecture with an upgraded set of functional requirements mapped to different elements of personalization. Combined teams should have the opportunity to pick and choose modules that support content delivery, creation, and authentic learning opportunities—to name a few—that can operate seamlessly within an LMS structure and integrate complex processes and functions in support of unique personalized learning practices.

There is still much work to be done to move the education technology market to a place where it will become a no-brainer investment for combined teams. Until this day arrives, we must manage and improvise with the options before us, which are steadily improving. Selecting products that support priority practices and offer efficient workflow solutions for teachers will take due diligence and creativity. Here are a few recommended tactics for combined teams to consider:

- *Define your ideal tools and resources.* Build on the concept of defining curriculum non-negotiables and research critical features and capabilities of ideal learning platforms. Describe what an excellent set of tools would look like to support your personalized learning model.
- *Make investments with the understanding that upgraded tools are coming.* While we cannot be sure about specific timeframes, we are pretty confident that the next generation of learning platforms will enable districts to eliminate many current products and barriers.
- *Consider investing in human capital over tools and resources.* Current learning management systems can become a huge value-add if teachers can access everything they need in one place. This can happen when curriculum coordinators are available to unbundle and digitize existing and open-source curriculum and upload it into an LMS (see the Fraser case study at the end of this section).
- *Leverage R&D classrooms.* Teachers leading these classrooms are well-positioned to help craft short-term solutions to a curriculum challenge, and/or determine the value of new tools and resources.
- *Focus on workflow first.* Consider a solution from a user perspective and work to leverage technology solutions that are compatible or efficient from a teacher's point of view. Curriculum or technology additions that decrease a teacher's workflow efficiency will not move your initiative in the right direction.

As combined teams contemplate how to attack curriculum and technology challenges emerging from their personalized learning pilots, the story of Fraser public schools in Fraser, Michigan, offers some helpful insights.

A Pathway Toward Personalized Curriculum

Led by Superintendent Dr. David Richards and Assistant Superintendent Carrie Wozniak, Fraser public schools launched personalized learning cohorts across the district in 2014. Initial work focused on developing a vision and common language around competency-based learning and emphasizing high-impact classroom practices.

Early in the initiative, Dave and Carrie recognized their personalization priorities were immersed in a complex and pervasive curriculum problem. In order to support competency-based learning, teachers required vertically aligned learning progressions across content areas; current textbooks and curriculum programs were not going to cut it. Their work began with an inventory of the current curricula, which helped the Fraser team identify significant gaps within existing curriculum resources. They acknowledged they could not ask their faculty to comb through the internet and navigate multiple websites and software programs to supplement current materials. In response, they committed to purchasing learning management systems and creating a curriculum foundation that would meet up to 90 percent of their teachers' instructional needs.

Based on the unique needs and data requirements present within elementary and secondary systems, different learning management systems were purchased to support each level. While existing options had various pros and cons, Dave and Carrie looked for platforms that could integrate existing student information and scheduling at the expense of options with data management and assessment features. As a non-negotiable, each LMS had to be interoperable with current systems.

Their curriculum strategy leveraged current teacher expertise across the district as well as an exceptional infrastructure for professional learning communities (PLC) already in place. The plan also required the designation of two full-time curriculum leaders, one to support elementary teachers and one to support middle and high school teachers. Teachers with demonstrated interest and expertise in standards-based curriculum were invited to join a new cohort of PLC groups that centered on four grade-level bands: K–second, third through fifth, sixth through eighth, and ninth through twelfth. Curriculum leaders designed the protocols that framed the initial work, which focused on identifying core competencies, big ideas, and essential questions tied to grade-level standards. From there, learning progressions across content areas were outlined for each grade-level band. This was a particularly challenging task at the high school level, where college and career pathways—as well as a multitude of electives—forced the PLC to look carefully at standards and objectives and determine priorities.

Next, curriculum leaders loaded the learning progression outlines into respective learning management platforms and established a tagging system. Existing curriculum and instructional units, aligned to newly developed learning progressions, were sent to curriculum leaders who were responsible for uploading and tagging all content. In some cases, curriculum leaders engaged in the additional tasks of unbundling, digitizing, and scaffolding printed materials and PDFs before uploading and tagging could begin. Unit by unit, and grade band by grade band, curriculum began to populate each learning progression.

A carefully developed protocol guides the creation of new content to maintain consistency through grade-level bands. New strategies and resources go through a vetting process. Curriculum leaders act as the gatekeepers, ensuring new materials meet quality standards before being added to an LMS. New additions are routinely reviewed by all PLC members.

The system is organized around the creation of master classes with anchors to identified competencies, core instructional materials, and supplementary resources. Teachers download a master course and adapt or supplement as needed. A protocol for suggested revisions continues to capture new thinking and provides a mechanism for continuous improvement. As new resources are added to master course folders, they can be directly copied into downloaded teacher versions.

Within each master class, curriculum is organized to facilitate instruction in a blended learning classroom. Resources and activities can be assigned to specific students and supplemented with teacher-created materials. Over time, courses have expanded to include more robust materials for scaffolding instruction and to offer teachers and students more choice in the various directions they can take through a unit.

Over the course of three years, PLCs and curriculum leaders have worked diligently to establish the 90 percent curriculum threshold across grade-level bands. These days, it is common to find students working on different competencies and modules within the same classrooms. Student agency and engagement continue to rise, and there are fewer behavior issues each year.

Dave and Carrie's approach to curriculum has honored the fact that teachers want to have input into their teaching content without being saddled with the huge responsibility of building content and systems on their own. Articulating the 90 percent curriculum goal has given teachers with different proclivities for iteration the freedom to adapt while relying on a significant foundation from which to build.

Both Dave and Carrie emphasize the critical role their two curriculum leaders have played through this process. Allocating the tasks of uploading and tagging content to the district has enabled PLC members to engage in deep conversations and focus on their personal areas of expertise. It has also ensured that content has a consistent look and feel within grade-level bands. Dave and Carrie believe this model is cost effective and the investment into two full-time curriculum leaders has been truly invaluable.

Dave does not hesitate to acknowledge the complex problem curriculum presents within personalized learning environments and is quick to point out it is a district—not a teacher—problem to solve. "If you want to extend the reach of personalized learning models, you can't send teachers back to their classrooms of thirty students and tell them to figure out a way to build their own curriculum."

With a handle on curriculum, Dave and Carrie are ready to push elements of pacing, which disrupts deeply entrenched grade-level constructs that are uncomfortable for stakeholders to abandon. Communication continues to be a priority as leaders engage a variety of stakeholders in ongoing conversations about the future of Fraser public schools. From all accounts, it looks like future iterations will continue to be designed around student learning rather than the system.

● ● ●

Across varied personalized learning initiatives, establishing a personalized curriculum represents a significant challenge. For the time being, combined teams sit in a gray area where traditional curriculum products are not well suited for personalized classrooms and next-generation products are currently under development. There are no easy answers, but there is one essential consideration that was well articulated by Fraser superintendent Dave Richards: curriculum is a district problem, not a teacher problem. We encourage teams to consider external partnerships and network opportunities to help accelerate solutions. We explore networking as a strategic focus in chapter 12, but first we shift gears to consider how professional learning is best supported when rolling out blended and personalized learning at scale, which is the subject of chapter 11.

PERSONALIZING PROFESSIONAL LEARNING

I n 2013, Patrick Welsh wrote an opinion article for the *Washington Post* reflecting on his forty-three-year career as an English teacher. Titled "Four Decades of Failed School Reform," the article takes readers on his journey from integration reforms in the 70s to edicts resulting from the 1983 "A Nation at Risk" report, through the standards-based era of the 90s, the small schools initiatives of the mid 2000s, and the expectations linked to "No Child Left Behind" over the past fifteen years.[1] Welsh is brutally honest about the impact of these initiatives, stating that "more than four decades of education reforms didn't make me a better teacher and haven't made T.C. Williams a better school. Rather, the quick fixes promulgated by headline-seeking politicians, school administrators and self-styled education gurus have in some cases done more harm than good."[2] Simultaneously, readers can feel Welsh's passion for teaching and relate to his teaching philosophy: "to make students care about what they're studying and understand how it's relevant to their lives."[3] Throughout his reform-laden teaching career, Welsh has been frank about the fact that many of the initiatives implemented at his school failed to include guidance around how teachers were supposed to operationalize the concepts in their classrooms, and none measured up to the professional development opportunity he found most valuable: exchanging ideas and best practices with his colleagues. Hundreds of teachers commented on the article. One of the more poignant responses questioned, "When will education stop being appropriated by ideological power mongers from the top down who want to ignore individual teachers and classroom experience in favor of abstractions that don't work?"[4]

In order to prevent blended and personalized initiatives from becoming just another abstraction with a similar fate, design teams and district leadership teams must focus their combined efforts into empowering, supporting, and engaging individual teachers in their own professional learning. Just as instructional efforts in classrooms move toward more student-centered models, change management processes surrounding professional learning should be teacher centered and tailored to the strengths and needs of individual teachers.

While this concept may sound obvious, it flies in the face of traditional professional learning methods and requires deep commitment on the part of leaders to provide the right levels of information, support, and agency to teachers in different categories of Roger's adoption curve. Too often we assume less talented, savvy, or engaged educators desire less input into their own professional learning or instructional design. In the same way we seek to engage reluctant learners in the classroom, leaders must find new and novel ways to give reluctant teachers more agency and support so they feel as if they are part of the reform instead of feeling like a reform effort is happening to them. This approach is much easier to talk about as a hypothetical than it is to implement, but in this chapter we describe strategies and processes combined teams can take to improve professional learning opportunities for a range of adults across a building or district.

BLENDED AND PERSONALIZED PROFESSIONAL LEARNING

As teams prepare to launch replication efforts across a school or district, we picture an idealized professional learning environment where money, talent, and time are not limiting factors. In a perfect world, districts could leverage implementation pathways to build a scope and sequence of teacher competencies that are attached to each new instructional practice, including authentic performance tasks that enable teachers to demonstrate mastery and the ability to add their work to a growing bank of district knowledge. Teachers would be able to establish goals around their selected priority practice and determine how, where, and when their own learning experiences would take place. In this perfect world, teachers could even select from a menu of personalized support options, such as online modules, face-to-face coaching or week-long trainings, to help them achieve mastery of new practices. Sadly, these concepts generally remain elusive in our current education space. As an organization, we continue to identify and document schools and institutions chasing these ideals. We imagine a day when just-right levels of support and information could exist for all teachers; in the meantime, we offer some current examples of best practices as well as insights from trailblazers to guide teams in the creation of more blended and personalized professional learning opportunities.

As we discussed in chapter 9, scaling decisions depend on the availability of time, resources, and human capital. Every ounce of energy the design team, pilot teachers, and district leadership have invested into carving a personalized pathway has generated clarity about what teachers across the adoption curve need in order to be successful implementers. For this reason, it is essential to align professional development planning with scaling strategies. This becomes even more important for schools and districts choosing to scale across multiple cohorts or through a full implementation model.

There are more frameworks, strategies, and methods for professional learning than there are species of birds in the rainforest. Every educator has a favorite book, guru, or theory regarding professional development. The goal of this section is not to convince you to drop your current process and start from scratch, but to show how professional learning relates to our framework and to showcase successful approaches we have identified when supporting scaling efforts.

At the Highlander Institute, we have built our reputation on our coaching and professional development services. We understand the power and importance of ongoing adult learning and how difficult it can be to reclaim teacher trust when their time is wasted with poorly organized professional learning experiences. For this reason, we build our professional development activities on three key tenets. First, we acknowledge personalized learning shifts are new for teachers. Most have never experienced any learning model other than traditional instruction. For this reason, we start by exposing teachers to new models through the simulation of blended and personalized learning experiences. We want all teachers to experience personalized learning before launching into the work in their own classrooms. Second, we center all our trainings, modules, playlists, and coaching around locally crafted implementation pathways or our priority practices tool. Even when we introduce digital tools or software, our focus remains on practices, not hardware or software. Third, we emphasize embedded coaching whenever possible, with an intentional shift away from workshops or full-group trainings. By focusing on embedded classroom coaching, we increase the opportunities we have to co-plan and co-teach with educators in a way that is responsive to their classroom situations. In this chapter, we explain how these three principles can support the scaling strategy of any team. We end this chapter by reiterating the importance of a strong school culture, driven by capable principals and guided by cycles of continuous improvement.

Inspiring Change Through Simulated Experience

"You can't teach what you don't know. And you can't lead where you won't go."[5] This famous quote from the Reverend Jesse Jackson is as true for making complex shifts in teaching and learning as it is for leading societal change. We know traditional instruction like we know how to breathe. It is instinctual, and the stress or discomfort of new approaches can push us to cling to this model like a security blanket. A staff-wide or system-wide shift toward blended and personalized learning requires teachers to build a level of familiarity and comfort around new practices. Teachers need to understand the unease of being assessed in a mastery model where feedback and persistence is more important than a final grade. They need opportunities to experience differentiated learning and evaluation. They need a chance to feel what it is like to have choice, agency, and ownership of their learning as well as opportunities to experience learning with a partner, in a small group, and by watching a video. Educators need to process and debrief these new experiences so they can build empathy for students who struggle and encourage those who need it. All simulation experiences should align to the strategies outlined in implementation pathways, connecting teachers more deeply to the approaches they will be encouraged to leverage in their own classrooms.

Any time we onboard a new school or district as part of a Highlander Institute cohort, we kick off the engagement with what we affectionately call a boot camp. Our boot camps are opportunities to immerse teachers in multiple blended learning models, scenarios, and examples of personalized learning practices. Our boot camps work best when we already know the priority practices a team is hoping to implement in their own school or district; when the district is just getting started with this work, we include a diverse mix of delivery models. Here are some of our favorites:

Station rotation model: As the most popular and well-worn model for blended and personalized learning, it is fairly easy to deliver content and skills through a station rotation model. We start simulations with a whole-group, online formative assessment to demonstrate how to run formative data collection and how to regroup based on real-time assessment data. Once teachers are grouped in stations, we explain all three center activities and then rotate participants every fifteen to thirty minutes. One of our centers typically features an online playlist or hyper-doc in which teachers select from a menu of short videos, blogs, and podcasts before building their own lesson plan or artifact. The second center includes a collaborative task in which the teachers discuss, design, build, or perform something as a pair or a group. When we have a local strategy rubric in hand, we can turn the collaborative center into a performance task aligned to a specific strategy. The final center features small group work with the facilitator and includes a quick, auto-graded exit ticket at the end. Usually, our small-group facilitator slightly adapts the content for each group, responding to questions, comments, and concerns that are common to the interests or needs of the group.

Playground model: This professional learning model requires multiple leaders and is a great way to engage local early adopter or pilot teachers as professional learning facilitators. This model also works well with large groups over a longer period of time (we have run a playground model with 350 teachers during a full-day training). The model demonstrates a personalized approach by empowering participants to decide what they want to learn and how they want to learn it.

The model requires significant planning and preparation. It relies on a large choice board of discrete tasks that are typically connected to implementation pathways. In figure 11.1, we utilize a bingo board theme to make it fun, but you do not need twenty-five tasks to successfully run this model. Usually divided into categories with increasing levels of challenge, each square includes a hyperlink to a task with a description of the assignment, links to resources teachers can explore and use to complete the assignment, optional scaffolds for teachers who need support or a push, and a process for teachers to submit their work. We have focused bingo boards on priority practices, strategy sets, general introductory topics, and practices associated with a set of tools, such as G Suite and Google Classroom.

We introduce the concept and set parameters in a whole-group setting. For example, over the course of three hours, teachers may be expected to explore and complete at least four tasks. We then describe a range of learning modalities that are available to support participants. We set up a lab environment—typically the school library—where teachers can work independently or in small groups with a few experts on hand to answer questions as they arise. Concurrently, we offer

FIGURE 11.1   **Sample bingo board**

B	I	N	G	O
1 B1: Using Google Drive, create a "PD Playground" folder. Create subfolders and keep all PD notes/task submissions in these folders. Google Apps 101	I1: Create a Google classroom for one of your classes. Create two resource folders for students. Google Classroom	N1: Develop at least three classroom expectations (norms) as they relate to technology. Create an audio clip using Vocaroo or Audioboo to explain them. Tools for self-directed learning	G1: Create a homepage with your class bookmarks using Symbaloo or Sqworl. Tools for self-directed learning	O1: Create a multiple-choice assessment using Socrative. Tools for assessment
2 B2: Create a shortened link and QR code using Google Shortener. Tools for productivity	I2: Run a Plickers assessment from your phone. Tools for assessment	N2: Create a Padlet and have at least three colleagues post on it. Tools for collaboration	G2: Download "choice eliminator" and embed questions into a Google form. Google Apps 101	O2: Create five cards on Quizlet. Tools for assessment
3 B3: Create a playlist for your class using Blendspace. Tools for self-directed learning	I3: Create an Evernote account, create two to three notebooks, and sync the notebooks across various platforms (desktop, online, phone). Tools for productivity	N3: Complete the blended learning basics playlist and submit the assessment via Socrative. (Room Code: HIGHLANDER)	G3: Create a Twitter account and tweet at least three ideas or links worth sharing with other educators using #edchat. Tools for collaboration	O3: Set up a Remind 101 account to keep in touch with your students. Tools for productivity
4 B4: Develop at least three classroom expectations as they relate to technology. Create a document in Google Docs and share the link. Google Apps 101	I4: Annotate an image using ThingLink. Tools for collaboration	N4: Create a ClassDojo (beginner) or Classcraft (advanced) account to manage behavior and explore gamification. Tools for productivity	G4: Choose any YouTube video and embed questions in it using EdPuzzle or EduCanon. Tools for assessment	O4: Record yourself sharing your classroom expectations as they relate to technology using Screencastify or Screencast-O-Matic. Tools for collaboration
5 B5: Create a two-minute whiteboard presentation using Educreations or ShowMe. Tools for collaboration	I5: Browse through resources on Gooru Learning and create a playlist. Tools for self-directed learning	N5: Create a multiplayer quiz using Quizizz or Kahoot. Tools for assessment	G5: Organize your files in Google Drive by uploading existing files on your computer. Create a "Playground" folder. Google Apps 101	O5: Watch a lesson on TED-Ed and personalize it for your students. Tools for self-directed learning

(Beginner Column)

> *Completing a Task:*
> Use the provided link to review playlists of resources to support you
> Fill out the Google Form at: _____ (click send copy of my responses)
> Show and discuss the task with a colleague and ask them to sign off on the box

small-group facilitated sessions for educators who want to engage in deeper conversations about a task or strategy with colleagues and also run scheduled stand-and-deliver tutorial sessions for anyone who wishes to receive direct instruction. The goal is to expose teachers to a range of classroom design options and encourage them to experience as many as they can during the course of a day, at their own pace, and based on tasks or information they are most interested in learning. At the end of the session, we reconvene as a whole group to debrief the learning experience.

Project-based learning: This model is tailored to teachers who are focused on priority practices centering on rigor, mastery, and collaboration. The approach requires a discrete but authentic problem for participating teams to solve. This model follows the Buck Institute's project-based learning framework and is often used by the Buck Institute, High Tech High, and other deeper learning organizations when working with adults around these classroom shifts. The entire professional learning experience takes place in a collaborative group setting that simulates a student classroom experience. The session begins by establishing group norms and group roles that will help teachers effectively replicate practices with students. Then, participants are presented with an authentic design problem and the parameters for developing a solution. We ran this model at our Highlander Institute office when we were contemplating how to design a high functioning, fully featured professional learning space. We walked teams through the empty area, gave them a scaled drawing of the space, a budget for furniture and technology, and a blurb about our aspirations for the room. Each team worked collaboratively for the majority of the morning to create a plan and then used time after lunch to practice their pitch. Rubrics were used to evaluate their final exhibitions. In the end, we selected a winner and two runners up. Most participants in our project-based learning sessions have never taught in a project-based learning environment but report feeling ready to try this type of task with their students after experiencing it themselves. Teachers love the authentic nature of the design work, which helps spark ideas for authentic extensions they can incorporate into their classrooms.

The most important aspect of each of these simulation models is the facilitated debrief. Sometimes we have whiteboards or chart paper available for participants to record their feelings as they engage in these models. Some feel energized by certain tasks or directions while others feel frustrated. It is important to pause throughout the simulation to check in and encourage participants to articulate their thoughts and feelings. Teachers need to understand how different aspects of personalized models may be received by different learners. Good facilitators can model real-time adjustments as they hear teachers express frustration or confusion. This helps participants build strategies for when things go wrong in their own classrooms. Finally, we model the practice of asking for specific feedback on the experience, which helps us iterate for future audiences and demonstrates how teachers can solicit feedback from students to improve on their own instructional shifts.

Aligning Content and Delivery to Implementation Pathways

Too often in education we subject teachers to random professional development with no anchors or connection to ongoing district vision or initiatives. According to a 2014 research study conducted by the Boston Consulting Group, few teachers are highly satisfied with current professional development offerings. "In interviews, teachers say that too many current professional development offerings are not relevant, not effective, and most important of all, not connected to their core work of helping students learn."[6] Sometimes trainings are just point-and-click software demos without any additional context. Sometimes trainings are skills focused but lack alignment with the core initiatives being led by the school or district. We call these types of trainings "additive professional learning" as they require teachers to make sense of the information and determine how it might fit into their practices and routines.

Our framework aspires to offer "integrated professional learning" that is directly aligned to implementation pathways, which should serve as the foundation for all professional learning for teachers on the other side of the chasm. No longer are we training teachers using stock definitions or national frameworks absent of background and context. Instead, we approach teachers who are new to this work with targeted practices already subjected to a rigorous and localized improvement process. Experiences are led by pilot teachers ready to offer testimonials and examples of how these priority practices have made a difference in their instruction and within their classrooms. Implementation pathways are brimming with a range of strategies connected to quantitative and qualitative data from the pilot phase. Including elements of choice and agency in integrated professional learning activities also increases teacher ownership and investment.

Let's look at an example from Greeley-Evans School District 6, which we profiled in chapter 9. District leaders asked all teachers to select one out of four priority practices as a central focus each year and empowered teachers to develop a personalized learning plan around their selected practice. Teachers could leverage the support of a coach, attend workshops, or craft their own approaches as long as they were aligned to priority practices. Offering choice and allowing teachers to establish a relevant and compelling focus builds trust and makes teachers feel valued as they face the uncertainties of new challenges.

Choice and multiple pathways can be overwhelming and counterproductive for some teachers, just as they can be overwhelming for some students. When teachers are not ready to engage in professional learning activities centered on implementation pathways, it is important to meet them where they are through introductory activities. We sometimes leverage our Highlander Institute priority practices tool (appendix C) to offer novice teachers an initial exploration of various practices and strategies. We have created playlists centered on practices and related sets of strategies that include a curated list of articles, videos, tools, guidance, and performance tasks. Based on the needs of a particular group, we decide how to disseminate the content, which often includes some combination of stations, the playground model, presentations, peer learning, and online work. Introducing teachers to the concept of blended and personalized learning through a focus on practices and strategies provides them with context for why their own implementation pathways are important. Our growing number of playlists can be accessed on our resource website.

In some cases, teachers must first attend to classroom culture indicators before tackling aspects of implementation pathways. When a leader or coach notices a deficiency with regard to the current status of student behavior or classroom systems, it must be addressed directly. Oftentimes these challenges require an exploration of the root cause to get at the barrier or impediment. Sometimes a simple solution can go a very long way. An uncomplicated but powerful breakthrough occurred when one of our coaches, Mike, was supporting teachers at a local elementary school. The principal and teachers wanted to increase student self-direction during project time in the classroom but struggled to combat the precedent of teacher-centered directions and troubleshooting that was disrupting small-group instruction. Mike noticed that teachers were assigning independent, small-group tasks with a range of complexity and expecting students to figure out what to do. When students were confused, teachers were taking one of two approaches. Either they spent an incredible amount of time at the start of class explaining directions to the full class, or they abandoned their targeted instruction group to answer questions as they arose. Mike's solution was simple but game changing. He went to the local party store and bought class sets of clear, plastic table tents. Mike then helped the teachers transition from writing paragraphs of instructions to writing bullet points with clear directives. Mike coached the teachers to emphasize the *why* behind the task and clarify the purpose and endgame, worrying less about compliance with each specific step. This helped build student self-direction relatively quickly and allowed the teachers to gradually increase the rigor and complexity of tasks, moving from simple collaborative games to longer challenge problems. The table tents were added to the implementation pathway for self-directed learning as an entry point for creating more effective classroom systems.

The Power of Embedded Coaching

The previous example leads us to the third component of our professional development philosophy, which centers on embedded coaching that is responsive to the needs of individual teachers. We believe, and research shows, that coaching is a high-impact professional learning strategy as teachers along the adoption curve begin to implement validated practices. In a 2010 report on a four-year longitudinal study, Biancarosa and colleagues found that instructional coaching contributed to a 32 percent increase in value-added student learning gains.[7] While there is widespread support for the concept of instructional coaching, nuanced differences in approaches and meeting frequency matter quite a bit.

Critical roles of the coach include observing classroom instruction, co-planning, brainstorming, troubleshooting, debriefing, modeling, and listening. Building strong, trusting relationships with teachers is at the heart of the coaching approach, and can make or break the impact of coaching effectiveness. There really is no better resource for establishing universal coaching skills and effective coaching practices than Elena Aguilar's book, *The Art of Coaching: Effective Strategies for School Transformation*.[8] The strategies outlined in this book can help coaches leverage any implementation pathway to support a range of teachers and advance a personalized learning vision.

In our framework, coaches can be experts, but they can also be school leaders, mentor teachers, district leaders, retired teachers—essentially any individual with a deep understanding of teaching, a belief in the potential of personalized practices, and the capacity to intentionally examine and reflect on instruction. Coaches are particularly important to our framework because they empower teachers to select their own starting points for this work, which are ideally connected to a problem of practice and aligned with an implementation pathway. As the research shows, there is greater impact when the work focuses on "*figuring out* an instructional solution that produces a detectable improvement in learning, [rather than] just *trying out* a variety of instructional activities."[9] Offering choice around priority practices and entry points is important but sometimes limits collaboration opportunities between teachers who are scaling the work through a cohort model. A strong, embedded coaching program affords districts the ability to offer both choice and tailored support to every teacher.

The number of teachers being supported by a coach impacts the effectiveness of professional learning, and we recommend limiting a coaching cohort to between eight and twelve teachers. We acknowledge the crazy math involved: onboarding two hundred teachers into the initiative would require an army of twenty coaches, which is a completely infeasible plan in many districts. Each of the schools/districts in our profiled case studies (chapter 9) responded creatively to this dilemma: Kristen (the principal) split coaching responsibilities with her pilot teachers in our school example; Colleen acted as a liaison, meeting with pilot teachers as a cohort for two hours each week in our charter network example; and Deagan sacrificed devices for coaches in early budgets and gave teachers options for professional learning that included but did not mandate coaching in our larger district example.

In our model, a coach works through cycles of embedded support that begin with a twenty-minute planning session around a selected entry point from an implementation pathway. The coach and teacher build a lesson and schedule a time to co-teach it, which is followed by a debrief. When a coaching cohort includes teachers in the same grade level, or even building, larger group debriefs are helpful for sharing successes and addressing pain points, as well as for promoting inter-classroom visits. In addition to building teacher capacity, improving practice, and promoting stronger student outcomes, coaching systems create coherence and alignment within a school and across a district. As design team liaisons, coaches are important for managing teacher accountability around specific professional goals as well as leadership accountability around reducing barriers and improving conditions for success. Ongoing and consistent feedback loops between implementing teachers, coaches, the principal, and the design team are critical. We explore the importance of communication between the coach and principal in more detail at the end of the chapter. As part of their ongoing role, coaches should collect artifacts to add to implementation pathways and gather and summarize process, outcome, and balance measures to share with teachers as well as the design team.

We have seen strong coaching efforts drive many successful and sustainable personalized learning initiatives across Rhode Island. At a local elementary school in Providence, Rhode Island, the Highlander Institute launched embedded coaching cycles with grade-level teams, in partnership with a committed building coach and a strong principal. Over the course of five years, the coaching spread from kindergarten to grade four with a deepening commitment to priority practices across the building. Our gradual release process has empowered the internal school coach who is now driving the effort. The coach meets weekly with grade-level teams during common planning time to discuss individual needs as well as content-specific curriculum and assessment challenges. The coach is incredibly accessible to teachers and is an essential driver of the successful implementation underway at the school.

While we emphasize the power and importance of establishing a strong coaching infrastructure, we also acknowledge the budgetary constraints within schools and districts. The next section explores lighter touch, lower-cost options for supporting new, implementing teachers through the difficult task of shifting practice.

Complementary Professional Learning Opportunities

In many high functioning design teams, a professional learning subcommittee of teachers coordinates components of a comprehensive professional learning plan. There are several relatively low maintenance but high-impact strategies that support ongoing professional learning for teachers with diverse strengths and needs.

Unconferences are becoming prominent components of blended and personalized learning initiatives. These teacher-led professional learning opportunities are structured around teacher interest and can be leveraged to dive deeply into an implementation pathway and explore how various teachers are approaching each strategy. The unconference format is centered on participant voice, and the agenda is typically built at the beginning of the session through a protocol that is inclusive of all ideas and interests. Sessions focus on relevance, collaboration, and creativity.

Pineapple charts are being leveraged by teachers to encourage and welcome colleagues into their classrooms (pineapples are considered an international symbol of warmth, welcome, friendship, and hospitality). Posted in central locations, such as faculty rooms, charts detail when a teacher is trying something new or is interested in peer feedback around a practice or strategy. Teachers consult the board regularly and informally visit a class of interest—for five minutes or a whole class period. In the most successful instances, lead teachers have worked closely with building administrators to support the effort. This has often meant creating effective communication systems to establish a fully populated list of interesting opportunities each week, as well as organizing flexible and responsive classroom coverage options. Aligning these charts to implementation pathways is also a helpful adaptation, supporting focused visits around the integration of a specific strategy.

Twitter chats have proven incredibly powerful as a free, highly engaging professional learning activity in Rhode Island. School leaders, coaches, and teacher leaders have led Twitter chats to share best practices and crowdsource ideas at all times of day and night. Requiring only a hashtag and an appointment, Twitter chats are great for building excitement around a personalized learning initiative and demonstrating the power of networking and collaboration. Launch an initial chat during a staff meeting when everyone can participate together and get acclimated to the concept. When teachers are comfortable, Twitter chats (connected to hashtags) can become an accessible archive of ideas, resources, and practices shared during chats—and updated over time. We have seen leaders build strong culture through the development and cultivation of their own Twitter hashtags. Hashtags are a great way for disseminating vision, priority practice, and personalized learning messaging to stakeholders with Twitter accounts.

Professional Learning for Leaders

As we referenced in chapter 9, the culture and climate of schools is a critical factor in predicting the success of scaling efforts. Strong culture is apparent in the emotional support present within a building, as well as the extent of social relationships between teachers, students, and administrators. In one particularly memorable consulting project at the Highlander Institute, we supported a cohort of eight early adopter teachers across two elementary schools in the same district. Four teachers at each school met with the same Highlander Institute coach each week for guidance around lesson planning, tools, resources, routines, and practices. Student demographics across both schools were almost identical. Teachers leveraged the same planning documents and engaged in a similar process of gradual release in partnership with their coach. Over the course of the year, each group of teachers received seventy hours of embedded support. In both schools, the academic year ended with significant progress in pilot classrooms—strong growth rates on student benchmark assessment data and enthusiastic feedback from both teachers and students, as noted on our walkthrough tool.

Yet, as we began to organize planning for year two, we noticed stunning differences in the number of teachers at each school who were interested in being part of the second cohort. At one school—call it Keenville Elementary—all eighteen of the remaining classroom teachers in the school signed up to be part of the second cohort. At the other school—let's say Stallfield Elementary—we struggled to identify four new teachers who wanted coaching support during year two. After talking to teachers at both schools and compiling additional observation notes, it was clear the fundamental difference between schools was the role of the principal.

At Keenville, the principal was deeply involved in supporting the early adopter cohort. She visited classrooms often and praised the shifts as they began to emerge. She acted as a trusted thought partner and actively worked to solve problems and reduce obstacles. She attended all meetings and participated alongside the Highlander Institute coaches during formal walkthroughs. She tweeted classroom photos and links to artifacts from pilot classrooms and encouraged teachers to be both creative and innovative without reprisal for failed attempts. At Stallfield, the principal was always preoccupied with a crisis or student behavior issue when the Highlander Institute coach was present. His focus on discipline was his primary connection to classroom initiatives. Both students and teachers actively avoided him and he was most often found in his office. The distinct differences in school culture between these two schools was a game changer at Keenville and a deal breaker at Stallfield. Keenville teachers wanted to be part of work that was considered valuable and innovative by their leader; Stallfield teachers simply wanted to be left alone.

The ramifications of this disparity are important. Even if a crack design team pulls together an incredible pilot, demonstrates strong evidence, establishes user-friendly implementation pathways, and works to overcome roadblocks, a building principal can accelerate or bury any replication effort. As the lead evangelizer within school buildings, the role of the principal is key for supporting, scaling, and sustaining personalized learning initiatives. In cases where principals are lead change agents or naturally skilled in the methods described throughout this book, principal professional learning may not be necessary. However, in districts or schools where the principal has not been involved in the design team process, additional training for school leaders is as necessary as embedded coaching for teachers. In fact, we see the coach, the teacher, and the principal as an essential triumvirate for scaling any personalized learning initiative. These three entities must work together in what we describe as a knowledge transfer model.

Efficient knowledge transfer exponentially increases the effectiveness of an implementation as well as the likelihood of sustaining and scaling this work over time. Scaling implementations will get an expected "1x" result when teachers and the coach are collaborating to operationalize implementation pathways. In this model, the coach directly transfers knowledge about blended and personalized learning implementation to the teacher through co-planning and co-teaching strategies, as described earlier in this chapter. This model is effective at getting an initiative up and running in a classroom but can have limited ongoing impact, as we saw in the Stallfield example. Alternately, a scaling implementation could get a "2x" result when the coach is transferring knowledge to both the classroom teachers and the principal. In this model, the classroom teachers and principal deepen their knowledge and understanding of priority practices and implementation pathways, and the coach receives feedback from both around strategies for iteration and improvement. While "2x" is good, in this situation the teacher and principal are reliant on the coach for communication, placing strains on coaching capacity. The ideal scenario generates a "3x" result by adding a reciprocal and ongoing transfer of knowledge, skills, and support directly between the classroom teachers and the principal. In this model, the coach works with the teachers and communicates with the principal, but the overall goal is to transition the relationship to a point where the principal and teacher are able to develop their own feedback loops and the coach can move on to support new teachers or build new capacities. This will result in greater sustainability and ongoing innovation as implementation pathways become a common language between teachers and principals, and resources are consistently shared, discussed, vetted, and analyzed by both educators and administrators.

For principals, developing several key priorities can have a significant impact on the success of blended and personalized scaling efforts.

Key priorities:

- Maintain a strong and consistent presence in classrooms: Visit classrooms and ask students questions while they work. Don't offer feedback, just participate.
- Consistently celebrate teacher successes: Create a video or an electronic newsletter or make an announcement celebrating something amazing you saw in a classroom. Make it public.
- Connect to a larger community of education innovators: Connecting with like-minded professionals outside of the school day, in a social context, is a great way to unwind and network with folks who are sharing the same challenges.
- Promote student and teacher innovation and risk-taking: Acknowledge students and teachers who are trying something new. Being supportive of

innovative practices and risk-taking helps create a school community where teachers and learners feel it is safe to step out of their comfort zones and potentially fail.

The final priority is so important it warrants additional explanation. The most important role of a building leader is to foster a climate of trust and transparency through relationships. We all have a strong human need "to know and be known" and "to see and be seen." When principals prioritize communication, empathy, and a desire to build community, they exponentially improve their chances of successful replication.

To know: Teachers, parents, and students will own this initiative when they feel communication efforts are authentic and transparent.

Be known: Teachers, parents, and students who feel valued as individuals, (culture, interests, and identities) and who feel their perspectives are relevant to the decision-making process will trust leaders and buy into the initiative.

To see: Teachers, parents, and students who observe priority practices in action will increase their understanding of and investment in the effort.

Be seen: Teachers, parents, and students who are recognized for great work connected to the vision and priority practices, regardless of how small the action may be, will feel they are part of the solution and double down on their efforts to support this work.

We have found value in having principal candidates self-assess their comfort and competency levels with these key priorities and in securing references from former colleagues who can speak to these actions. We have also seen districts use these key priorities to create a 360-degree assessment of their building leaders, integrating feedback from students and teachers with principal self-assessments and using the combined data to shape ongoing goal-setting and professional development with building leaders. Combined teams can collaborate to develop professional learning plans tailored to the unique strengths and needs of principals, which can include principal shadowing, mentoring, developing specific competencies, and working toward various performance assessments to demonstrate growth. The role of building leaders in establishing strong school culture and learning environments cannot be overstated.

•   •   •

As we come to the end of our grow phase, we would like to issue one last reminder to continually leverage process, outcome, and balance measures as your personalized learning initiative begins to expand to new teachers and new classrooms. Walk through as many classrooms as possible with strategy rubrics. Track outcome measures to ensure student achievement continues to accelerate across subgroups. Lastly and most importantly, make an effort to understand the perspectives of teachers, students, and parents through conversations, focus groups, and feedback surveys.

While our framework supports design teams through the process of visioning, piloting, and creating implementation pathways, successful scaling depends on the extent of ongoing barriers, the strength of implementation pathways and bounded solutions, and the relationships established between teachers, coaches, students, and leaders. The design team should continue to meet on a regular basis to check in on the status of implementation efforts, ongoing R&D testing, and the reduction of obstacles. At this point, the work centers on being responsive to needs and spreading successes. As replication efforts begin to gain traction, design teams are often ready to pursue common solutions with external partners who are facing similar challenges. Just like your R&D engine will drive ongoing classroom innovation, a strong network of like-minded leaders can drive innovation at the systems level. We dive deeper into the concept of networked improvement communities in chapter 12.

NETWORK

Pathway to Personalization Framework

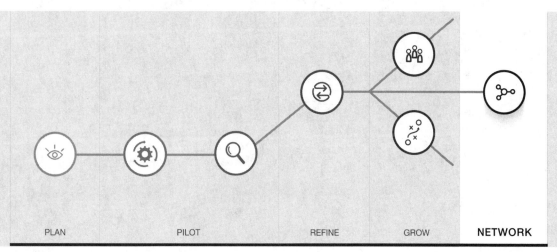

PLAN   PILOT   REFINE   GROW   **NETWORK**

Accelerate through
collaboration

ACCELERATING THROUGH COLLABORATION

Every summer the Highlander Institute hosts multiple, two-day blended and personalized learning boot camps. The liveliest and most well-attended session we run is our Fuse RI pilot classroom boot camp. The program convenes early adopter teachers who have spent the last year participating on their district design teams and launching their own pilot classrooms. For sixteen hours, these growth-oriented educators identify common challenges, discuss bounded solutions, and share lessons learned from their experiences in different classrooms across the state. As an organization, we learn a lot from these cross-district conversations. While these early adopters are implementing different priority practices and using different metrics of success, they often find themselves battling similar challenges:

- "How do I run a self-paced model when the students who are behind continue to need more time? When do they catch up?"
- "Where do I go to find high quality projects and performance tasks aligned to our state standards?"
- "What is the best way to incorporate student voice into district-mandated math curriculum?"
- "What is the most efficient process for one-on-one goal-setting conversations with students?"

The conversations help participants develop a more sophisticated understanding of implementation options while providing some group therapy around the collective challenges they face. They support each other with new ideas and resources but also acknowledge when their thinking leads to dead ends. There is a lot of power in cross-district networking. As teams deepen their understanding of the complexities within personalized learning initiatives and begin to scale, they should initiate networking opportunities with partners or mentors to solve common problems, study common data sets, and begin to codify the conditions in which promising practices can thrive across various contexts.

If you have persevered to the final stage of our development framework, you should celebrate your resilience and endurance. What started as a single spark is hopefully blazing across your school or district. While it is important to celebrate successes, in education we can never take our foot off the gas. Even as you win over new advocates and identify new exemplars, your barriers and impediments will persist. The scaling challenges described in chapters 10 and 11 are common and pervasive. Ongoing evidence collected from implementing classrooms will continue to uncover pain points. At this stage, macro-level data analysis protocols can help leaders understand what challenges are unique to certain teachers and what challenges are common across classrooms. Common challenges are often the impetus for leveraging a network of partners.

The final phase of our framework provides a rationale for collaboration as a mechanism for addressing sticky system problems plaguing multiple combined teams across a city, region, or state. We begin by defining the characteristics of a networked improvement community. Then we discuss the evolution of the blended and personalized learning movement in Rhode Island, describing how the progression from isolated classroom efforts to statewide meetings and collaboration took two decades to realize. While we do not encourage replication of this imperfect trajectory, we hope that distilling critical turning points and lessons learned can expedite networking opportunities for your team. Finally, we explore a state-level partnership in Rhode Island that reflects an aspiring networked improvement community. The goal of this chapter is to underscore the importance of external networking in this emerging field and to encourage combined teams to approach replication and scaling efforts with one eye on internal implementation and the other eye on how regional colleagues and leaders are approaching common challenges.

NETWORKED IMPROVEMENT COMMUNITIES

The concept of an improvement community was crafted by Douglas Engelbart, an American engineer, inventor, and technology pioneer best known for his founding work in the field of human-computer interaction in the late 1960s. Engelbart defined an improvement community as "any group involved in a collective pursuit to improve a given capability."[1] This concept is different than a role-based organization, such as the National Association of Secondary School Principals, that convenes building leaders to share ideas, learn new strategies, and discuss policy implications. An improvement community centers on a specific, common challenge; a networked improvement community (NIC) convenes leaders across schools, districts, regions, or states to focus on a common challenge, leveraging "networking as a scientific strategy to extend human capabilities in pursuit of shared interests."[2] NICs collectively engage in defining solutions and leverage disciplined inquiry to develop, implement, and study a common approach across their diverse district or school environments. This allows new methods to be tested with greater reliability and attention to variance, raising the combined IQ of all network participants. For teams that have made it to the grow phase of our framework, the NIC concept will feel familiar. NICs leverage the six core principles of improvement science and the establishment of continuous learning cycles as standard operating procedures. In his 2015 blog post, "Why a NIC," Paul LeMahieu from the Carnegie Foundation further defines a NIC through four essential characteristics.[3]

Focused: A networked improvement community requires members to focus on a common problem and collaborate to test a common solution. The ability to clearly define and communicate implementation successes and challenges at a local level is a precursor for successfully initiating or joining a NIC. Your specific vision, priority practices, and implementation barriers will help you identify schools or districts on a parallel path who are struggling with similar obstacles.

Knowledgeable: Effective members of a NIC bring a deep understanding of a central problem and can define root causes of the problem within their local context. The process of studying the district problem space and building a scaling strategy during the grow phase has positioned combined teams to be thoughtful and effective members of a NIC. Together, members share their various perspectives to develop a theory of improvement and discuss possible solutions.

Disciplined: NICs that leverage improvement science to define and study a problem have the best chance of accelerating improvements across the field. The goal is to establish a well-defined and evidence-based solution and to test this solution across diverse contexts. Your experience establishing continuous learning cycles in pilot classrooms and framing data collection through a family of measures will position you as a leader within your network. Your ability to leverage R&D classrooms will also be invaluable for testing a solution.

Coordinated: The process of developing and testing a solution across diverse districts requires careful coordination. A local point person is often required to manage the process for each partner and collect data and artifacts. Similarly, a point person within the NIC is essential for organizing and sharing data sets, reflection, and implementation details across diverse partner efforts.

At this point in the framework, the elements of disciplined inquiry should be very familiar if not second nature. Adding an additional layer of data-driven learning to the mix will require an investment of time and energy, but the investment yields a high payoff when resulting solutions are effective and widely applicable. We know this because we have slogged through the hard work in Rhode Island. Our story of growth, iteration, and ultimately collaboration in the process of building a movement spans more than two decades. We are just starting to reap the benefits of our collective efforts. We share our story as an example of a long arc toward statewide networked improvement.

THE RHODE ISLAND STORY

The Rhode Island story demonstrates the importance of partnership and key tactics in the evolution of blended and personalized learning, such as identifying organizations with the capacity to coordinate and convene, building the capability of interested educators to engage in this work, and coordinating the efforts of innovative leaders through targeted collaboration. This section explores the movement toward blended and personalized learning that began in the late 1990s and is now percolating with energy and enthusiasm.

Catalysts for Change: 1995–1997

Before the complicated arrival of modern devices, internet, and software in classrooms, the conversation about personalized learning was sparked in Rhode Island by Dennis Littky and Elliot Washor when they launched Big Picture Learning (BPL) in Providence in 1995. The premise of BPL was radical: eliminate courses, design curriculum around individual students, recast teachers as advisors and facilitators, and value individual differences through a holistic approach to learning based on relationships. With a focused mission of putting students at the center of their own learning, Littky and Washor created a movement promoting fundamental education reform. In 1996, BPL launched the first school of its kind—the Metropolitan Regional Career and Technical Center (MET)—in Providence. Operating outside of the constraints of a traditional district school, the MET cultivated parent involvement, authentic learning, hands-on experiences, and a nurturing community, completely altering the concept of a high school education and demonstrating the potential of a truly personalized learning environment.

Soon after the MET was launched, efforts to integrate technology in Rhode Island classrooms centered on building grassroots educator leadership and empowering teachers to find value in the potential of technology-enabled classrooms. In 1997, the Rhode Island Foundation launched the Rhode Island Teachers and Technology Initiative (RITTI), a four-year, $5-million effort to bring hardware and training to approximately 2,500 public school teachers in Rhode Island (one quarter of state classrooms). Working in collaboration with the Rhode Island Department of Education (RIDE), the University of Rhode Island, the state teachers unions, the Office of the Governor, the General Assembly, and business partners, this initiative was an early and ambitious effort to integrate the potential of personal computing into teaching and learning.[4] The project trained over 150 state teachers to lead two-week summer trainings for fellow educators.

By enabling teachers to invest in classroom hardware, the RITTI project started the movement that would ultimately eliminate the computer lab. In these early days of the internet, teachers leveraged classroom devices and projectors to open the world to students with the help of evolving search engines. Students began to incorporate word processing, PowerPoint presentations, graphics, and spreadsheets into their work across content areas. RITTI teachers were the first informal pilot teachers, experimenting at the intersection of curriculum and technology, supporting colleagues, and pushing administrators to embrace the power of digital learning resources.

Building on Successes: 2005

The RITTI project evolved through Enhancing Education Through Technology (E2T2) grants that were funded through the federal No Child Left Behind Act of

2001. In 2005, RIDE leveraged RITTI teacher-trainers to support the Model Classroom Initiative. This school-based project was structured to increase ownership and investment in the work. The opportunity required local matching funds, multiple participants to attend trainings together, and explicit alignment with district and school strategic plans. School cohorts attended a two-week summer professional development session and received $6,000 (including a 50 percent local match) to purchase enough devices to maintain a four to one student-to-device ratio inside classrooms. While the initiative supported an investment in hardware, it also enabled teachers to explore newly developed software applications. Teachers were able to experiment with software programs to support small- and whole-group instruction, streamline formative assessment practices, and experiment with new apps to engage students as well as deepen their learning. The Model Classroom Initiative also continued to build on the RITTI professional network; participating teachers likened the experience to a professional learning community that encouraged them to share and learn from each other.

Raising the Bar: 2012

In 2012, the Rhode Island Department of Education established a $20 million capital bond project to improve school and classroom wireless infrastructure across the state. Over three years, the Wireless Classroom Initiative increased Internet access and bandwidth to approximately 350 schools in fifty-seven districts, enabling teachers to leverage class sets of devices simultaneously with reliable wifi performance in any classroom across Rhode Island. A year later, RIDE created master price agreements to facilitate cheaper purchasing of new technology, including agreements between professional development providers.[5] By expanding high-speed wireless access and reducing purchasing barriers, RIDE sent a message to school committees, superintendents, principals, teachers, and parents that state leaders were serious about supporting technology integration in schools.

Formalizing an Early Adopter Network: 2012

The onset of wireless access bolstered the excitement of a growing number of tech-savvy teachers. At the time, the Highlander Institute affectionately dubbed this group "wild horses looking for their herd" and created several free, monthly opportunities for this talented bunch to convene for exploration, research, and development, as well as new edtech product vetting. By 2012, Highlander Institute had formalized three professional learning communities to engage and expand this growing network. EdUnderground focused on making coding, media, and design accessible to early adopter teachers for use in classrooms; EdCampRI sparked teacher-to-teacher professional development events across the state; and EdTechRI meetups facilitated dialogue and collaboration between edtech entrepreneurs and educators. Emerging best practices and processes across these communities were shared at our first annual blended learning conference, drawing sixty educators in a school cafeteria in the spring of 2012.

Offering various strands of accessible professional learning opportunities enabled early adopters to develop and hone new practices outside of the more formal and traditional professional development activities required by their schools. It also united like-minded, early adopter educators from different corners of the state in professional learning communities driven by teacher interest. Within a year, we developed a roster of more than three hundred teachers who were interested in pursuing various blended and personalized learning approaches.

Establishing New School Models: 2013

In the spring of 2012, RIDE announced a $470,000 school grant opportunity to establish a state proof point for leveraging technology to fundamentally transform teaching and learning. Highlander Institute supported the development of the winning application submitted by Pleasant View Elementary School, a Providence public school with 83 percent of students eligible for free or reduced lunch and 36 percent of students receiving special education services. Serving a dramatic range of learning profiles and proficiency levels, the Pleasant View staff found immediate value in leveraging technology to support a model centered on small-group differentiated instruction. Within two years, Pleasant View students had the most statistically significant growth on state math and reading assessments in the city of Providence and the second highest in the state of Rhode Island.

Simultaneously, two innovative charter high schools opened in Providence, offering new choices to high-need student populations. Village Green Virtual Charter School was launched as a fully blended high school, with students spending 50 percent of their time working with teachers to advance their individual skills and knowledge and 50 percent of their time working on online courses at their own pace. The Skip Nowell Leadership Academy developed a model aimed at supporting pregnant and parenting teenagers, combining flexible scheduling with specialized services and multiple learning pathways. Both schools leveraged their nimble school environments to iterate quickly and experiment with bold new blended learning models.

Up to this point, the best examples of blended and personalized learning in Rhode Island were relatively buried within the individual classrooms of early adopters. These three school models offered an opportunity for leaders to understand the intention, pain points, and early successes behind whole-school efforts at transformation. All three schools garnered significant statewide attention and hosted school visits for hundreds of state educators and leaders, which catalyzed the launch of a variety of blended learning pilots over the next two years. As the only school engaged in the redesign of a previously traditional model, Pleasant View offered additional lessons to existing schools. The varied responses of the faculty underscored the importance of differentiated and embedded classroom coaching for teachers, allowing teachers to control the pace of their initial shifts while being supported around their individual needs. Teachers across the school appreciated these personalized efforts, becoming vocal advocates for their new instructional practices as their comfort levels increased.

Inspiring a Movement: 2014

The Rhode Island State Department of Education closely watched the evolution of these school models and leveraged early promising results to double down in support of blended learning efforts. In 2014, RIDE established a five-year strategic plan to expand the implementation of blended and personalized learning models to all schools across the state. This included a communications campaign to help develop stakeholder awareness of new learning models and the creation of a free statewide conference dedicated to showcasing high quality examples of technology integration and blended learning approaches. Credit for this state-level push was given to the educators and leaders on the ground who pioneered the movement. When asked why Rhode Island was pursuing this work, former state Commissioner of Education Deborah Gist replied:

> Without question it's because of the enthusiasm of our educators. We have a growing group of teachers and principals and superintendents who recognize the power of this movement. . . . [t]hey are rethinking the way education is delivered and making it more personalized and seeing how technology helps them get there. It has taken off in our state organically, led by educators who are . . . breaking new ground and sharing what they are doing with each other.[6]

For the first time, the work of teachers and leaders in classrooms and schools was triggering top-down support. The state was not issuing directives in hopes that stakeholders would buy in; leaders recognized the promising practices being undertaken in the field, and their strong support added increased legitimacy and needed capacity to the growing movement. Teachers, principals, and superintendents around the state were curious and interested in learning more about the potential value of this work.

Fuse RI: 2014

Rhode Island's early blended learning momentum drew national attention to the state. In 2013, a national funder reached out to the Highlander Institute to brainstorm how we could support a statewide push for personalized learning in Rhode Island. After considering our state assets, which included a strong and networked early adopter teacher population, a supportive department of education, robust wireless infrastructure, and a history of cross district collaboration, we designed the Fuse RI program to help increase the breadth and depth of blended and personalized learning implementation. The theory of action behind Fuse RI centered on recruiting early adopters of blended and personalized approaches as Fuse fellows (current teachers and occasionally principals), training them in change management, coaching and consulting strategies, and then matching them with partner districts outside of their home districts to facilitate personalized learning shifts. In the process of supporting district design teams, we were also building state capacity by cultivating a pipeline of experienced blended and personalized learning teacher-leaders.

Fuse RI has recruited and trained 108 fellows across five cohorts who have teamed up to support forty-six Rhode Island districts and charter schools—over 60 percent of the sixty-six public local education agencies (LEA) in the state. Fellows have facilitated design teams and coached pilot teachers in partner LEAs while supporting their home districts as design team members and/or pilot teachers. Having highly engaged and deeply knowledgeable educators with the skillsets of trained coaches and consultants has triggered immeasurable professional learning growth and activity across the state. Many fellows have moved into district- or building-level coaching positions and are now managing their own pilot teacher cohorts after graduating from the fellowship. Graduates have spearheaded their own statewide efforts, such as project-based learning meetups, middle school unconferences, or a map of maker spaces across Rhode Island. The Fuse RI fellowship has led to spin-off programming in support of model classrooms, principals, and high school redesign. The project has offered us incredible insight into district challenges and has kept us connected to the realities of what is happening on the ground through the course of complex change initiatives.

New Leadership Moves: 2015–2017

Early in her gubernatorial term, Governor Gina Raimondo attracted two leaders with knowledge and experience in personalized learning to the state of Rhode Island. First, she appointed Dr. Ken Wagner as the new state commissioner of education. The former senior deputy commissioner for education policy for the state of New York, Ken coordinated education technology, data collection, and management for New York public schools and oversaw the development of the popular EngageNY.org curriculum website. With a deep understanding of curriculum, content, and assessment, Ken is a cautious proponent of personalized learning and highly skeptical of efforts that attempt to quickly scale "solutions." Within six months, the governor also hired Richard Culatta to lead the newly created Rhode Island Office of Innovation. The former director of the US Department of Education's Office of Educational Technology, Richard is a strong advocate of personalized learning and was tasked with developing cutting-edge approaches to streamline and improve government operations. In his new role, Richard was given the latitude and autonomy to launch initiatives, partner with the public sector, and collaborate with local nonprofits—coordinating high-impact partnerships. One of Richard's most important legacies during his brief tenure was the creation of Rhode Island's first personalized learning white paper, which created a common language and shared definitions for leaders and educators around the state.

Through the hiring of these two leaders, Governor Raimondo sent a message to educators, legislators, nonprofits, and families regarding her confidence in blended and personalized learning to improve Rhode Island schools. The endorsement and support of the governor, the commissioner of education, and the chief innovation officer sparked a new level of discussion among administrators, pushed new districts into the conversation, and emboldened new pilot efforts. It also helped galvanize multiple nonprofits to refocus, expand, or launch services related to this new demand.

The Missed Opportunity

One particularly critical lesson in the Rhode Island story is who has been missing from the evolving conversation. Educators, principals, administrators, nonprofits, funders, universities, and politicians have all served as leverage points for advancing the work. However, student and parent voice has been grossly absent from the conversation. State and district leaders and policy makers are still making well-intentioned changes on behalf of our main stakeholders without deeply and authentically involving them in the process. There are a myriad of reasons why we have collectively missed the mark on this, but it is mostly due to the time and effort involved in credible community outreach. Without the establishment of new strategies or models to increase our capacity, we rationalize student and family engagement as the cherry on top instead of the ice cream base. This is why we have included student and parent voice in our design team structure even though we have very few exemplars of how this has played out over time. We encourage you to build on this important lesson learned by looking for national best practices in this domain and infusing student, parent, and community perspectives within your change initiative from the beginning.

The Current Inflection Point

In Rhode Island, the conversation has evolved from a focus on technology to a focus on blended learning, to a focus on personalization. This is a promising progression that has been accompanied by a slow transformation of classroom pedagogy across pockets of the state, but it has taken twenty years. The good news is teacher-centered, one-size-fits-all instruction is generally recognized as an unsatisfactory approach. Models promoting student voice, choice, and agency are starting to become mainstream concepts, engaging a greater proportion of teachers and leaders. State-level efforts over the past twenty years would not have been possible without strong organizations working together to support even stronger networks of teachers and leaders.

The Carnegie Foundation's definition of networked improvement communities leverages different levels of activities first characterized by Douglas Engelbart. A-level activities center on classrooms and the teaching and learning done by educators on a daily basis. Networked improvement at this level typically occurs during common planning time, staff meetings, or professional development. B-level activities occur at the building or district level and are designed to improve on-the-ground work. B-level pursuits could include a focus on improving horizontal or vertical alignment within a system, policies, strategy, resource allocation, or professional learning. C-level activities are "inter-institutional," where multiple districts or organizations collaborate to design, develop, and test improvements and learn

FIGURE 12.1   Networked improvement across three levels

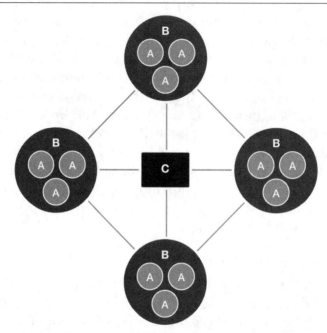

Source: A.S. Bryk, L.M. Gomez, A. Grunow, and P.G. LeMahieu, *Learning to Improve: How America's Schools Can Get Better at Getting Better* (Cambridge, MA: Harvard Education Press, 2015).

from one another. C-level work is important for understanding variability between contexts and developing a common understanding of a problem that could eventually lead to a shared solution (figure 12.1).

For over two decades in Rhode Island, opportunities to collaborate within the blended and personalized learning realm have evolved along these lines. Early on, activities focused on A-level initiatives with individual RITTI teachers and the Model Classroom Initiative. As technology improved, the wireless bond initiative passed, blended learning became a more established classroom practice, and the focus shifted to B-level initiatives such as the model school grant and the two initial blended learning charter high schools. Over the past three years, B-level initiatives have expanded to the point where most schools and districts in the state are engaged at some level with concepts including blended, personalized, competency-based, student-centered, or deeper learning. These labels are helping our schools and districts self-organize and find like-minded colleagues for collaboration. Our

108 Fuse RI fellows are part of a larger, active network of educators engaged in multiple statewide fellowships, meetups, nonprofits, and professional learning communities. Best practices at the classroom, school, and district level are being disseminated, further and faster than ever before. We are close to breaking down the walls that separate district-based professional learning. However, in order to really engage in C-level activity across the state, we need a process for organizing around the central problems facing our schools and districts.

The Network of College Success (NCS), out of the University of Chicago, is a great example of how something as simple as a collective metric can forge C-level relationships across multiple districts. NCS created a research and development network focused specifically on the challenge of keeping high school freshmen "on track" to graduate by organizing around common essential questions and metrics.[7] By developing the "freshman on-track" indicator and providing guidance around data collection and reporting, NCS united seventeen high schools in the Chicago public school (CPS) system around this data point. Implementing a common metric attached to a detailed rationale and process allowed CPS and NCS to collaborate in powerful ways. Comparing the data across schools highlighted patterns in the performance of various student subgroups and identified specific conditions that impacted the data for certain students and schools. Insights from the project have created the opportunity for meaningful action planning with the potential to impact all Chicago high school students. This C-level example represents what is possible for Rhode Island and other regions as we work to establish NICs.

NETWORKING DRIVEN BY DEMAND

As multiple schools and districts have begun grappling with common problems through their personalized learning journeys, the state has become fertile ground for assembling networked improvement communities. As we learn more about improvement science, we are working toward infusing young partnerships with a more disciplined approach to identifying solutions. In the next section, we explore how one nascent network is evolving in Rhode Island.

Revisiting the Curriculum Challenge

Universally, our Fuse fellows—and the pilot teachers they coach—continue to struggle amidst legacy curriculum designed for whole-group consumption and a dearth of bounded solutions. Some partner districts allow their early adopter teachers to augment, replace, or abandon district curriculum but leave teachers alone to develop a more personalized option. None of the district design teams we have supported through Fuse RI have had the capacity to create fully personalized and blended curriculum for their teachers. While there are some benefits to offering teachers autonomy in this realm, we have watched this pattern unfold across multiple districts and, as we have mentioned before, do not consider the "isolated-teacher-as-curriculum-builder" strategy to be sustainable.

As a partner working in multiple districts, we saw potential in combining efforts to address this challenge. Highlander Institute has been following the Open Education Resource (OER) movement with interest and has been waiting for the concept to mature to a point where it could frame a possible low-cost solution for districts looking to personalize their curriculum. Launched in early 2016, the #GoOpen initiative sought to create an ecosystem where districts could leverage organized sets of high quality, openly licensed curriculum materials without restrictions. The effort convened district and state leaders, entrepreneurs, and nonprofit organizations to contemplate solutions and create prototypes.[8]

Connecting a significant need with a timely opportunity, we convened teachers and leaders from eight partner districts in Rhode Island who were interested in forming a state-level design team around OER. Bringing deep knowledge, experience, and understanding of the curriculum need within personalized classrooms, this group was committed to designing and testing prototypes within their home districts. Our goal was to develop a state-level solution that could form the foundation of personalized curriculum for any interested classroom.

We began by creating a common understanding and vision for the work, including this vision statement: "Rhode Island teachers will have access to an organized, comprehensive array of quality, free materials that are easy to leverage and repurpose within local contexts." We then identified a realistic solution we all could rally behind: the building of a state-level OER repository. We engaged a product team currently funded through the Rhode Island Department of Education and worked together to create a slimmed-down, OER-specific, beta version of their already functioning platform. With the ability to upload and tag high quality digital tasks, lessons, and projects, we expanded the team to twelve partner districts who are currently uploading resources into the system. Our next step is to pilot the platform with classroom teachers across partner districts to understand the strengths and limitations of the resource. We are in the process of identifying common metrics that will compare the relative success of the tool across various district classrooms.

While a viable and fully operational platform is still a ways off, each participating district is further developing its understanding of the complex and nuanced elements that define an effective personalized learning curriculum. Together, we are moving more efficiently toward a solution than any district could by working in isolation.

Finding a Networked Improvement Community

Leaders who can clearly articulate the persistent challenges within their school or district are poised to be active NIC members. However, with the concept of networked improvement communities still in the early stages, the larger dilemma is finding a NIC to join. The rationale for NICs is compelling, but the process for initiating, joining, and sustaining a NIC remains unclear. Currently, there is no system for finding like-minded external partners. As the work of the Carnegie Foundation expands, we are hopeful that NIC activity will also increase across the country. Every year, the Carnegie Foundation runs a national education summit in the spring that focuses on improvement science and is a good place to find potential NIC collaborators. Meanwhile, connecting with state-level organizations to identify potential collaborative partners is also a good place to start. This could include state departments of education; regional service agencies, such as BOCES in New York; area education agencies in Iowa; or educational service units in Nebraska. State or national nonprofit education organizations may also help you tap into larger networks of like-minded leaders. Some options include the Massachusetts Personalized Learning Network, the District Reform Support Network, Next Generation Learning Challenges, or the School Improvement Network. The other option is to initiate your own NIC by slowly and purposefully uniting like-minded leaders around a common challenge.

•   •   •

We are extremely grateful for the many bold, creative, trailblazing Rhode Island leaders at the classroom, building, district, community, and state levels who have worked tirelessly to establish our strong foundation of blended and personalized learning knowledge and experience. We will continue to support and learn from the incredible leaders in our state, collecting new examples of best practices as design teams increase their capacity through a collaborative problem-solving approach.

The objective behind our Pathway to Personalization Framework is to empower educators to rethink change management as much as it is to support sustainable blended and personalized learning models. It is our hope that lead change agents, design teams, and pilot teachers who participate in all five phases of our framework will find their mentalities toward change fundamentally altered, never settling for subpar student experiences or lackluster school performance. NICs are a logical next step for teams who are hooked on disciplined inquiry and recognize the potential of networked improvement. We look forward to following the growing NIC movement as it continues to evolve.

EPILOGUE

As we contemplated writing this book we sat down with many educators across the country including Shawn's parents, Barry and Rochelle Rubin. Both have been educators for more than forty years. Shawn's father worked as an elementary teacher and principal and Shawn's mother was a middle school science teacher and district science coordinator. In the fall of 2017, we had breakfast with both of them at a diner in southeastern Michigan. After several embarrassing stories about Shawn's high school years, the topic turned to "innovations" in education. Rochelle took a deep sip of her black, decaf coffee and uttered a statement that, while simple, encapsulated their combined eighty years of education perspective and wisdom.

> Shawn, innovations are nothing new or special in education. Educators have been coming up with new and innovative ways to educate students for centuries. I remember when your father brought one of the first Macintosh computers into his elementary classroom and taught kids how to program in the 1980s. As educators we've always been great at innovation. Our problem is that we're terrible at implementation, and we're even worse at researching whether what we're doing is working and adapting when it isn't.

This triad of innovation, implementation, and continuous improvement is so simple and yet so powerful as a schema for thinking about scaling new initiatives across schools and districts. In education, just like in business or commerce, we tend to worship shiny new innovations. Articles about virtual reality, coding boot camps, and essay-grading software easily grab our attention while we ignore the fact that we have yet to make good on the promises of the last decade—such as SMART

Boards, tablets, and streaming video. We struggle to get all teachers onboarded, trained, and effective at using an innovative product and then fail to study whether the innovation is actually an improvement when used consistently over time. Our models for implementing and measuring what works across our K–12 system are sorely ineffective, and while the promise of new innovations is exciting, our real challenge is identifying what works—and bringing those practices to scale for the benefit of all students.

If you are still reading, you are most likely a workhorse who understands the persistent challenges we face in education but still believes the struggle is worth the reward. Like us, you pine for school to be something students love, and you can picture incredible classrooms in any neighborhood regardless of race, class, or income. The good news is there are a lot people out there who think like you. We have named some of them in previous pages, and for each amazing practitioner we have named, there are hundreds more with comparable and compelling stories. The Pathway to Personalization Framework connects all the wisdom, guidance, and ideas we have collected through the leadership of countless teachers, principals, and district administrators. As the field continues to evolve, these trailblazers will continue to provide glimpses of what is possible for the rest of us.

Through the expected evolution and iterations of personalized learning that lie ahead, we hope this book will help center future efforts on the challenges of implementation, measurement, replication, and scaling and that it will persevere as a guide for authentic and purposeful change in schools. Continued rapid change is a certainty. The next generation will not tolerate the traditional system as the status quo for its own children. Our preschoolers, born into an age where everything is personalized, customized, and designed for ease of use, will not stand for a one-size-fits-all learning model. The timeline for supporting a productive and sustainable shift in education will hinge on the ability of early adopter teachers and leaders to collaborate and accelerate learning across city, state, and country lines.

If you are chasing this dream with us, let us be your Graceland. Join us at our annual Blended and Personalized Learning Conference (BPLC), share your stories of design and redesign with us, brag to us about your measurement tools, and share your personalized curriculum. Let us share your breakthroughs with hundreds and thousands of teachers and leaders who can continue to build on your foundation. Let's realize the dream of personalized learning together and ensure that a sustainable, rigorous, relevant, high quality approach spreads with equity to support every student in our care.

SAMPLE MEMORANDUM OF UNDERSTANDING FOR DESIGN TEAM MEMBERS

Design Team Memorandum of Understanding

OVERVIEW

Our district's design team aims to leverage the expertise and enthusiasm of our educators to support blended and personalized learning in our schools. Design team members were selected based on interest, willingness to support data collection and transparency, ability to convene for frequent meetings, and willingness to both host and send educators on site visits.

Our work will begin with a self-study, completed by the full district design team, to determine where we are as we begin this process. We will leverage results to engage in the following activities:

- Building knowledge
- Laying the groundwork
- Designing our plan
- Recruiting pilot teachers
- Structuring the learning process
- Evaluating the pilot
- Creating pathways
- Aligning communication and strategic scaling
- Contemplating the curriculum challenge

- Personalizing the professional learning
- Accellerating through collaboration

Together, we will engage in a deep level of reflection and strategic planning through the creation of tailored resources and the establishment of a customized change process.

LEAD CHANGE AGENT RESPONSIBILITIES

Our district is making a commitment of resources, time, and staffing in order to further blended and personalized learning within our schools. As the lead change agent for this work, _____, agrees to do the following:

1. Organize, facilitate, and oversee all design team meetings and activities
2. Provide design team members with knowledge and support to effectively design a tailored blended and personalized learning model for our district
3. Lead the communication effort to ensure that all stakeholders are informed about this work and regularly update the district leadership team
4. Create and facilitate opportunities for networking within our district and across other innovative districts

RESPONSIBILITIES OF PARTICIPATING DESIGN TEAM MEMBERS

The success of this initiative will be contingent on the strength of our partnership and mutual commitment.

We expect that as a design team member, _____, will do the following:

INITIALS

1. Attend meetings (up to four hours per month) to engage in design team work _____
2. Designate up to two hours a month to asynchronously building knowledge and exploring tools and resources relevant to district priorities _____
3. Help identify, support, and expand on the work of pilot teachers _____
4. Participate in a district self-study, including a student shadowing exercise to build context and identify current problems of practice _____

INITIALS

5. Provide timely responses to reasonable requests for information   _____
    to ensure maximum impact (including but not limited to surveys,
    interviews, etc.)

6. Aid in the development, deployment, collection, and summary of   _____
    data surveys and focus groups for pilot students and teachers

7. Review district, school, teacher, and classroom data to support   _____
    data-driven action plans to guide our work

8. Build relationships with students, parents, teachers, leaders, and   _____
    community stakeholders to gain a full perspective on community
    opinion regarding blended and personalized learning work (through
    surveys, focus groups, interviews, etc.) and share information about
    the initiative

9. Agree to follow the team norms developed collaboratively at the   _____
    beginning of the initiative

10. Provide open communication and feedback regarding any and all   _____
    aspects of the design team work

You were invited to be on the design team based on your demonstrated interest and commitment. However, recognizing the limited resources available and the high interest of other educators in our district, we reserve the right to reevaluate our partnership together if design team responsibilities are unmet. Should this become necessary, the lead change agent will communicate proactively to remedy any problems prior to taking this step. In addition, as a design team member, you reserve the right to terminate the partnership at any time if you no longer recognize a need for the support and/or if the support does not meet your expectations.

As a design team member, _____, will be recognized as a leader in our blended and personalized learning implementation.

Signed,

_____   _____

Lead change agent   Date

_____   _____

Design team member   Date

HUMAN CAPITAL ASSESSMENT

Scoring criteria	0 = No evidence	1 = Some evidence	2 = Growing evidence	3 = Strong evidence	
ROLE	**INDICATOR**			**PLAN PHASE (0–3)**	**REFINE PHASE (0–3)**
School board	Willing to green-light pilots without school board approval				
	Curious and interested in learning more about pilots				
	Willing to walk through pilot classrooms more than once during the pilot process				
	Willing to fund ongoing work when district leadership, principals, or teachers show value or promise through pilots				
	Willing to participate in the shadow-a-student challenge				
Superintendent	Willing to engage in design teamwork				
	Curious and interested in learning more about pilots				
	Expresses willingness to discuss barriers to personalized learning implementation				
	Is adept at cultivating and building relationships across stakeholder groups				
	Willing to walk through pilot classrooms more than once during the pilot process				
	Willing to participate in the shadow-a-student challenge				

ROLE	INDICATOR	PLAN PHASE (0–3)	REFINE PHASE (0–3)
District leadership team	Willing to engage in design team work		
	Curious and interested in learning more about pilots		
	Expresses willingness to discuss barriers to personalized learning implementation		
	Willing to walk through pilot classrooms more than once during the pilot process		
	Willing to give early adopter teachers autonomy/waivers from curriculum and training		
	Willing to participate in the shadow-a-student challenge		
Building principal (of potential pilot classrooms)	Spends significant time in classrooms as an instructional leader		
	Has background in pedagogy, instruction, and assessment		
	Has established a strong culture of collaboration, sharing, and experimentation		
	Understands and values data-driven decision making		
	Willing to give early adopter teachers autonomy/waivers from curriculum and training		
	Willing to participate in the shadow-a-student challenge		

PRIORITY PRACTICES TOOL

Note: The reference codes listed in column two help facilitate the discussion of priority practices. The number and letter combination allows meeting participants to immediately pinpoint the domain and specific practice being discussed.

DOMAIN		PRACTICES
Classroom culture	1A	Tasks are supported by clear instructions
	1B	Students' behavior is appropriate for the task
	1C	Transitions between activities are efficient
	1D	Systems are in place to assist students in solving problems independently
	1E	Interactions between students are positive and productive
	1F	Interactions between students and teachers are positive and productive
	1G	Students have the opportunity to provide input and feedback on learning experiences
	1H	Students are collaborating

DOMAIN		PRACTICES
Identity, interest, and agency	2A	Physical classroom environment reflects a wide range of diverse experiences
	2B	Students have choice over how they learn
	2C	Students have choice over what they learn
	2D	Students have choices in how they demonstrate their understanding
	2E	Students set goals for their learning tasks
	2F	Teacher creates connections between the subject matter and students' identities
	2G	Teacher encourages student ownership of learning
Differentiation	3A	Small-group instruction is differentiated based on students' needs
	3B	Tasks are differentiated based on students' needs
	3C	Teacher uses a variety of techniques to assess student progress toward learning goals
	3D	Teacher provides opportunities for students to reflect on their own data
	3E	Teacher uses data to inform instruction
	3F	Classroom experiences allow students to progress through learning tasks or content without waiting for the teacher
Rigor and mastery	4A	Students are given the opportunity to apply learning from one task to another
	4B	Students present evidence that supports their thinking
	4C	Students design or create a product to demonstrate their understanding
	4D	Students are engaged in work that is authentic
	4E	Students are engaged in work that requires higher-order thinking skills
	4F	Feedback process is kind, specific, and helpful
	4G	Teacher provides students with a clear vision of what mastery looks like

SAMPLE MEMORANDUM OF UNDERSTANDING FOR PILOT TEACHERS

In states and school districts across the country, interest in and adoption of blended learning is on the rise. This movement involves the strategic integration of teaching, technology, and data to increase personalization, engagement, and mastery of all essential skills for all students. We envision a movement toward student-centered learning environments in which students of all ages have increased agency and ownership. We believe that the following classroom practices are essential to creating effective blended classrooms:

- Instruction is differentiated to meet student needs
- Teachers use frequent formative assessments to engage learners in their own growth (moving ownership and analysis of data to students to promote independent learning)
- Students show their learning in a variety of ways
- Students are actively collaborating to solve complex problems

In order to better understand the transition from traditional instruction to blended learning, we are embarking on a pilot classroom initiative. Through a readiness survey distributed to the entire faculty throughout the district, eight classrooms will be selected (K–12) as pilot classrooms. These teachers will explore new strategies and tools to broaden our understanding of the following:

- How to best implement our blended learning vision
- Which competencies and skills teachers need to make the transition from traditional to blended learning classrooms
- Which tools and resources are needed to support blended classrooms
- Which models and strategies best reflect our vision

At the end of the 2016–2017 school year, we hope that these classrooms will be open to district teachers for observations and offer a foundation from which we can scale blended learning across the district.

SUPPORT

Pilot classrooms in each building will be offered the following:

- Devices for each student in the class
- One additional planning period per week
- Opportunity to request software licenses/equipment/conference tickets (selections must be approved by district administrators)
- Release time to observe teachers in other districts/attend conferences
- Embedded coaching; meetings with the entire pilot cohort coaches to share progress (see attached coaching support schedule)
- Opportunity to debrief with building/district leaders once a month

EXPECTATIONS

In addition to meeting district expectations, pilot teachers will be accountable for the following:

- Participating in a formal professional learning community with other pilot teachers (format and logistics to be determined by participants and administration; see attached coaching support schedule)
- Agreeing to an open-door policy for district visitors for observations and feedback
- Implementing the priority classroom practices previously outlined
- Exploring meaningful ways to leverage classroom technology on a regular basis
- Documenting and sharing learning
- Attending design team meetings every eight weeks to provide updates

- Leading building professional development/share-outs (format and logistics to be determined by participants and building administration)
- Collecting and sharing specific data metrics

I am excited about the support I will receive as a pilot classroom and agree to the expectations outlined.

Pilot classroom teacher:

Name:	Phone:
Signature:	Date:

I agree to support pilot classrooms in my building as outlined.

Building administrator:

Name:	Phone:
Signature:	Date:

Received by central administration: _____
Date: _____

Coaching Support Schedule for Pilot Teachers

November	Memo of understanding signed by pilot teachers and principals Baseline classroom walkthroughs conducted and baseline data collected by design team Coaches and pilot teachers meet to discuss goals, timelines, systems, and getting started
January *(1 date)*	Site visits to see model classrooms by district administrators and pilot teachers Debriefing meeting Introduction to lesson plan template and any relevant tools, resources, or articles (playlist)
February *(2 dates)*	Coaching observation and planning session Debriefing, planning, and learning
March *(2 dates)*	Coaching observation and planning session Debriefing, planning, and learning
April *(2 dates)*	Coaching observation and planning session Debriefing, planning, and learning
May *(3 dates)*	Coaching observation and planning session Reflecting, planning, and learning for year two Data collection (outcome, process, and balance measures) Reflection forms completed by pilot teachers Design team check-in meeting with pilot teachers
Summer	Invitation for pilot teachers to attend a summer boot camp in August Additional professional development opportunities to meet needs/goals sought out by pilot teachers Cohort, design team, and coaches meet to set goals for the year in August
October *(2 dates)*	Collection of beginning-of-year data (outcome, process, and balance measures) Coaching observation and planning session Debriefing, planning, and learning
November *(2 dates)*	Coaching observation and planning session Debriefing, planning, and learning
January *(3 dates)*	Coaching observation and planning session Debriefing, planning, and learning Reflection forms completed by pilot teachers Design team check-in meeting with pilot teachers
February *(2 dates)*	Coaching observation and planning session Debriefing, planning, and learning
March *(2 dates)*	Coaching observation and planning session Debriefing, planning, and learning
April *(3 dates)*	Coaching observation and planning session Debriefing, planning, and learning PD day 4/27—pilot teachers present
May	Final data collection (outcome, process, and balance measures) Formal pilot evaluation with design team and pilot teachers

PRIORITY PRACTICES TOOL WITH STRATEGIES

DOMAIN		PRACTICE	STRATEGIES
Classroom culture	1A	Tasks are supported by clear instructions	• Each station or task has clear instructions posted • Instructions are accessible to students of all languages and reading abilities represented • Instructions are concise with few grammatical errors • Instructions reach a variety of learning modalities (e.g., in words, pictures, through a read-aloud) • Students can complete the task based on the instructions given
	1B	Students' behavior is appropriate for the task	• Teacher provides students with visuals that help them monitor their own behavior • Student behavior is consistent with expressed expectations for a task (e.g., volume level, engagement level, what we should see, anchor chart) • Students are working consistently on assigned tasks
	1C	Transitions between activities are efficient	• Teacher provides students with visual and auditory cues about where, when, and how they should move • Students transition from task to task safely and efficiently (as instructed) • Teacher provides tools that help students manage time (e.g., stopwatch, time warning)
	1D	Systems are in place to assist students in solving problems independently	• Students have a method to follow if a problem arises (e.g., re-read directions, ask a neighbor, ask a teacher) • Students can use instructions to solve problems • Visuals in classroom support systems in place • Systems are student-friendly and easily accessed (e.g., labeled accessible areas/bins for materials) • Students play a role in the running of classroom logistics

DOMAIN	PRACTICE		STRATEGIES
Classroom culture	1E	Interactions between students are positive and productive	• Students communicate using positive language and a level tone with each other • Students adhere to classroom rules and expectations with respect to each other • Students utilize accountable talk stems with each other • Students help each other • Students do not interrupt when peers are speaking • Teacher facilitates problem solving between students • Teacher models and reinforces positive and productive interactions
	1F	Interactions between students and teachers are positive and productive	• Teacher communicates with students using positive language and a level tone • Teacher reinforces classroom rules and expectations • Teacher adheres to classroom rules and expectations • Students communicate with the teacher using positive language and a level tone • Students adhere to classroom rules and expectations with respect to the teacher • Students' positive interactions with adults are recognized and reinforced • Teacher fosters an environment where failure is embraced as part of the learning process
	1G	Students have the opportunity to provide input and feedback on learning experiences	• Students have opportunities to provide feedback throughout the class period • Teacher uses student feedback to inform his or her practice • Teacher uses a portion of the class period to debrief the lesson experience with students
	1H	Students are collaborating	• Teacher provides opportunities for students to share roles and responsibilities to complete work • Teacher creates accountability systems for all types of roles/responsibilities (e.g., checklist, posters, protocols) • Teacher models and debriefs around meta-cognitive skills and traits involved in collaboration • Students are engaging in meaningful collaboration • Students collaborate with an equitable division of work and effort
Identity, interest, agency	2A	Physical classroom environment reflects a wide range of diverse experiences	• Space is inclusive of students' identities and needs (mirrors) • Space includes materials and content that are reflective of a wide range of diverse experiences (windows) • Students' personal artifacts and work are reflected in the classroom

DOMAIN		PRACTICE	STRATEGIES
Identity, interest, agency	2B	Students have choice over how they learn	• Teacher gives students a choice of multiple modalities for learning a concept (e.g., video, slide deck, website to explore) • Teacher provides students with opportunities that allow choice over when to do each task (e.g., choice board, playlist)
	2C	Students have choice over what they learn	• Students can choose their own topic for a project or task • Students can ask and then answer their own questions or work to solve a self-identified problem
	2D	Students have choices in how they demonstrate their understanding	• Students can choose to demonstrate their understanding from a variety of equally rigorous tasks • Teacher designs rubrics/scales for a single skill that can allow for a range of student products • Teacher designs tasks that encourage students to show mastery in a variety of ways
	2E	Students set goals for their learning tasks	• Students set and articulate goals • Students reflect on progress toward goals
	2F	Teacher creates connections between the subject matter and students' identities	• Teacher collects rich data on students (e.g., surveys, student conferences, family interviews) • Teacher uses knowledge of students' identities (e.g., individual, social) to activate prior knowledge or select resources • Students have space (e.g., physical, emotional) to share their identities/ experiences
	2G	Teacher encourages student ownership of learning	• Teacher provides opportunities for students to assess their own learning (e.g., reflection, journal) • Teacher provides opportunities for students to analyze and interpret ideas from multiple perspectives
Differentiation	3A	Small group instruction is differentiated based on students' needs	• Data is used to inform student groupings • Teacher varies content by group or individual • Teacher varies delivery (instructional strategies) by group or individual
	3B	Tasks are differentiated based on students' needs	• Scaffolds are in place to support students as needed (e.g., sentence stems, math references) • Student tasks are varied by content for group or individual (degree of difficulty) • Student tasks are varied by process for group or individual (e.g., highlighting words, manipulative materials vs. paper)
	3C	Teacher uses a variety of techniques to assess student progress toward learning goals	• Teacher uses formative assessment to track student achievement in assigned tasks (e.g., exit tickets) • Formative assessment is directly linked to learning goals/content • Teacher uses informal assessments (e.g., "fist to five," checklists) to track student understanding

DOMAIN		PRACTICE	STRATEGIES
Differentiation	3D	Teacher provides opportunities for students to reflect on their own data	• Teacher models how to reflect on learning • Teacher provides routines/structures to support student self-reflection • Teacher conferences with students to discuss their data • Students record progress or track their own data (e.g., a data journal where they log data and reflect on their work)
	3E	Teacher uses data to inform instruction	• Teacher groups students or adjusts instruction based on formative assessment • Teacher regroups students or adjusts instruction in the moment based on formative assessment
	3F	The classroom experience allows students to progress through learning tasks or content without waiting for the teacher	• Teacher creates structures such as playlists/agendas that students can progress through as they complete tasks (e.g., Hyperdocs, Google Classroom) • Teacher plans a variety of tasks for an extended period of time • Students are held accountable for tasks completed (e.g., activity logs, assessments, journals)
Rigor and mastery	4A	Students are given the opportunity to apply learning from one task to another	• Tasks within stations, playlists, or projects connect to a central focus • Students have learning opportunities that build on previous classroom experiences • Students apply knowledge/skills to make decisions, draw conclusions, or solve problems within a content area without being prompted (transfer)
	4B	Students present evidence that supports their thinking	• Students use evidence to support written/oral responses • Students' responses include clear reasoning (e.g., "because" statements) • Tasks or questions demand rigorous responses from students (e.g., using textual evidence) • Teacher provides opportunities for students to share their thinking throughout the lesson
	4C	Students design or create a product to demonstrate their understanding	• Teacher provides clear, student-friendly rubrics that students can reference as needed • Teacher monitors students' progress (individual or team) throughout the process • Teacher communicates clear expectations to guide students' process and product • Students create/design a product that aligns with task instructions or project expectations • Students give and receive feedback during the creation process
	4D	Students are engaged in work that is authentic	• Teacher presents "real world" or relevant tasks • Students are provided with opportunities to pursue topics relevant to their specific interests • Students present to an authentic audience (e.g., shark tank, community organizations, professionals, peers, families) • Teacher balances authentic tasks with content-specific objectives

DOMAIN		PRACTICE	STRATEGIES
Rigor and mastery	4E	Students are engaged in work that requires higher-order thinking skills	• Students have the opportunity to create (e.g., design, assemble, develop, formulate, construct, author, investigate) • Students have the opportunity to evaluate (e.g., critique, value, appraise, argue, defend, judge, select, support) • Students have the opportunity to analyze (e.g., differentiate, organize, experiment, test, question, examine, relate, compare, contrast) • Students have the opportunity to apply (e.g., execute, implement, solve, use, demonstrate, interpret, operate, schedule, sketch)
	4F	Feedback process is kind, specific, and helpful	• Feedback is specific to task • Teacher uses students' actions and work as exemplars • Teacher utilizes a protocol to provide feedback • Teacher provides visual references to support positive feedback (e.g., sentence stems, anchor charts) • Feedback provides students with specific action(s) they can take to improve the work • Students utilize a protocol to provide peer feedback • Students are responsive to feedback provided by peers or teacher • Teacher models how to give feedback
	4G	Teacher provides students with a clear vision of what mastery looks like	• Teacher provides students with a process to achieve mastery with checkpoints along the way • Teacher creates and shares work exemplars • Teacher translates standards to student-friendly language (e.g., "I can" statements) • Students can articulate key standards/skills/"I can" statements • Students can describe a process or path to achieve mastery

COMMON BLENDED AND PERSONALIZED ENTRY POINTS

Station Rotation

Teams that are designing around differentiation as their main personalized learning challenge and are moving from a traditional model to macro differentiation on our Personalized Learning Progression (chapter 2, figure 2.2) may be interested in leveraging the station rotation model. This approach supports the movement of students between at least three learning stations during instructional time: a teacher-directed station for tailored small-group instruction, a computer-based station for self-paced work on adaptive software programs, and an independent/collaborative station for students to apply knowledge or solve more complex problems. This model supports differentiated learning across each center while establishing smaller learning communities in the classroom. The station rotation model can be aligned to priority practices such as small-group differentiation, task differentiation, using data to inform instruction, student grouping, student collaboration, and higher-order thinking skills. Teachers leveraging this model have the opportunity to adapt the concept of learning centers to meet their needs, deciding whether all students rotate through all centers or on a targeted center schedule. Some classrooms rotate students on a fixed schedule; some allow students to complete a task before rotating or spend different amounts of time with the teacher.

Project-Based Learning

Project-based learning is an entry point that sits at the intersection of agency and differentiation. Design teams interested in rigor, self-directed learning, authentic audiences, or engagement can consider integrating problem- or project-based learning models in pilot classrooms. The concept centers around connecting students with a real-world task or problem that interests them and provides them the freedom and resources to find a solution. Project work requires teachers to clarify aligned academic/socio-emotional competencies and build learning plans that articulate indications of mastery. Associated priority practices include student collaboration, student choice over what they learn and how they demonstrate their understanding, student ownership of learning, opportunities for applying learning, engagement in authentic work for real audiences, and a focus on higher-order thinking skills.

Choice Boards

Choice boards afford students the opportunity to select activities they will complete to practice a skill or demonstrate mastery. Often delivered as a menu, a bingo board, or a tic-tac-toe grid, choice boards also offer teachers options as they consider types of activities to include. Choice boards can focus on a particular skill or standard, or on opportunities for exploration once students complete class work. Teachers can design and tag choice boards around different levels of complexity, different learning modalities, different deliverables, or various student interests. Choices are often scaffolded based on student readiness to propose and deliver rigorous work. Design teams focusing on aspects of student agency may find value in the concept of choice boards. Choice boards align with the following priority practices: students have choice over both how and what they learn, students have choice in how they demonstrate understanding, tasks are differentiated to meet student needs, students create a product to demonstrate understanding, and students are engaged in work that requires higher-order thinking skills.

Flipped Classroom

Pilot classrooms that launch with a focus on pacing often begin by leveraging the flipped classroom model. Within flipped classrooms, students access lectures on new topics via video, at home or at school, with the chance to digest the material at their own pace. In this model, class time is best used for concept application through activities such as discussions or collaborative problem solving. Teachers either video themselves teaching a new concept or utilize a growing library of open-source videos to introduce a topic. During class, teachers have the opportunity to address misconceptions in a small group setting, answer specific questions with individual students, and support more student-centered exploration. Leveraging digital content and addressing specific student needs enables teachers to assign work based on student proficiency levels and allows students to progress without waiting for their peers. The flipped classroom model supports several critical teacher practices and student goal setting, including student ownership of learning, allowing students to progress without waiting for the teacher.

Learning Profiles

Pilot classrooms that are focusing on elements of student identity, interest, or agency sometimes launch by creating student learning profiles. One could argue the most important step toward personalizing learning is truly knowing all the students in a classroom and giving students the opportunity to know themselves and each other. Learning profiles help teachers and students collect and update information on student interests, strengths, needs, identities, learning preferences, and achievement levels. This initial information enables teachers to tailor learning activities and choices, set periodic goals, and determine relevant curriculum resources that actively include the varying perspectives of students in the room. Teachers can also use initial information to create classrooms that respect and value the different ethnicities, religions, languages, gender definitions, and other identifiers important to how students view themselves as well as the larger world. Learning profiles are typically housed on a platform that can be regularly updated and expanded as students build skills and explore new interests. The creation of learning profiles aligns to key priority practices such as student goal setting, student ownership of learning, student reflection on their progress, and creating connections between student identities and curriculum.

Socio-Emotional Learning

As new frameworks and tools are emerging that help educators focus on the whole child, some teams are launching personalized learning initiatives by focusing on how students think and feel about themselves, get along with others, and self-regulate. Socio-emotional learning (SEL) centers on the set of skills that include cognitive, intrapersonal, and interpersonal awareness and provides a more comprehensive approach to understanding how students develop foundational skills they need to be successful. Design teams prioritizing elements of student agency and focusing on issues of school culture and building relationships often find alignment with SEL frameworks and school models. Instructional approaches that emphasize SEL competencies focus on building empathy to develop student confidence. At the school level, this can take the shape of climate building and integrating opportunities for teamwork and collaboration throughout all aspects of the school day. In the classroom, teachers model SEL competencies and directly teach SEL skills across content and subject areas. A related focus centers on trauma-informed instructional strategies for schools in which large percentages of students have faced adverse childhood experiences (ACEs). Research has shown that children who have endured multiple ACEs have experienced cognitive losses as well as physical, emotional, and social delays, all of which impact learning. Key responses include routine screening for trauma exposure, culturally appropriate treatment for symptoms, strengths-based instruction, coordination among interventionists, and support for teachers.

Once again, design teams should carefully consider which facets of popular approaches translate well within existing priorities. Teams can reframe or restructure established models to align with local conditions or meet the needs of specific students. For example, in a classroom with a diverse range of learners, a teacher may run a rotation model to provide students with tailored small-group instruction and use a choice board in the collaborative center to offer students some degree of agency, while also flipping instruction for students who are capable of moving at their own pace through online content. The role of the design team is to adapt and iterate—not to settle for stock solutions.

NOTES

Introduction

1. Eric Ries, *The Lean Startup: How Today's Entrepreneurs Use Continuous Innovation to Create Radically Successful Businesses* (New York, NY: Crown Business, 2011).
2. Geoffrey A. Moore, *Crossing the Chasm: Marketing and Selling High-Tech Products to Mainstream Customers* (Oxford, UK: Capstone Publishing, 2008).
3. Anthony S. Bryk, Louis M. Gomez, Alicia Grunow, and Paul G. LeMahieu, *Learning to Improve: How America's Schools Can Get Better at Getting Better* (Cambridge, MA: Harvard Education Press, 2015).
4. Christian Seelos and Johanna Mair, *Innovation and Scaling for Impact: How Effective Social Enterprises Do It* (Stanford, CA: Stanford University Press, 2017).
5. John P. Kotter, "Leading Change: Why Transformation Efforts Fail," *Harvard Business Review*, January 2007, https://hbr.org/2007/01/leading-change-why-transformation-efforts-fail.

Chapter 1

1. Motoko Rich, Amanda Cox, and Matthew Bloch, "Money, Race and Success: How Your School District Compares," *The New York Times*, April 29, 2016, https://www.nytimes.com/interactive/2016/04/29/upshot/money-race-and-success-how-your-school-district-compares.html.
2. Benjamin Wallace-Wells, "The Hard Truths of Ta-Nehisi Coates," *New York Magazine*, July 12, 2015, http://nymag.com/daily/intelligencer/2015/07/ta-nehisi-coates-between-the-world-and-me.html.

Chapter 2

1. Robert Guisepi, "The History of Education," World History International: World History Essays from Prehistory to the Present, http://history-world.org/history_of_education.htm; Joe Ventura, "The History of Personalized Learning," *New Classrooms*, http://blog.newclassrooms.org/the-history-of-personalized-learning.
2. John Dewey, *The Project Gutenberg e-Book of Democracy and Education*, July 26, 2008, http://www.gutenberg.org/files/852/852-h/852-h.htm.

3. "Yale Child Study Center," Comer School Development Program, https://medicine.yale.edu/childstudy/comer/.

4. MIT Media Lab, "Professor Emeritus Seymour Papert, Pioneer of Constructionist Learning, Dies at 88," *MIT News*, August 01, 2016, http://news.mit.edu/2016/seymour-papert-pioneer-of-constructionist-learning-dies-0801.

5. An "effect size" is simply a way of standardizing the size of the difference between two groups. It allows us to move from individual, outcome-specific understandings of the magnitude of group mean differences to a more sophisticated, broader, comparable understanding of the magnitude of group difference. In other words, looking at a standardized difference (the "effect size") allows us to look across studies that may have been conducted in a range of settings and with a range of participant types—and even allows us to combine these differences where appropriate—to give us a more general understanding of whether or not an intervention works. For these reasons, effect size is an important tool in reporting and interpreting effectiveness.

6. Shaun Killian, "Hattie Effect Size 2016 Update," The Australian Society for Evidence Based Teaching, July 21, 2017, http://www.evidencebasedteaching.org.au/hattie-effect-size-2016-update/.

7. Saro Mohammed, "Blended Learning Research Clearinghouse 1.0," The Learning Accelerator Learning Commons, May 2015, https://practices.learningaccelerator.org/artifacts/blended-learning-research-clearinghouse-1-0-may-2015.

8. Bruce Friend, Susan Patrick, Carri Schneider, and Tom Vander Ark, "What's Possible with Personalized Learning? An Overview of Personalized Learning for Schools, Families, and Communities," iNACOL, February 2017, https://www.inacol.org/resource/whats-possible-personalized-learning-overview-personalized-learning-schools-families-communities/.

9. Jason Kazi, "Personalized Learning Considered a Critical Element of the Country's Changing Classrooms," *Education Week*, September 21, 2016, http://blogs.edweek.org/edweek/Digital Education/2016/09/personalized_learning_consider.html.

10. Catalina Gonella, "20 Percent of Millennials Identify as LGBTQ, GLAAD Survey Finds," *NBC News*, March 31, 2017, https://www.nbcnews.com/feature/nbc-out/survey-20-percent-millennials-identify-lgbtq-n740791.

11. Emily Gasoi, "How We Define Success: Holding Values in an Era of High Stakes Accountability," *Schools: Studies in Education* 6, no. 2 (2009): 173–86. doi:10.1086/605886.

12. Dan French and Diana Lebeaux, "A Vision for Personalized Learning in Massachusetts," Center for Collaborative Education, May 2017, 4–7, http://cce.org/files/A-Vision-for-Personalized-Learning-in-Massachusetts.pdf.

13. National Research Council, *How People Learn: Brain, Mind, Experience, and School* (Washington DC: National Academies Press, 1999); Dylan William and Paul Black, *Inside the Black Box: Raising Standards Through Classroom Assessment* (London, UK: King's College, 1998).

14. Antonia Rudenstine, Sydney Schaef, and Dixie Bacallao, "Meeting Students Where They Are," iNACOL, June 2017, https://www.inacol.org/wp-content/uploads/2017/06/CompetencyWorks-MeetingStudentsWhereTheyAre2.pdf

15. Allison Zmuda, Diane Ullman, and Greg Curtis, *Learning Personalized: The Evolution of the Contemporary Classroom* (San Francisco, CA: Jossey-Bass, 2015).

16. Allison Powell, Kathryn Kennedy, and Susan Patrick, "Mean What You Say: Defining and Integrating Personalized, Blended, and Competency Education," iNACOL, October 2013, 6, https://www.inacol.org/resource/mean-what-you-say-defining-and-integrating-personalized-blended-and-competency-education/.

17. "Framework for 21st Century Learning," Partnership for 21st Century Learning, http://www.p21.org/our-work/p21-framework.

18. Bev Campbell et al., "CTE Model Curriculum Standards—Standards and Framework," California Department of Education, February 14, 2017, http://www.cde.ca.gov/ci/ct/sf/ctemcstandards.asp.

19. "Core SEL Competencies," CASEL, January 2, 2017, http://www.casel.org/core-competencies/.

20. "The ISTE Standards for Students," ISTE, 2016, https://www.iste.org/standards/for-students.

21. "Stanford Center for Assessment, Learning, and Equity (SCALE)," Stanford Graduate School of Education, https://scale.stanford.edu/; "Teaching Performance Assessments and Rubrics," SCALE, https://scale.stanford.edu/teaching/assessment-system/teaching-performance-assessments.

22. "The Three Principles," National Center On Universal Design for Learning, http://www.udlcenter.org/aboutudl/whatisudl/3principles.

23. "UDL Examples and Resources," National Center On Universal Design for Learning, http://udlguidelines.cast.org/.

24. Jon Deane, Chief Information Officer at Summit Public Schools, in discussion with attendees during a Summit school tour, May 2016.

25. "Blended Learning Models," Blended Learning Universe, http://www.blendedlearning.org/models/.

26. Personal interview, Jason Appel, Math Teacher/Technology Integration Fellow at Barrington High School (Rhode Island), June 1, 2017.

27. Allison Powell, Beth Rabbitt, and Kathryn Kennedy, "iNACOL Blended Learning Teacher Competency Framework," October 2014, https://www.inacol.org/wp-content/uploads/2015/02/iNACOL-Blended-Learning-Teacher-Competency-Framework.pdf.

Chapter 3

1. Heather Lattimer, "Agents of Change: Teacher Leaders Strengthen Learning For Their Students, Their Colleagues, and Themselves," *The Australian Educational Leader* 34, no. 4 (2012): 15–19 (internal citations omitted). doi:10.1107/s0108768107031758/bs5044sup1.cif.

2. Anthony S. Bryk, Louis M. Gomez, Alicia Grunow, and Paul G. LeMahieu, *Learning to Improve: How America's Schools Can Get Better at Getting Better* (Cambridge, MA: Harvard Education Press, 2015), 113.

3. "Deeper Learning," William and Flora Hewlett Foundation, 2016, https://www.hewlett.org/strategy/deeper-learning/.

4. "IDEO," https://www.ideo.com/.

5. John Kotter, "Building the Team You Need to Drive Change," *Forbes*, May 24, 2011, https://www.forbes.com/sites/johnkotter/2011/05/24/building-the-team-you-need-to-drive-change/#275864ca4979.

6. Michael B. Horn and Heather Staker, *Blended: Using Disruptive Innovation to Improve Schools* (San Francisco, CA: Jossey-Bass, 2011).

7. Everett M. Rogers, *Diffusion of Innovations*, 5th ed. (New York, NY: Free Press, 2003), Kindle edition.

8. "Diffusion of Innovation Theory," http://www.ou.edu/deptcomm/dodjcc/groups/99A2/theories.htm.

9. Christopher Emdin, *For White Folks Who Teach in the Hood . . . and the Rest of Y'all Too: Reality Pedagogy and Urban Education* (Boston, MA: Beacon Press, 2016).

10. Alex Cortez and Yordanos Eyoel, "Want Great Schools, First Work With Parents to Create 'Actionable Demand,'" May 10, 2017, http://the74million.org/article/notes-from-the-field-if-you-want-great-schools-first-work-with-parents-to-create-actionable-demand.

11. Ibid.

12. Eric Ries, *The Lean Startup: How Today's Entrepreneurs Use Continuous Innovation to Create Radically Successful Businesses* (New York, NY: Crown Business, 2011).

13. John F. Pane et al., *Informing Progress: Insights on Personalized Learning Implementation and Effects*, (Santa Monica, CA: RAND Corporation, 2017), e-book, https://www.rand.org/pubs/research_reports/RR2042.html.

14. John F. Pane et al., *Continued Progress: Promising Evidence on Personalized Learning: Survey Results Addendum* (Santa Monica, CA: RAND Corporation, 2015), 1–40, e-book, https://www.rand.org/pubs/research_reports/RR1365z2.html.

15. "ATLAS—Looking at Data Protocol," School Reform Initiative: A Community of Learners, https://toandthrough.uchicago.edu/sites/default/files/uploads/documents/NCS_FOT_Toolkit_ISBT_SetB_ATLAS%20Data%20Protocol.pdf.

16. Grant Wiggins, "A Veteran Teacher Turned Coach Shadows 2 Students for 2 Days—A Sobering Lesson Learned," *Granted and . . .* October 10, 2014, https://grantwiggins.wordpress.com/2014/10/10/a-veteran-teacher-turned-coach-shadows-2-students-for-2-days-a-sobering-lesson-learned/.

17. Julia Carson, "A New Perspective from an Authentic Classroom Experience," Shadow a Student Challenge, http://shadowastudent.org/stories/a-new-perspective-from-an-authentic-classroom-experience.

18. "School Retool," schoolretool.org.

Chapter 4

1. Anthony S. Bryk, Louis M. Gomez, Alicia Grunow, and Paul G. LeMahieu, *Learning to Improve: How America's Schools Can Get Better at Getting Better*, (Cambridge, MA: Harvard Education Press, 2015).

2. Greg Pilewski, "Learning to Improve Fast and Implement Well," *Education Closet*, January 29, 2015, https://educationcloset.com/2015/01/29/steam-leadership-learning-to-improve-fast-and-implement-well-as-you-transition/.

3. Alicia Grunow, "Improvement Discipline in Practice," Carnegie Foundation for the Advancement of Teaching, July 21, 2015, https://www.carnegiefoundation.org/blog/improvement-discipline-in-practice/.

4. Eric Ries, *The Lean Startup: How Today's Entrepreneurs Use Continuous Innovation to Create Radically Successful Businesses* (New York, NY: Crown Business, 2011), 22.

5. Valerie von Frank, "Group Smarts Elevate Collective Intelligence through Communication, Norms, and Diversity," *The Learning System* 8, no. 4 (Summer 2013): 6–7, https://learningforward .org/docs/default-source/learning-system/lsystem-sum-2013.pdf.

6. David Ferrabee, "Change Management: 5 Rules for Building a World-Class Guiding Coalition," Chartered Management Institute, February 29, 2016, http://www.managers.org.uk/insights/ news/2016/february/change-management-5-rules-for-building-a-world-class-guiding-coalition.

Chapter 5

1. Geoffrey A. Moore, *Crossing the Chasm: Marketing and Selling High-Tech Products to Mainstream Customers* (Oxford, UK: Capstone Publishing, 2008).

2. Allison Powell, Beth Rabbitt, and Kathryn Kennedy, "iNACOL Blended Learning Teacher Competency Framework," October 2014, https://www.inacol.org/wp-content/uploads/2015/02/ iNACOL-Blended-Learning-Teacher-Competency-Framework.pdf.

3. Ibid.

4. Ibid.

5. "Educator Competencies for Personalized, Learner-Centered Teaching," Jobs for the Future and the Council of Chief State School Officers, 2015, https://jfforg-prod-prime.53.amazon.aws.com/ media/documents/Educator-Competencies-081015.pdf.

6. Ibid.

Chapter 6

1. Benjamin Herold, "Personalized Learning: Modest Gains, Big Challenges, RAND Study Finds," *Education Week*, July 11, 2017, http://blogs.edweek.org/edweek/DigitalEducation/2017/07/ personalized_learning_research_implementation_RAND.html.

2. Kevin L. Meyer, *The Simple Leader: Personal and Professional Leadership at the Nexus of Lean and Zen* (Morro Bay, CA: Gemba Academy LLC, 2016).

3. Anthony S. Bryk, Louis M. Gomez, Alicia Grunow, and Paul G. LeMahieu, *Learning to Improve: How America's Schools Can Get Better at Getting Better*, (Cambridge, MA: Harvard Education Press, 2015).

4. John Hattie, "Hattie's Index Of Teaching and Learning Strategies: 39 Effect Sizes In Ascending Order," TeachThought, May 16, 2016, https://teachthought.com/pedagogy/hatties-ascending-order/; National Research Council, *How People Learn: Brain, Mind, Experience, and School* (Washington DC, National Academies Press, 1999).

5. Elizabeth City, Richard F. Elmore, Lee Teitel, and Sarah E. Fiarman, *Instructional Rounds in Education: A Network Approach to Improving Teaching and Learning* (Cambridge, MA: Harvard Education Press, 2014), 3.

6. Caitrin Wright, Brian Greenberg, and Rob Schwartz, "All That We've Learned: Five Years Working on Personalized Learning," August 2017, 9, http://www.siliconschools.com/wp-content/ uploads/2017/09/All-That-Weve-Learned-Silicon-Schools-Fund-1.pdf.

7. Sarah McKay, "Quality Improvement Approaches: The Networked Improvement Model," Carnegie Foundation for the Advancement of Teaching, February 23, 2017, https://www.carnegiefoundation .org/blog/quality-improvement-approaches-the-networked-improvement-model/.

Chapter 7

1. Cristina Mele, Jacqueline Pels, and Francesco Polese," A Brief Review of Systems Theories and Their Managerial Applications," *Service Science* 2, no. 1–2 (February 15, 2010): 126–35, doi:10.1287/serv.2.1_2.126.

2. Christian Seelos and Johanna Mair, *Innovation and Scaling for Impact: How Effective Social Enterprises Do It* (Stanford, CA: Stanford University Press, 2017).

3. Geoffrey A. Moore, *Crossing the Chasm: Marketing and Selling High-Tech Products to Mainstream Customers* (Oxford, UK: Capstone Publishing, 2008).

4. Caitrin Wright, Brian Greenberg, and Rob Schwartz, "All That We've Learned: Five Years Working on Personalized Learning," August 2017, 24, http://www.siliconschools.com/wp-content/uploads/2017/09/All-That-Weve-Learned-Silicon-Schools-Fund-1.pdf.

Chapter 8

1. Christian Seelos and Johanna Mair, *Innovation and Scaling for Impact: How Effective Social Enterprises Do It* (Stanford, CA: Stanford University Press, 2017), 5.

2. "Loudoun County Personalized Learning in Our Schools: 2016–2017," Loudoun County Public Schools, https://docs.google.com/document/d/1xNr0Rav60m25vBmyRLn9rn_D1E8teSLgt9PrmVGTRas/edit?ts=57c5c898.

3. Anthony S. Bryk, Louis M. Gomez, Alicia Grunow, and Paul G. LeMahieu, *Learning to Improve: How America's Schools Can Get Better at Getting Better* (Cambridge, MA: Harvard Education Press, 2015), 61.

4. Geoffrey A. Moore, *Crossing the Chasm: Marketing and Selling High-Tech Products to Mainstream Customers* (Oxford, UK: Capstone Publishing, 2008), 51–52.

5. "Performance Assessment Resource Bank," Stanford Center for Opportunity Policy in Education, https://www.performanceassessmentresourcebank.org/; "BIE's Project Search, Project Based Learning," Buck Institute for Education, http://www.bie.org/object/tools/project_search.

6. Steven Leinwand, "Four Teacher-Friendly Postulates for Thriving in a Sea of Change," *100 Years of Mathematics Teacher* 100, no. 9 (May 2007): 580–83, http://ljournal.ru/wp-content/uploads/2017/03/a-2017-023.pdf.

7. Caitrin Wright, Brian Greenberg, and Rob Schwartz, "All That We've Learned: Five Years Working on Personalized Learning," August 2017, 22, http://www.siliconschools.com/wp-content/uploads/2017/09/All-That-Weve-Learned-Silicon-Schools-Fund-1.pdf.

Chapter 9

1. Eric Ries, *The Lean Startup: How Today's Entrepreneurs Use Continuous Innovation to Create Radically Successful Businesses* (New York, NY: Crown Business, 2011), 267.

2. John P. Kotter, *Leading Change* (Boston, MA: Harvard Business School Press, 1996), 5.

3. Christian Seelos and Johanna Mair, *Innovation and Scaling for Impact: How Effective Social Enterprises Do It* (Stanford, CA: Stanford University Press, 2017), 211.

4. "Princess Bride Official Site," Princess Bride Forever, http://princessbrideforever.com/.

5. KaiEminence, "You Keep Using That Word. I Do Not Think It Means What You Think It Means," YouTube video, 0:22, September 14, 2009, https://www.youtube.com/watch?v=YIP6EwqMEoE.

6. "Communications Planning for Innovation in Education: New Guide and District Profiles," Alliance for Excellent Education, https://s3-us-west-1.amazonaws.com/tla-craft-assets/images/companyResources/CommunicationsGuide.pdf.

7. Ibid., 7.

8. Ibid., 9.

9. "Personalized Learning," Fulton County Schools, October 28, 2015, http://www.fultonschools.org/en/divisions/acd/personalizedlearning.

Chapter 10

1. Beth Rabbitt, "Analysis: Teaching, Technology, Transformation—5 Ways to Talk (and Think) About Personalized Learning," *The 74*, December 12, 2017.

2. Thomas J. Kane, "Never Judge a Book by Its Cover—Use Student Achievement Instead," *Brookings Institute*, March 3, 2016, https://www.brookings.edu/research/never-judge-a-book-by-its-cover-use-student-achievement-instead/.

3. National Research Council, *How People Learn: Brain, Mind, Experience and School* (Washington DC: National Academies Press, 1999), 10.

4. "Find What Works," What Works Clearinghouse, https://ies.ed.gov/ncee/wwc/; EdReports, https://www.edreports.org/.

5. Daniel Willingham, "Three Versions of Personalized Learning, Three Challenges," *Daniel Willingham—Science & Education Blog*, November 14, 2017, http://www.danielwillingham.com/daniel-willingham-science-and-education-blog/three-versions-of-personalized-learning-three-challenges.

6. Ibid.

7. Liz Arney, *Go Blended!: A Handbook for Blending Technology in Schools* (New York, NY: Jossey-Bass, 2015), 90.

8. Victoria McDougald, "Finding the Right Tool for the Job: Improving Reading and Writing in the Classroom," *The Thomas B. Fordham Institute*, September 14, 2016, https://edexcellence.net/articles/finding-the-right-tool-for-the-job-improving-reading-and-writing-in-the-classroom.

9. Arney, *Go Blended!*, 89.

10. V. Darleen Opfer, Julia H. Kaufman, and Lindsey E. Thompson, *Implementation of K–12 State Standards for Mathematics and English Language Arts and Literacy: Findings from the American Teacher Panel* (Santa Monica, CA: RAND Corporation, 2016), https://www.rand.org/pubs/research_reports/RR1529-1.html.

11. Julia H. Kaufman et al., *Use of Open Educational Resources in an Era of Common Standards: A Case Study on the Use of EngageNY* (Santa Monica, CA: RAND Corporation, 2017), 14–16. https://www.rand.org/pubs/research_reports/RR1773.html.

12. Ibid. xii.

13. Khan Academy, https://www.khanacademy.org/.

14. "About BIE," BIE, http://www.bie.org/about.

15. "Educating For a Diverse Democracy," Teaching Tolerance, https://www.tolerance.org/.

16. PhET, https://phet.colorado.edu/.

17. OER Commons, https://www.oercommons.org/.

18. Alfie Kohn, "The Overselling of Education Technology," *EdSurge*, March 16, 2016, https://www.edsurge.com/news/2016-03-16-the-overselling-of-education-technology?utm_content=buffer974fc&utm_medium=social&utm_source=twitter.com&utm_campaign=EdSurgeBuffer.

19. Molly B. Zielezinski, "What a Decade of Education Research Tells Us About Technology in the Hands of Underserved Students," *EdSurge*, May 19, 2016, https://www.edsurge.com/news/2016-05-19-what-a-decade-of-education-research-tells-us-about-technology-in-the-hands-of-underserved-students?utm_content=buffercca52&utm_medium=social&utm_source=facebook.com&utm_campaign=buffer).

20. Julia Freeland Fisher, "5 big ideas for education innovation in 2018," *Christensen Institute*, January 10, 2018, https://www.christenseninstitute.org/blog/5-big-ideas-education-innovation-2018/?_sft_topics=social-capital

21. Liz Glowa and Jim Goodell, "Student-Centered Learning: Functional Requirements for Integrated Systems to Optimize Learning," *iNACOL*, May 2016, https://www.inacol.org/wp-content/uploads/2016/05/iNACOL_FunctionalRequirementsForIntegratedSystems.pdf.

Chapter 11

1. Patrick Welsh, "Four Decades of Failed School Reform," *The Washington Post*, September 27, 2013, https://www.washingtonpost.com/opinions/four-decades-of-failed-school-reform/2013/09/27/dc9f2f34-2561-11e3-b75d-5b7f66349852_story.html?utm_term=.e5a9ec977b8c.

2. Ibid.

3. Ibid.

4. DesireforTruth, comment to author, September 30, 2013.

5. Reverend Jesse Jackson and Roger D. Hatch, *Straight from the Heart* (Minneapolis, MN: Fortress Press, 1987), 77.

6. K–12 Education Team, "Teachers Know Best: Teachers' Views on Professional Development," *Bill & Melinda Gates Foundation*, 2015, http://k12education.gatesfoundation.org/resource/teachers-know-best-teachers-views-on-professional-development/.

7. Gina Biancarosa, Anthony S. Bryk, and Emily S. Dexter, "Assessing the Value-Added Effects of Literacy Collaborative Professional Development on Student Learning," *Elementary School Journal* 111, no. 1 (2010): 7–34.

8. Elena Aguilar, *The Art of Coaching: Effective Strategies for School Transformation* (San Francisco, CA: Jossey-Bass, 2013).

9. Ronald Gallimore, Bradley Ermeling, William Saunders, and Clyde Goldenberg, "Moving the Learning of Teaching Closer to Practice: Teacher Education Implications of School-Based Inquiry Teams," *Elementary School Journal* 109, no. 5 (2009): 537–553.

Chapter 12

1. Christina Engelbart, "About Networked Improvement Communities (NICs)," Doug Engelbart Institute, http://www.dougengelbart.org/about/nics.html.

2. Paul LeMahieu, "Why a NIC?" Carnegie Foundation for the Advancement of Teaching, August 18, 2015, https://www.carnegiefoundation.org/blog/why-a-nic/.

3. Ibid.

4. "Teachers and Technology," Rhode Island Foundation, http://www.rifoundation.org/Transforming RhodeIsland/100YearsofCommunity/TeachersandTechnology.aspx.

5. "Connecting Kids to Their Future," Gumet Consulting, June 2014, gumet.com/wp-content/uploads/2014/06/Gumet-CS-RIDE-FINAL.pdf.

6. Jennifer D. Jordan, "Q & A with Rhode Island Education Commissioner Deborah A. Gist: Our goal is to be the first state to fully blend technology into all schools," *The Hechinger Report*, August 13, 2014, http://hechingerreport.org/q-rhode-island-education-commissioner-deborah-gist-goal-first-state-fully-blend-technology-schools/.

7. Mary Ann Pitcher et al., "The Network for College Success: A Capacity-Building Model for School Improvement," October 2016, https://consortium.uchicago.edu/sites/default/files/publications/A%20Capacity-Building%20Model-Nov2016-Consortium.pdf.

8. "#GoOpen Districts," Office of Educational Technology, https://tech.ed.gov/open/districts/.

ACKNOWLEDGMENTS

Pathways to Personalization: A Framework for School Change is our attempt to build a more efficient and effective process for personalizing education for all students. We began this work together in 2000 as founding faculty members of a startup charter school in Providence, Rhode Island. For more than ten years, we worked to find new and novel ways to engage and educate urban students with a range of talents and special needs through interest- and inquiry-driven projects. Never satisfied with our approaches to the work, we continued to refine both our classroom practices and our systems tactics until we found ourselves reunited again in 2012 at the Highlander Institute, attempting to bring high quality classroom strategies to the larger Providence and Rhode Island community. Six years later, with a staff of thirty-five and a growing footprint across the country, we find ourselves humbled at the opportunity to share our story with a wider audience.

We are truly blessed to work, collaborate, and laugh alongside the dedicated and talented team at the Highlander Institute. Our framework has emerged from their ongoing commitment to empowering students and teachers through new education models. Without their insights and thought partnership, this book would never have been possible. We offer heartfelt thanks to Stephanie Castilla, Eric Butash, Laura Jackson, Kara O'Connell, Erin Brouillette, Maeve Murray, Dawn Manchester, Michael Klein, Michaela Comella, Maureen Sigler, Mike Miele, Melinda Lopez, Christina Corser, Emily Grant, Nick Vockerodt, Vera Dejesus, Malika Ali, Karina Rodriguez, Danielle Blasczak, Nicole Lanni, Meg Smallidge, and our interns Zachary Charette and Charlotte Thompson.

Special thanks to our fearless leader, Dana Borrelli-Murray, who has given us the time, space, and inspiration to complete this ambitious project. We also owe extensive thanks to our social coordinator and book designer extraordinaire, Roshni Lakhi, for the beautiful artwork and graphics that were instrumental in helping us tell our story. And, we will forever appreciate the precision and organization of Jennifer Polexi, who provided invaluable support with our endnotes.

Thank you to the dedicated and inspirational Highlander Institute staff who supported our work before moving on to new endeavors: Joshua Marland, Jonathan Santos Silva, Karla Vigil, and Theresa Moore. Thank you to our board of directors for your unending support, especially our board chair, John Muggeridge. Thank you to our former colleagues at the Highlander Charter School, including early mentors Jim Donahue, Gigi DiBello, and Rose Mary Grant, as well as past and current staff who saw potential in our work before we even saw it ourselves.

A huge shout-out to all of the practitioners leading this work on behalf of students across Rhode Island, especially the 108 talented Fuse RI fellows who possess endless energy and enthusiasm for new ideas and continuous improvement. We are grateful for our growing Fuse family, expanding in Syracuse, New York; Orange County, California; and in 8 other districts across Massachusetts. A special shout-out to all of the Rhode Island district administrative teams and principals who pioneered, tested, and scaled the great ideas that helped establish our framework, particularly Gara Field, Cameron Berube, Edda Carmadello, Michael Barnes, Barry Ricci, Paula Dillon, Bill Black, Denise Missry-Millburn, Victor Capellan, and Chris Maher.

This book is filled with stories of real educators and leaders implementing blended and personalized learning models. In some cases, the school or educator names are pseudonyms. Special thanks to these Rhode Island educators who shared their inspirational stories with us: Jason Appel, Deb Ramm, Mike Miele, Simona Simpson, Yanaiza Gallant, Douglas Nelson, Beccy Siddons, Leslie Tirocchi, Melissa Trevitt, Val Seveney, Maya Chavez Akin, Julia Carlson, Hilary Lundgren, Rachel Salvatore, Kristen Danusis, and the incredible team of teachers at Pleasant View elementary school in Providence, Rhode Island. Thank you to the Rhode Island Department of Education, including Commissioner Ken Wagner and former commissioner Deborah Gist for their support and partnership over the years. Thank you to Governor Gina Raimondo, former chief innovation officer Richard Culatta, and current director of education Daniela Fairchild for being incredible advocates for personalized learning across the state.

We stood on the shoulders of giants as we wrote this book. Thank you to our national partners, especially the esteemed professionals who shared their stories with us: Deagan Andrews from Greeley-Evans School District 6 in Greeley, Colorado; Dr. David Richards and Carrie Wozniak from Fraser Public Schools in Fraser, Michigan; and Scott Frauenheim and Colleen Collins from Distinctive Schools in Chicago, Illinois. There are too many national thought leaders and researchers for us to thank, but we must give special shout-outs to our conference partners, Julia Freeland-Fisher, Beth Rabbitt, and Juliana Finegan, as well as Learning Assembly collaborators Phyllis Lockett and Chris Liang-Vergara. Thank you to Paul LeMahieu at the Carnegie Education Foundation for deepening our understanding of improvement science, and thank you to organizations such as iNACOL, Silicon Valley Education Fund, Digital Promise, ISTE, Future Ready, and the many others who are documenting, collecting, and building fantastic content to support blended and personalized learning.

We are extremely grateful for the expertise of our team at the Harvard Education Publishing Group. Our editor, Nancy Walser, was both patient and supportive as we navigated this process as rookies. Huge thanks to Jonathan Santos Silva, David Swank, and Kara O'Connell for their careful reading of early drafts and thoughtful revision suggestions.

There is no way this book would be possible without the tremendous support of our friends and family.

To my incredibly tolerant and loving wife Laura, who has done everything in support of this book; from editing the first drafts to long weekends with the kids, thank you for being a kind, thoughtful, and hilarious partner throughout this adventure. To my parents, who have given me the education bug and fostered it through loud and lively dinner table debates, these pages are yours as much as they are mine. Thank you to my brother Eric, my most loyal fan and first best friend. Thank you John Lavall for unending avuncular wisdom, and thank you Glenn Robertelli for teaching me there's always a better option. Thank you to Cauley, Rachel, and the children for all the lovely, warm Shabbos meals that I needed more than you could ever imagine. And finally, to my boys, Asher and Asa, thank you for being my inspiration and constant feedback loop. You push my thinking and challenge my assumptions daily. Thank you for being the sunshine of my life.

—Shawn

To my wonderful husband Eric, your love and support make the impossible possible. Thank you for picking up the slack, attending all the games, doing all the dishes, volunteering for all the pick-ups, and patiently waiting to watch the next episode of *Breaking Bad* until I could take an evening off. Thank you Bill and Katie for anchoring me to reality with your hilarious stories of toddler antics. To Mom and Dad, thank you for your steadfast belief in me and for providing me with the mentality and fortitude to always challenge the status quo. Thank you Gimi and Papa for your constant encouragement of my work and your generous support of the institute for so many years. To the many Sanford authors in the extended family, it is a privilege to now sit on the fringe of this esteemed group.

To my friends, near and far, I am incredibly grateful for your love, comradery, and support through thick and thin. Gratitude is definitely a central theme this year and I am blessed to have you all in my life. Special shout-out to Dawn, who can always be relied on to locate the best craft cocktails within a three-mile radius. And last but certainly not least, love and gratitude to Charlotte and Ally, who learned to tolerate an empty fridge, a distracted mom, and a kitchen corner draped with books and papers. Our many conversations about education and life and hopes and dreams propelled me through this year and grounded me in the belief that this work really matters.

—Cathy

ABOUT THE AUTHORS

SHAWN C. RUBIN is chief education officer at Highlander Institute in Providence, Rhode Island. Shawn designs and manages the institute's blended and personalized learning initiatives. He is a national thought leader around coaching and consulting approaches to personalized learning and has been an integral driver of personalized learning growth in Rhode Island. His ten years in the classroom have informed his insider's view into the challenges and limitations teachers face on a daily basis.

Shawn is the architect of the institute's Fuse program, which trains educators to become change agents for personalized learning in schools and districts looking to accelerate this work. He is the co-founder of Rhode Island's bi-monthly EdTechRI meetups, which brings educators together to share ideas about edtech products and how they can help improve learning for students.

Shawn earned his undergraduate degree at the University of Michigan and his master's in Education at Lesley University in Cambridge, Massachusetts. Shawn co-founded an international nonprofit called Longitude in 2006 to support grassroots human rights efforts in Ghana and India. He is also the co-founder and CEO of a competency assessment startup called Metryx.

Shawn is the winner of iNACOL's Outstanding Individual Contribution to Personalized Learning award for 2017. Shawn has also won MassCue's 2015 Pathfinder award and the Americorps Alums 2009 Eli Segal Entrepreneurship award.

Shawn lives in Providence, Rhode Island with his wife and two boys. He is the son of two career educators and an avid Detroit sports fan. Follow Shawn on Twitter @ShawnCRubin.

CATHY SANFORD is an experienced educator, education consultant, and nonprofit administrator. She has consulted as an adjunct faculty member of the Brown University Graduate School of Education, participated as a board member of Breakthrough Providence and the Rhode Island branch of the International Dyslexia Association, and currently sits on the board of trustees for Boon Philanthropy and Camp Onaway.

Currently, Cathy leads research and development efforts at Highlander Institute. She coordinates several initiatives across the institute's portfolio and supports the creation of frameworks, tools, and project plans that align with the overall mission and vision of the organization. Cathy is the also the lead writer on white papers, project proposals, and grants.

Before her move to the institute, Cathy supported the launch of the Highlander Charter School, a preK–12 urban school that specializes in supporting the unique learning needs of students. Prior to joining the Highlander family, Cathy co-directed Breakthrough Providence, a nonprofit committed to creating a pathway to college for academically motivated middle school students in Providence public schools and to encouraging talented secondary and college students to pursue careers in education. Cathy also spent seven years in the classroom teaching math.

Cathy holds a bachelor's in psychology from the University of Virginia and a master's in education policy analysis from Stanford University. She resides in southeastern Massachusetts with her husband and two daughters. Cathy is an outdoor enthusiast and can often be found on a paddleboard, cross-country skis, or somewhere in the woods when she is not working or attending youth sporting events. Follow Cathy on Twitter @csanford42.

INDEX